RECLAIMING THE FOREST

RECLAIMING THE FOREST

The Ewenki Reindeer Herders of Aoluguya

Edited by
Åshild Kolås and Yuanyuan Xie

berghahn
NEW YORK · OXFORD
www.berghahnbooks.com

First published in 2015 by

Berghahn Books

www.berghahnbooks.com

© 2015, 2020 Åshild Kolås and Yuanyuan Xie
First paperback edition published in 2020

Library of Congress Cataloging-in-Publication Data

Reclaiming the forest : the Ewenki reindeer herders of Aoluguya / edited by
Åshild Kolås and Yuanyuan Xie.
    pages cm
    Includes index.
    ISBN 978-1-78238-630-8 (hardback) — ISBN 978-1-78238-631-5 (ebook)
    1. Evenki (Asian people)—China—Genhe Shi. 2. Evenki (Asian people)—
Ethnic identity. 3. Reindeer herders—China—Genhe Shi. I. Kolas, Ashild,
editor of compilation. II. Xie, Yuanyuan (Sociologist) editor of compilation.

DS731.E85R44 2015
951.7′7004941—dc23

                                                                    2014033524

British Library Cataloguing in Publication Data

A catalogue record for this book is available from the British Library

Printed on acid-free paper.

ISBN: 978-1-78238-630-8 hardback
ISBN 978-1-78920-762-0 paperback
ISBN: 978-1-78238-631-5 ebook

Contents

⏺𝕎 Figures

ꙮ Foreword

In the taiga there is a proverb: "Where people ride reindeer, that's where the last paradises are." In the northern regions of what today are the provinces of Inner Mongolia and Heilongjiang in northeast China, one little-known such paradise once harbored the hunting grounds of the Reindeer Ewenki. The area's flora and fauna should be considered part of the Siberian subregion, as the area and its continental climate are, practically speaking, an extension of the Siberian taiga onto Chinese territory.

The Reindeer Ewenki, a tiny splinter group of the Tungusic reindeer breeders who inhabit a vast expanse of eastern Siberia, are the only reindeer breeders in China. As speakers of an eastern dialect of northern Tungus, they are classed as a Manchu-Tungusic people in the Altaic ethnic and linguistic groups. They are also a circumpolar population.

The nomadic family groups (Ewenki: *urilen*) and their reindeer began to roam the mountain taiga in the Great Amur Bend in the 1820s. Yielding to pressure from the demographically and economically stronger Yakut (Sakha), they had moved southward from their old homelands on the upper reaches of the Lena River system in Yakutia, seeking fresh hunting grounds. For a time they lived as nomads and hunters along the Amazar west of the upper Amur, but eventually they crossed the border from Russia into China by taking their herds across the Amur (Chinese: *Heilong Jiang* = black dragon). On the Chinese side of the river, they discovered an area of almost untouched forests offering vast hunting grounds rich in game. Here one could find bear, elk, red deer, roe deer, musk deer, hare, and boar, as well as large populations of precious furbearers like sable, ermine, and fire- or Siberian weasel. Game birds such as wood grouse (*Capercaillie*), black grouse (moorhen), hazel grouse (hazel hen), and various kinds of duck abounded. Crucially, the area's tundra vegetation offered the reindeer—who not only served as pack and riding animals but also provided milk—the right kind of nourishment: a sufficient amount of lichen of the *Cladonia* species (Ewenki: *onko* or *jagel*). Thanks to the relatively high altitude of the Great Hinggan range extending through the region from north to

south, this environment allowed the recently arrived hunters to preserve their traditional economy and lifestyle, supported by their reindeer, without interruption.

Those first nomadic groups were soon followed by further arrivals.
By 1890 members of about twelve clans (Ewenki: *hala* or *chala*) lived in
this area on the fringe of what was then the Chinese Empire. Some of
these nomadic groups later moved farther south to the river Gen (also
known as Gan) or east to the Emur (Albazicha), Huma (Kumara), and
Gan (Gen) Rivers. In the west the Tungusic taiga dwellers hunted on
the upper reaches of the river Mo'erdaoga (Marekta) and on the lower
Aba (Apa). Through this huge and theretofore uninhabited wilderness
flowed the taiga's rapid, enchanting Jiliu (Bystraja) and its numerous
tributaries, all providing the clearest water imaginable. The richest
hunting grounds lay in their vicinity.

Even before migrating to the Chinese side of the border, Tungusic
hunters had engaged in barter with the border Cossacks on the Argun
and upper Amur Rivers. They now continued this trade in their new
forest homeland, having already come to depend on certain goods
offered by civilization, such as hunting rifles and ammunition, flour,
sugar, salt, cloth, and (not least) alcohol and tobacco. In their old Siberian homeland they had been members of the Russian Orthodox
Church, but Christianity had never significantly influenced or in any
way displaced their former religious ideas, worldview, or belief in
shamanism.

Traditionally, hunting families' trading relations were based on personal acquaintance with Russian Cossacks, with whom Tungusic taiga
dwellers shared economic interests. Without exception, the Russians
engaged in such trading relations were ordinary peasants. The partners
called one another *andak,* meaning "friend" or "comrade." Families of
hunters and peasants maintained this *andaki* barter over generations.
Han Chinese were only rarely involved in *andaki* trade, and never as
professional traders. Money had no role to play; the exchanges were
pure barter. *Andaki* trading meetings (Ewenki: *bogžor*), took place four
or five times a year. In return for precious furs and other natural products from the taiga as well as handicrafts, the hunters received the products of civilization that they needed. These friendly trading relations
with border Cossacks persisted after the Russian Revolution and the
civil war in eastern Siberia, as most of these Cossacks had emigrated to
Chinese territory and settled in the region close to the border.

In 1932, northeast China was occupied by Japanese troops who subsequently installed the puppet state Manchukuo. At first, this had little effect on the taiga dwellers in the Hinggan Mountains. Manchukuo

rulers who attempted to monopolize barter with taiga nomads met with only limited success. However, as the ravages of World War II reached the Hinggan Mountains young Ewenki males were organized into a ranger unit to support the Japanese war effort. After the Japanese armed forces' capitulation and the end of World War II in the Far East in August 1945, Soviet Russian forces occupied northeast China and Ewenki-Russian barter was revived.

With the founding of the People's Republic of China in 1949, the Reindeer Ewenki were registered for the first time and put under Chinese administration in the early 1950s. Now, the store of a state cooperative in Qiqian (also known as Cigan) monopolized their trading in products of the forest and the hunt. This ended not only the traditional *andaki* trade with Russian emigrants but also an absolutely free, independent existence as hunters and nomads that had lasted more than 125 years. Throughout that period, now in the past, the hunters of the Hinggan Mountains had never put themselves under any country's administration. Under Chinese rule, however, the Reindeer Ewenki were subject to politicians responsible for the area, who wanted to experiment with Marxist social and economic theories. Few of the measures they imposed ultimately had positive, enduring effects for the taiga dwellers. One of the first administrative regulations, for example, essentially reduced the area where the population was allowed to hunt and pursue their nomadic lifestyle. This insensitive, shortsighted administrative measure caused many reindeer to die from lack of fodder, and the Ewenki were struck by disease. In 1953, they suffered from an epidemic of typhoid fever due to the sudden and unfamiliar density of families of hunters, and lack of medicine. Furthermore, the so-called Great Proletarian Cultural Revolution (1966–1976) brought the small group of Tungusic reindeer breeders much suffering and distress. Many died from extreme measures of suppression.

In 2003, the hunting families suffered a fourth, forced (re-)settlement. From Aoluguya, the center of their established hunting grounds, where they had lived since 1967, they were moved 250 km south to the outskirts of the city of Genhe, where the Chinese state had built them a settlement called New Aoluguya. An order prohibiting hunting was issued, and the hunters had to turn in their rifles. Reindeer breeding was restricted to the surroundings of Genhe. Once again, many reindeer died from lack of lichen fodder, and the bureaucrats responsible for the situation finally conceded that their hasty action had been a serious mistake. To save at least some reindeer, mobile reindeer breeding camps were set up in areas with sufficient lichen resources.

Today, only about 700 reindeer remain in northeast China. This means the Chinese Reindeer Ewenki cannot continue on the path they have followed so far. Hopefully, they can find a new path linking their ancient forest culture to the new times and changed conditions, and thereby manage to preserve their traditions—not only their handicraft skills, but also their particular dialect, songs and dances, folk poetry, and shamanistic traditions as well as their customary social relations and original worldview. This field offers young scholars satisfying topics for research. The present book, the fruit of an initiative by my research colleagues Åshild Kolås and Yuanyuan Xie, presents the beginnings of such research. This first volume to cover exclusively this group in a Western language also launches an effort to make the Reindeer Ewenki of China known to the world.

I hope the reader will pardon my use of this foreword mainly to summarize the history of the Reindeer Ewenki. With this presentation of this ethnic group's eventful fate, I aim to spur interest in the life of this small population with their reindeer in the taiga on the margins of the Chinese world. Having myself studied the cultural history and the life of the Reindeer Ewenki in the mountain forests of the Great Hinggan range for the last forty years, I accepted the invitation to contribute a foreword to the present volume with great pleasure. I thank my friend and research colleague Peter Knecht of Nagoya for translating this foreword from German into English.

The volume is the fruit of collaboration among an international group of scholars and researchers. Alongside scholarly contributions on Ewenki reindeer breeding, material culture, and cultural history, it features texts representing autochthonous voices of the Ewenki nationality in China, offering substantial opportunity to learn about the life, thoughts, and feelings of this southernmost branch of Tungusic taiga dwellers. I earnestly hope that readers of the following pages will come to admire this little-known ethnic group of hunters and reindeer herders in northeast China.

F. Georg Heyne
Bielefeld, Spring 2015

ꙮ Acknowledgments

We would never have been able to carry out the research presented in this book without the generous help and hospitality of the people of Aoluguya. Although they are too many to be named individually, we would like to express our deep gratitude to all of them on behalf of each of the contributors. This book is dedicated to them.

As the editors, we would like to thank the other contributors to this volume for their enduring confidence and unremitting efforts. We also appreciate the meticulous work of those who translated some chapters into English from Chinese and Japanese. Courteously hosted by the Association of Ewenki Studies of Inner Mongolia, the contributors got together in Aoluguya Ewenki Ethnic Township (29 June–2 July 2011) to revisit friends in the taiga, Aoluguya, and Genhe, and discuss our work. In Aoluguya we enjoyed the company of three other scholars who deserve thanks for their participation in these discussions. These were Bao Shengli (Institute of Ethnology and Anthropology, Chinese Academy of Social Sciences), Ivar Bjørklund (Department of Cultural Sciences, University of Tromsø), and Kalina (Ethnic Museum, Central University of Nationalities).

This book is an outcome of the research project "Pastoralism in China: Policy and Practice," a joint venture between the Peace Research Institute Oslo (PRIO) and the Institute of Ethnology and Anthropology (IEA) at the Chinese Academy of Social Sciences (CASS). Funded by the Research Council of Norway, the project investigated policies and programs targeting pastoralists in China, focusing on the local implementation of these policies. Exploring grassland management as well as programs to combat environmental degradation and sedentarize herders, the project took a broad look at the livelihoods, land use, herding practices, and socioeconomic situation of herders in contemporary China.

We are sincerely grateful to colleagues at IEA for their dedicated support and steadfast commitment over the years, and especially to then IEA Director Hao Shiyuan. Professor Hao initiated this project with his idea of carrying out a comparative study of Reindeer Ewenki in China and Sami reindeer herders in Norway. We extend our thanks also to the project reference group: Jon Pedersen (Fafo Institute for Applied International Studies), Kirsti Strøm Bull (University of Oslo and Sami University College), Vigdis Broch-Due (Department of Social Anthropology, University of Bergen), Joseph Fox (Department of Biology, University of Tromsø), Steinar Pedersen (Sami University College), and the late Aud Talle (Department of Social Anthropology, University of Oslo). We also appreciate our collaborators in the secretariat of the Association of World Reindeer Herders and the International Centre for Reindeer Husbandry based in Kautokeino, Norway.

We would also like to thank Hasibater, PhD in Mongolian Language and Literature from Inner Mongolia University and professor at the Research Center of Manchu Language and Culture, Heilongjiang University. Drawing on his comparative research on Mongolian, Manchu and Tungusic languages, Hasibater provided invaluable advice on translation and transliteration. In addition, we want to thank the three anonymous reviewers who took the time to go through our manuscript and give us their opinions. Their insightful suggestions were very helpful. Finally, we thank the editors at Berghahn Books for their excellent editorial guidance and support.

Location map, inset shows location of Aoluguya. Created by Zhang Rongde.

⟐ Introduction

WRITING THE "REINDEER EWENKI"

Åshild Kolås

This volume is the first English-language book devoted solely to the Ewenki[1] reindeer-herding community of Aoluguya, China, known locally as the Aoxiangren or people of Aoluguya Ewenki Ethnic Township. The Reindeer Ewenki (Chinese: *xunlu ewenke*), known as China's only reindeer-using tribe (*shilu buluo*), have also been identified as the country's "last hunting tribe" (*zuihou de shoulie buluo*). As nomadic hunters of the taiga, they once lived in cone-shaped tents similar to the North American tepee. As tall as ten feet, these dwellings were made of birch bark in the summer and the hides of deer or moose in the winter, supported by larch poles. The Ewenki used reindeer as pack animals to carry tents and equipment as their owners moved through the taiga forest. Women and children would ride the reindeer, and reindeer-milk tea was a favorite drink.

After the founding of the People's Republic, a "hunting production brigade" was established, and reindeer antlers started to be cut for the production of Chinese medicine. The Ewenki still hunted for subsistence, but as workers in the brigade they were expected to hand over game for "points," which was the only way they could acquire supplies at the store. Following Deng Xiaoping's economic reforms in the early 1980s, the brigade was turned into a hunting cooperative. Hunting remained an important source of income and subsistence until 2003, when the community was relocated to a new settlement far from their hunting grounds. Prior to the move, their guns were confiscated and a complete ban on hunting was imposed. The Aoluguya Ewenki thus lost a key aspect of their way of life, culture, and identity. After their relocation, reindeer herding was the last remnant of the Ewenki nomadic lifestyle, and since then the reindeer have become a key source of livelihood and symbol of the unique identity of the Reindeer Ewenki.

Chinese ethnologists and historians believe that as early as 2000 B.C., the ancestors of the reindeer-using Ewenki people lived around Lake Baikal and the upper reaches of the Nerchinsk River, northeast of Lake

Baikal. Between the sixteenth and mid seventeenth century, they moved to the areas near the Weile and Weitmu Rivers, branches of the Lena River northwest of Lake Baikal. During the eighteenth century they migrated further, along the Shilka River, and gradually crossed the Argun River (Chinese: E'erguna) into the forests of the Greater Hinggan Mountains,[2] currently known as Daxing'anling, in Hulun Bei'er League, Inner Mongolia Autonomous Region. According to a 1909 survey conducted by Zhao Chunfang, in the Amur River bend the Ewenki hunted mainly along the Bei'erci River (Russian: Bystraja), the Amur, and the upper reaches of the Genhe River. In the 1950s, their hunting grounds stretched from the banks of the E'erguna in the west (the border between China and the Soviet Union) to the estuary of the Kamalan River and the upper Huma'er River in the east, and from Enhehada and Xilinji in the north to the Genhe River in the south (Kalina 2006). Moving around in this area with their reindeer, they hunted deer, moose, boar, wild birds, and rabbits. In winter they also hunted and trapped squirrel, lynx, fox, and sable. Furs, hides, and meat were bartered with Russian traders known in Ewenki as *andak,* who supplied them with goods such as black tea, flour, salt, sugar, alcohol, clothes, guns, and ammunition (Heyne 2003). From the Russians they learned how to bake pan bread, called *lieba.* Many Ewenki hunters spoke Russian as a second language, and Russian names were popular. While continuing to adhere to Shamanism, some of their customs and beliefs, burial practices, and other rituals were also somewhat influenced by Russian Orthodox Christianity.

In 1932 the Japanese army occupied Manchuria and established the puppet state of Manchukuo (1932–1945). By 1942 the Japanese Secret Service had marshalled the young Ewenki men into camps to be trained as rangers or scouts (Heyne 2007). This was a time of violent killings among the Ewenki, especially after the death of the respected shaman Olga Kudrina, who had mediated in earlier conflicts. After the killing of a Japanese officer, one group of Ewenki, fearing retaliation, crossed the Amur River and stayed in Siberia. The Russian military took over the area after the Japanese defeat at the end of World War II.

Soviet administration continued until 1948, when the Communists emerged victorious in the civil war in China. After the People's Republic of China was founded, Ewenki hunters were given the choice of remaining in China or moving across the E'erguna River to the Soviet Union. In the 1950s the Chinese government constructed houses for the Ewenki hunters in the village of Qiqian, on the eastern bank of the E'erguna (the Chinese call it the "left bank"). Far from becoming sedentary, the Ewenki community continued its hunting lifestyle, living most of the year in cone-shaped tents transported by reindeer.

However, the deteriorating relationship between China and the Soviet Union in the early 1960s had far-reaching implications. Due to growing tension and tightened border control between the two regimes, a new settlement named Aoluguya was built in the interior of the Amur River bend, near the town of Mangui. The Ewenki community was relocated there, and for nearly four decades (1965–2003) Aoluguya was the seat of their "ethnic township" (Chinese: *minzu xiang*). Then the community was again relocated, this time to the "new Aoluguya" near the city of Genhe.

The Aoluguya Ewenki share many aspects of their hunting and reindeer herding culture with neighboring groups, including the Oro-qen (Chinese: Elunchun) in Heilongjiang Province (hunters who used horses for transportation), the reindeer-herding Dukha and Tuva in northern Mongolia and the Russian autonomous republics of Tuva and Buryatia, and the Evenki in the Zabaikalsky region and Amur Oblast across the border in Russia. Linguistically they are closely tied to the latter group, with whom they share a language classified as a branch of Manchu-Tungusic. In the past decades, these small groups of hunt-ers and herders inhabiting the border regions of Mongolia, Russia, and China have all undergone social and political transformations driven by Soviet and Chinese communism, followed by economic reforms and marketization leading to further marginalization. As a result, they all face similar challenges to their cultural survival today.

The Ewenki in the "New China"

After the founding of the People's Republic, scientists were recruited to identify China's "nationalities" (Chinese: *minzu*) in the "nationali-ties identification project" (*minzu shibie*). As a part of this exercise, the unique identity of the Reindeer Ewenki was acknowledged by their designation as "Yakut" (Chinese: Yakute) Ewenki, although they were not given the status of a separate nationality. The "Yakut" label reflected the belief that the Reindeer Ewenki originated in Yakutia, or what Lind-gren (1936) called the Iakut Administration, which was an independent polity at the time of the Russian Civil War. According to Heyne (2007: 166) the Reindeer Ewenki began immigrating in clan groups from Ya-kutia (modern Sakha) to the yet undisturbed taiga of northern Manchu-ria as of about 1825.

Besides the forest-dwelling Yakut, the nationalities identification project also placed two larger groups inhabiting the grasslands of Hulun Bei'er League in the Ewenki category. These were the "Solon" (Suolun) and the "Tungus" (Tonggusi) Ewenki, the latter also known by the Buriat-Mongolian term Khamnigan.[3] According to the project's scientists, the three groups all spoke related languages classified as Manchu-Tungusic and had histories of migration from Siberia and the Lake Baikal region. The other Ewenki groups differed from the Yakute in that they had adopted horse breeding and taken up livestock herding and farming as their main livelihoods. Their languages were different, and as the scientists perceived, the groups had different migration histories. Nevertheless, the scientists concluded that the two other groups shared the same ethnic origins as the hunting and reindeer-using Ewenki of Daxing'anling.

Before the founding of the People's Republic, Ewenki hunters moved back and forth across the Amur River relatively freely in a region alternately controlled by Russian and Manchu administrations. The victorious Communists in China were a force for integration and state expansion as well as increasingly strict border control. As soon as "minority nationalities" were identified, they were recruited into new forms of political organization through the Communist Party and its mass organizations. The Communist leadership also introduced a new production system based on communes and brigades, modern schooling, a new economic system relying on collective and state ownership, and completely new infrastructure (e.g., roads, railroads, power supply, concrete buildings). Frontier areas were simultaneously "opened up" to large-scale forestry, coal mining, and other extractive industries. After the establishment of communes, Ewenki hunters, as workers in the production brigade, were provided with rifles and regular supplies of ammunition. Over the years, the Aoluguya settlement was furnished with a school, a hospital, a post office, a bank, a store, a museum, a cultural center, a retirement home, office buildings for the township government, and a television ground receiving station. Meanwhile, excessive logging diminished the hunting grounds and gradually led to the depletion of wildlife. As the Aoluguya community became more integrated with mainstream Chinese society, dependency on the government also increased, leading to a sense of marginalization, loss of language, and widespread alcoholism.

Since the 1980s, the dismantling of communes and introduction of economic reforms have brought new challenges to the Aoluguya community while largely failing to address the weaknesses of earlier policies. According to one researcher, the root causes of high mortality rates among Ewenki adults are scarcity of resources, limited lands for reindeer herding, declining reindeer population, and unemployment, which lead to loss of livelihood, threats to cultural survival, spiritual confusion, and feelings of alienation (Kalina 2006). Current efforts to develop China's small ethnic groups seek to rectify issues of marginalization, but authorities continue to render minorities as passive subjects. As with other such groups, the agency of the Ewenki reindeer herders is at stake: once more written as "other," now they are also exhibited as a tourism resource and staged as cultural performance. Their material culture is carefully "protected" in the museum, but the Ewenki language and cultural heritage are gradually disappearing. The last Ewenki shaman, Njura Kaltakun, passed away in 1997. Their language was never written and was taught in school only from 1998 to 2001. According to surveys by Kong Fanzhi (1994) and Kalina (2006), 48 to 77 percent of Aoluguya households contain mixed marriages. The non-Ewenki spouses include Mongolians, Manchu, Daur, Han Chinese, and Russians. At present very few Ewenki children are able to speak their native language.

The government invested more than ¥13 million to resettle the Aoluguya community from the "old Aoluguya" settlement 17.5 km north of Mangui to the "new Aoluguya" 4.5 km southwest of the county capital. The new Aoluguya Ewenki Ethnic Township covers 17,672 square km of land, or 8.83 percent of the total area of Genhe County (Kalina 2006). As of 2009, the 243 Ewenki people living in the township made up 16 percent of the total township population of 1,548 people. According to the local government, the "hunters" increased their annual per capita income from ¥2,892 in 2003 to ¥5,512 in 2009. Each Ewenki household resettled in the new Aoluguya was provided with free housing. Refurbished in Finnish design in 2008–09, these have become comfortable houses with modern amenities such as central heating, cable TV, and indoor plumbing. Attempting to protect their native language from extinction, the inhabitants of new Aoluguya have organized evening classes in Ewenki language and culture. The newly constructed Aoluguya Ethnic Reindeer Resort is a potential source of employment opportunities, including hotel jobs, souvenir production, and tourism services such as "Ewenki home-stays." The master plan for the resort (developed by the Finnish consultancy firm Pöyry) says the concept is "to preserve the Aoluguya cultural heritage and old livelihoods by turning the old skills and unique lifestyle into a tourism product" (Pöyry 2008: 7).

The new Aoluguya settlement was built with central government funds for "ecological migration" (*shengtai yimin*), a government scheme to restore vulnerable ecosystems by moving herders out of "degraded" (*tuihua*) environments and into planned settlements, targeting most pastoral areas in China. In the case of Aoluguya, environmental concerns were clearly not the only grounds for the 2003 resettlement. According to Zhang Rongde and Bai Ying, a key goal of the government was to offer the former hunters a better standard of housing and infrastructure as well as a convenient administrative seat.

The 2003 resettlement also paved the way for creation of an ethno-tourist attraction where tourism could become a new livelihood for community members and a source of profit for investors and entrepreneurs. This raises the question of why a tourist resort was not constructed in the old settlement, where the natural scenery is far more beautiful than in the new site—especially when this was in fact precisely what happened to old Aoluguya after it was vacated. If relocation was required for the sake of environmental protection, why was the old Aoluguya site opened to further exploitation after its original inhabitants were moved out? As illustrated by several of the chapters of this volume, a political ecology story lurks beneath the propaganda surface. There is reason to doubt that resettlement was the only way to protect a fragile ecosystem, whether to save the wildlife from over-hunting or the taiga from overgrazing. It seems more plausible that the community was moved to protect the Ewenki and their reindeer from the environmental damage unleashed by an exploitive timber industry and an influx of Han Chinese poachers, as described by Siqinfu. A more critical interpretation would be that further exploitation was already planned, so the community was moved mainly to allow others to profit.

Another important question is whether the "unique lifestyle" of the Ewenki reindeer herders can be a viable tourism product if reindeer herding fails to survive outside the tourist-park parameters. As of 2009, reindeer herding was the livelihood of only twenty-four households in the new township. Herders received ¥35 monthly in "forest protection" compensation. A total of 275 people in the township (other nationalities included) received compensation for hunting restrictions and welfare in the form of poverty aid, ranging from ¥12.5 to ¥104 monthly (Kalina 2006). In 2009, the twenty-four reindeer-herding households held about 650 reindeer—an average of less than thirty reindeer per household, down from a reindeer population of 706 at the time of the 2003 resettlement as per government records. Meanwhile, community members who do not have reindeer face a serious unemployment problem. Even those who are educated have great difficulty making a living in the settlement, as they must compete for jobs with more qualified "outsiders." For many, welfare payments have become the main source of income.

The herders are well aware of the challenges they face in sustaining the health of their reindeer stock. They know the benefits of increasing the genetic diversity of their herds through interbreeding with reindeer from other stocks. There is no wild reindeer population in the area, so they have no option to deliberately interbreed their reindeer cows with wild forest reindeer. Restrictions against transporting live reindeer across international borders add to the difficulties. Given these challenges, the main compensatory strategy is to keep a relatively high number of male breeding reindeer. This also increases the reindeer horn harvest, as males have larger antlers than females.

Though acknowledging the serious difficulties facing Ewenki reindeer herders today, this book challenges the implicit pessimism in popular conceptions of the Reindeer Ewenki as a relic of the past, as in the epithet "the last hunting tribe." Without losing sight of the past, we primarily explore the present, reviewing current challenges and, even more importantly, responses to these challenges. The chapters of this book describe the reindeer herders' efforts to reclaim their forest lifestyle and develop new forest livelihoods in the aftermath of the hunting ban and resettlement. We also describe how the people of Aoluguya re-envision their identity as "keepers of reindeer" as they engage in ethnic tourism, exchange experiences with Evenki neighbors in Russia, and network with other reindeer herders across the circumpolar region.

The literature

A substantial English-language literature has described the Evenki of Siberia (Russia) (e.g., Abe 2005; Anderson 1991, 2000, 2006a, 2006b, 2010; Brandisauskas 2007, 2009; Ermolova 2003; Fondahl 1989, 1998; Istvan 2005; Lavrillier 2010; Sirina 2006; Vitebsky 1990, 2005), building on an even larger body of Russian literature. Until the early twentieth century, the scarce literature on their "little cousins" in the Amur River bend consisted of fragmented records by exiled bureaucrats, explorers, and ethnologists, mainly in Chinese, Russian, and Japanese (Kalina 2006; Siqinfu 1999, 2000). Monographs by Russian scholar Sergei Mikhailovitch Shirokogoroff (1929, 1935) were first to describe the "Tungus of Manchuria" in English. Shirokogoroff and his wife, both ethnographers, carried out research in the forests of the Amur River bend from 1915 to 1917. A few years later the Swedish-American anthropologist Ethel John Lindgren did extensive fieldwork in Daxing'anling (then known as the Greater Hinggan Mountains). Lindgren published several works on the "Reindeer Tungus of Manchuria," including her doctoral dissertation (Lindgren 1930, 1935, 1936, 1938).

With the Japanese invasion and founding of the state of Manchukuo, the area became largely inaccessible to researchers. In the New China, ethnographic studies of its northeastern region mainly mapped "minority nationalities," described their stage on the Marxist evolutionary ladder of societies, and investigated the social issues confronting their "socialist development." This situation prevailed until the departure of Mao Zedong, after which Deng Xiaoping embarked on his Reform and Opening Up campaign (started in 1979). The Japanese ethnographer Kazuyoshi Ohtsuka of Japan's National Museum of Ethnology was an early member of a new wave of foreign researchers conducting fieldwork in the region. His ethnography of the Ewenki, Oroqen, and other ethnic groups (Ohtsuka 1988) has become a valuable resource for Japanese scholars of the Aoluguya Ewenki.[4] Ethnologists Ingo Nentwig (1989, 1991, 2003), F. Georg Heyne (1989, 1994, 1999, 2003, 2007, 2009, 2013)[5] and Hugh Beach (2003, 2012) subsequently made field trips to Aoluguya in 1985, 1993, and 1997. Another important contribution to the English-language literature is an article by the Inner Mongolian anthropologist Naran Bilik (1996) based on research in Aoluguya in 1994.

There is of course no lack of Chinese (or Mandarin) writings on the Ewenki. Among the early ethnographies in Chinese was Qiu Pu's (1962) "The Primitive Social Organization of the Ewenki People."[6] The township government of Aoluguya later published "The Reindeer Oroqen," based on studies carried out in the 1930s by Haruka Nagata (1985). The Inner Mongolia Autonomous Region Editorial Team's "Survey of the Social History of the Ewenki" (Neimenggu Zizhiqu Bianji Zu 1986), part of a historical research series on China's various ethnic minority communities, is still among the most important Chinese works on the Ewenki published in the People's Republic. Works by Ewenki writers include Wure'ertu's (1998) edited book "Ewenki Narratives." Kong Fanzhi, a former government cadre in Aoluguya, has also contributed with several ethnographies (1994, 2002). In the past decade, and especially since the 2003 resettlement, renewed academic interest in the Reindeer Ewenki has resulted in several academic articles and books, still mainly in Chinese (e.g., Bai 2003; Chao and Wang 2002; Dong 2007; He 2007; Kalina 2006; Qi 2006; Xie 2010).

The authors contributing to this volume are either indigenous to the region or have carried out fieldwork among the Reindeer Ewenki since the late 1990s. One of the Chinese contributors is an ethnic Mongolian (Siqinfu), one belongs to the Oroqen minority (Bai Ying) and three are Reindeer Ewenki (Gu Xinjun, Gong Yu, and Weijia). Contributions originally written in Chinese have been translated and carefully edited. The book has four parts. The first, introductory part is a historical account based on fieldwork in old Aoluguya by Siqinfu. The second part, "Migrations: Reindeer Herding in Flux," comprises chapters by Tang Ge,

Åshild Kolås, and Aurore Dumont, all writing on contemporary practices and organization of reindeer herding. The third, "Representations:
Defining the Reindeer Ewenki Culture and Identity," consists of chapters by Zhang Rongde and Bai Ying, Xie Yuanyuan, and Richard Fraser,
all dealing with issues of identity and cultural representation. The final
part, "Local Voices," presents Ewenki contributions in the form of a
poem, an essay, and a short story.

Summarizing the recent history of the Reindeer Ewenki, Siqinfu
understands nomadic movement as both the Ewenki survival strategy
and their key response to the expansion of foreign forces. Toward the
end of the twentieth century this strategy became increasingly difficult,
however, as "ownerless land" ceased to exist and the influence of the
nation-state permeated all spaces. After the nationalization of land and
forests in the New China, sedentary lifestyles became the norm, and
movement was relegated to migration or resettlement. Siqinfu looks
back at the immense changes imposed on the Reindeer Ewenki while
they were based at what is now known as old Aoluguya from the mid
1960s until their relocation to new Aoluguya in 2003. Chinese mainstream writing on the Aoluguya Ewenki generally interprets their resettlement as part of their "development," but Siqinfu questions this
notion and instead grounds Ewenki experiences in the larger context of
China's rapid, unprecedented transformation during the past decades.

Forest pastures of the reindeer

In his chapter on contemporary reindeer herding, Tang Ge observes the
significant changes brought by the gradual transformation from hunting to reindeer herding. Not only has the main source of livelihood
changed, but the shift from hunting to herding has also greatly lowered
the rate of migration within the forest. Whereas hunting used to be the
main occupation of Ewenki men, now they work mainly in reindeer
management. In the past, Ewenki women looked after the reindeer
while the men went hunting; now, the women take care of the reindeer
in and around the campsite while men seek out the reindeer in distant
forest pastures, bringing them regularly back to the campsite. Tang Ge
argues that in addition to the predator attacks and poaching that directly cause high death rates among reindeer, the current lack of male
labor for herding is an important indirect cause for concern about the
future viability of reindeer herding.

Reindeer herding now centers on production of reindeer horn for use
in Chinese medicine, with a government-run enterprise still in charge

of cutting and marketing the reindeer horn (although restrictions on the marketing of antlers have recently been eased). As described in my own account of "ambiguities of the Aoluguya Ewenki,"[7] the nationwide decollectivization of farming and pastoralism was never fully implemented in Aoluguya, with vital implications for the reindeer herders' grazing rights and ownership of the reindeer. Ewenki reindeer herders find themselves in an ambiguous space where they are neither a hunting tribe (*shoulie buluo*) as they were in the past, nor true pastoralists (*mumin*). Meanwhile, different government departments' various handling of reindeer as domestic and wild animals is not just semantically significant but has very practical consequences for the management of reindeer husbandry.

In her chapter on "the many faces of nomadism," Aurore Dumont details how the Reindeer Ewenki have maintained and adapted their economy to the present situation. The Chinese state has significantly altered the mode of reindeer herding and use of land through planned economy and sedentarization. However, the author argues, adaptations of old economic forms still endure in the new environment. This chapter analyzes the continuities, changes, and substitutions that are now shaping the Ewenki economy and transhumant lifestyle. Taking into account the herders' sociocultural practices and adaptability to their natural environment, she explores how local people face the new challenges by developing their own adaptations and rearranging the social and spatial organization of nomadic camps. They do so with the help of the social and economic networks that Ewenki establish with Han people from the small towns and among themselves.

Representations of Reindeer Ewenki culture and identity

Writing on the Ewenki "passage from forest to state," Bai Ying and Zhang Rongde describe the museums that emerged and developed in Aoluguya Ewenki settlements as a government instrument intended to help a minority nationality realize modernization while simultaneously constructing the modernity of China. The advent of the museum thus reflects the passage of the Ewenki from the Daxing'anling forests into the fold of the multiethnic Chinese state. A review of museum development in the resettlement of the Reindeer Ewenki shows how a multiethnic state has realized its minority nationalities' unity and integrity while also constructing ethnic minorities as objects of governance. However, the role of the museum is changing, reflecting contemporary processes of social change. Since the late twentieth century, when China began socialist economic reforms and entered the global market, marketization has expanded its reach into minority areas, where museums have become an important resource in the production of ethnic visibility. Thus the role of museums for ethnic minorities has shifted from representation of a "development problem" in the modernizing China to market-driven production of visibility.

In her chapter on resettlement and Ewenki identity, Xie Yuanyuan describes how the 2003 relocation to new Aoluguya not only altered the hunting lifestyle as such but also significantly impacted notions of Ewenki identity. Contrary to the earlier relocations in 1957 and 1965, the hunters in 2003 were forced to lay down their guns and leave their hunting grounds behind. As described by Xie Yuanyuan, the Ewenki community falls into at least two different groups, in terms of their reactions to the resettlement. Modern hunters were strongly influenced by discourses of modernization and had thus already abandoned the traditional values of the forest lifestyle. Traditional hunters, however, still cherished their life in the forest and held the prospect of a modern life in disregard. In line with their preferences, traditional hunters never agreed with the ecological resettlement, whereas modern hunters not only agreed to it but conscientiously accepted mainstream values and conceptions of hunting and gathering as a backward, primitive relic of the past. They were therefore willing to support the ecological migration advocated by the local government and leave their seminomadic lifestyle behind for the promise of a modern life in the town. However, after the move they were dissatisfied with the conditions and facilities in the new settlement. The local government officials were aware of their views but also knew that these modern hunters would easily be placated by an offer of better services and conditions. They took a different approach to traditional hunters, who were merely ignored, largely because their views were more challenging and their complaints far more difficult to address.

In the final chapter on identity and representation, subtitled "Vernacular Ewenki Architecture and the State," Richard Fraser describes the use of the tent as an identity marker, offering insights into the changing nature of minority-state relations (see also Fraser 2010). Despite the state promulgation of the conical tent (Ewenki: *djiu*) as a marker of Reindeer Ewenki identity, the vernacular features of Ewenki architecture continue to be evident in the ridge tents adopted in recent decades (Figure 0.1). Unlike the state, Fraser finds, herders do not explicitly distinguish between traditional and nontraditional architecture.

Figure 0.1. Tents in the herding camp, January 2008, Alongshan. Photograph by Aurore Dumont.

Instead, transformations are experienced from within the exigencies of the reindeer-herding lifeworld, where herders make changes to their architecture when they see fit and acquire new materials if and when they become available. In this regard, the adoption of ridge tents and new houses should not be seen as a non-vernacular transformation, but rather as an inherent dimension of contemporary Ewenki architecture.

Local voices

Contributions by three members of the Aoluguya Ewenki community make up the final part of this volume. We shall let their words speak for themselves, briefly presenting the authors here. Weijia, who authored the poem in this volume, was born in 1965 in the Daxing'anling Forest and went to school in Aoluguya. His artistic talent was evident since childhood. Following in the footsteps of his older sister Ljuba, he was accepted as a student in the arts department of the Central University of Nationalities in Beijing in 1995. After studying traditional

Chinese painting for two years, he returned to the forest to live as a hunter-herder, poet, and painter. Weijia's paintings and poems portray the natural environment and wildlife of the forest, the Ewenki people, their campsites, and especially the reindeer.

Gong Yu, who wrote an essay for this volume, was born in 1981 in Aoluguya. Her Ewenki name is Niurika, after the last shaman. After graduating from secondary school, she left the settlement to attend teachers college, returning three years later to work as a teacher in the Aoluguya school. In 2001 she left again for studies at Inner Mongolia Normal University, graduating in 2009 with a master's degree in ethnic studies. Since then she has worked as a researcher at the Centre for Ethnicity, Culture and History, Hulun Bei'er College. She has also written for newspapers such as *Zhongguo Minzu* (China's Nationalities), *Zhongguo Qingnian Bao* (China's Youth Newspaper), and *Guangming Ribao* (Guangming Daily Newspaper). Her writings have focused on the traditional culture of her people, as a lifestyle attuned to the reindeer and the natural environment of the high cold mountain forest.

Gu Xinjun is the author of several short stories, including "Hunting along the Bei'erci River," reproduced here for the first time in English. Born in 1964 in Qiqian, he grew up in the hunting camps of the Daxing'anling taiga. After graduating from Inner Mongolia Agricultural College, he served as township leader of Aoluguya from 1992 until 2001, when he was offered a position in the United Front Work Department of China's Communist Party in Genhe County. He currently leads the Ethnic Affairs Committee of the Genhe National People's Congress. Gu Xinjun is also the deputy head of the Association of Ewenki Studies of Inner Mongolia. Several of his short stories have been published by the literary society in Genhe. "Hunting on the Bei'erci River" records the author's experiences in the spring of 1990, on a hunting trip down the Bei'erci River (Russian: Bystraja; also known as Jiliu) in a small wooden boat. Gu Xinjun's motivation for writing this story was to record the hunting practices of the Ewenki people, and in his own words, "let the Ewenki youth know about the old hunting culture."

As the editors of this volume, Xie Yuanyuan and I are happy to present a wide range of contributions, covering academic findings as well as the results of life experiences, including those of members of the Aoluguya community. We see this as the best approach to the book's objective, which is to raise interest in and awareness of the reindeer herders of China, and to let some of their voices reach out to a wider audience, offering a glimpse into the contemporary world of the people of Aoluguya.

Notes

1. We use the Chinese-mediated Latin transcription of the ethnonym, i.e., Ewenki, rather than a transcription directly from Tungusic, which would render the name as Evenki.
2. Alternative spellings of Hinggan are Hingan, Khinggan, and Khingan.
3. The term "Khamnigan" also defines a group of Tungus origin in Mongolia. According to the 2010 Chinese national census, Mongolians were still the largest ethnic minority group in Hulun Bei'er prefecture, with a population of 230,000. The total Ewenki population stood at 30,875 in 2010, of which the Reindeer Ewenki or Yakut was decidedly the smallest group, with a population of only around 250 people. The Solon was the largest Ewenki group, numbering about 27,000, while the Tungus was the second largest with about 2,000 members.
4. Two other notable contributions to the Japanese literature are *Dai koanreitan ken* (Daxing'anling Exploration), edited by Kinji Imanishi (1991), and *Hoppo kiba minzoku Orochon* (The Oroqen: The Northern Horsemen) by Haruka Nagata (1969), historical accounts of Ewenki culture and livelihoods as documented by the Japanese.
5. F. Georg Heyne has also drawn substantially on works by the Russian ethnographer Anatoliĭ Makarovich Kaĭgorodov (1927–1998) (see Kaĭgorodov 1968, 1970).
6. Qiu Pu also authored the monograph *The Oroqens: China's Nomadic Hunters,* published in English in 1983 by Beijing Foreign Language Press.
7. The chapter is based on the article "Ewenki Reindeer Herding as Exception," published in *Human Organization* (Kolås 2011).

References

Abe, Yoshiko. 2005. "Hunting and Butchery Patterns of the Evenki in Northern Transbaikalia, Russia." Ph.D. diss., Department of Anthropology, Stony Brook University, New York.

Anderson, David G. 2010. "Shamanistic Revival in a Post-Socialist Landscape: Luck and Ritual among Zabaikal'e Orochen-Evenkis." In *Landscape and Culture in Northern Eurasia,* ed. Peter Jordan. Walnut Creek, CA: Left Coast Press.

———. 2006a. "Dwellings, Storage and Summer Site Structure among Siberian Orochen Evenkis: Hunter-Gatherer Vernacular Architecture under Post-Socialist Conditions." *Norwegian Archaeological Review* 39, no. 1: 1–26.

———. 2006b. "Is Siberian Reindeer Herding in Crisis? Living with Reindeer Fifteen Years after the End of State Socialism." *Nomadic Peoples* 10, no. 2: 87–104.

———. 2000. *Identity and Ecology in Arctic Siberia: The Number One Reindeer Brigade.* Oxford: Oxford University Press.

———. 1991. "Turning Hunters into Herders: A Critical Examination of Soviet Development Policy among the Evenki of Southeastern Siberia." *Arctic* 44, no. 1: 12–22.

Bai Lan. 2003. *Bei zhongguo — na yuanqu de luqun* [North China: Faraway Reindeer]. Kunming: Yunnan renmin chubanshe [Yunnan People's Publishing House].

Beach, Hugh. 2012. "Milk and Antlers: A System of Partitioned Rights and Multiple Holders of Reindeer in Northern China." In *Who Owns The Stock? Collective and Multiple Property Rights in Animals,* ed. Anatoly M. Khazanov and Günther Schlee. Oxford: Berghahn Books.

———. 2003. "Milk and Antlers: Chinese Dual-Ownership System Remains a Hopeful Model Despite Forced Relocation from Olguya (Inner Mongolia)." *Cultural Survival Quarterly* 27, no. 1: 33–35.

Bilik, Naran. 1996. "Emotion Gets Lost: An Ewenki Case." *Inner Asia* 1, no. 1: 63–70.

Brandisauskas, Donatas. 2009. *Leaving Footprints in the Taiga: Enacted and Emplaced Power and Luck among Orochen-Evenki of the Zabaikal Region in East Siberia.* Ph.D. diss., University of Aberdeen.

———. 2007. "Symbolism and Ecological Uses of Fire among Orochen-Evenki." *Sibirica* 6, no. 1: 95–119.

Chao Ke and Wang Lizhen. 2002. *Ewenkezu zongjiao xinyang yu wenhua* [Ewenki Religion and Culture]. Beijing: Zhongguo minzu daxue chubanshe [China Nationality University Press].

Dong Liansheng. 2007. *Zhongguo zuihou de shoulie buluo* [The Last Hunting Tribe of China]. Hohhot: Neimenggu renmin chubanshe [Inner Mongolia People's Publishing House].

Ermolova, Nadezhda. 2003. "Evenki Reindeer-Herding: A History." *Cultural Survival Quarterly* 27, no. 1 ('The Troubled Taiga'): 23–24.

Fondahl, Gail. 1998. *Gaining Ground? Evenkis, Land and Reform in Southeastern Siberia.* Boston: Allyn and Bacon.

———. 1989. *Native Economy and Northern Development: Reindeer Husbandry in Transbaykalia.* Ph.D. diss., Department of Geography, University of California, Berkeley.

Fraser, Richard. 2010. "Forced Relocation amongst the Reindeer-Evenki of Inner Mongolia." *Inner Asia* 12, no. 2: 317–346.

He Meng. 2007. *Qianlun Aoluguya Ewenke liemin de shengtai yimin* [A Brief Discussion of Aoluguya's Ewenki Hunters Ecological Migration] *Ewenke yanjiu* 1, no. 1: 35–38.

Heyne, F. Georg. 2013. "On the Symbolism of the Shaman's Costume among the Reindeer Evenki in Manchuria." *Shaman* 21, nos. 1–2: 19–66.

———. 2009. "Among Taiga Hunters and Shamans. Reminiscences Concerning my Friend, the Scholar of Manchuria, Anatoliĭ Makarovich Kaĭgorodov (1927–1998)." *Shaman* 17, nos. 1–2: 53–78.

———. 2007. "Notes on Blood Revenge among the Reindeer Evenki of Manchuria (Northeast China)." *Asian Folklore Studies* 66, nos. 1–2: 165–178.

———. 2003. "Frauen, die Geister beherrschen. Geister und Schamaninnen bei den Rentier-Ewenken in den Grossen Hingan Bergen (Nordostchina)." *Anthropos* 98, no. 2: 319–340.

———. 1999. "The Social Significance of the Shaman amongst the Chinese Reindeer Evenki." *Asian Folklore Studies* 58, no. 2: 377–395.

———. 1994. "Bärenjagd und Bärenzeremoniell bei den Rentier-Ewenken in der Taiga Nordost-Chinas." *Jahrbuch des Museums für Völkerkunde zu Leipzig* 40: 122–135.

———. 1989. "Die Jagd in den Wäldern des Großen Hinggan. Ein Beitrag zur Wirtschaftsethnologie der chinesischen Rentier-Ewenken." *Jahrbuch des Museums für Völkerkunde zu Leipzig* 38: 32–100.

Imanishi, Kinji, ed. 1991. *Dai koanreitan ken* [Daxing'anling Exploration]. Asahi Bunko.

Istvan, Santha. 2005. "Somewhere in Between: Social Ties on the Borderland between Taiga and Steppe to the West of Lake Baikal." In *Rebuilding Identities: Pathways to Reform in Post-Soviet Siberia*, ed. E. Kasten. Berlin: Dietrich Reimer Verlag.

Kaĭgorodov, Anatoliĭ Makarovich. 1970. "Svad'ba v tajge." [Wedding in the Taiga] *Sovetskaja Etnografija*, no. 3: 153–161.

———. 1968. "Evenki v Trechrec'e (Po lichnym nabliudeniiam)" [The Ewenki of the Three Rivers Area (Personal Observations)] *Sovetskaja Etnografija*, no. 4: 123–131.

Kalina. 2006. *Xunlu ewenkeren wenhua yanjiu* [Studies of the Culture of Ewenki Reindeer Herders]. Shenyang: Liaoning renmin chubanshe [Liaoning People's Publishing House].

Kolås, Åshild. 2011. "Reclaiming the Forest: Ewenki Reindeer Herding as Exception." *Human Organization* 70, no. 4: 397–404.

Kong Fanzhi. 2002. *Aoluguya ewenke ren de wenhua bianqian* [The Cultural Change of the Aoluguya Ewenki]. Tianjin: Tianjin guji chubanshe [Tianjin Ancient Books Publishing House].

———. 1994. *Aoluguya de ewenke ren* [The Ewenki of Aoluguya]. Tianjin: Tianjin guji chubanshe [Tianjin Ancient Books Publishing House].

Lavrillier, Alexandra. 2010. "The Creation and Persistence of Cultural Landscapes among the Siberian Evenk: Two Conceptions of Sacred Space." In *Landscape and Culture in Northern Eurasia*, ed. Peter Jordan. Walnut Creek, CA: Left Coast Press.

Lindgren, Ethel J. 1938. "An Example of Culture Contact without Conflict: Reindeer Tungus and Cossacks of North-Western Manchuria." *American Anthropologist*, n.s. 40, no. 4, part 1: 605–621.

———. 1936. *Notes on the Reindeer Tungus of Manchuria. Their Names, Groups, Administration and Shamans*. PhD diss., Cambridge.

———. 1935. "The Reindeer Tungus of Manchuria." *Journal of the Royal Central Asian Society* 22, no. 2: 221–231.

———. 1930. "North-Western Manchuria and the Reindeer-Tungus." *Geographical Journal* 75: 518–536.

Nagata, Haruka 1985. *Xunlu Elunchunzu* [The Reindeer Oroqen]. Aoluguya: Aoluguya ewenke minzu xiang zhengfu [Aoluguya Ewenki Ethnic Township Government].

———. 1969. *Hoppo kiba minzoku orochon* [The Oroqen: The Northern Horsemen]. Mainichi Shinbunsha.

Neimenggu Zizhiqu Bianji Zu [Inner Mongolia Autonomous Region Editorial Team]. 1986. *Ewenkezu shehui lishi diaocha* [Survey of the Social History of the

Ewenki]. Hohhot: Neimenggu renmin chubanshe [Inner Mongolia People's Publishing House].

Nentwig, Ingo. 2003. "Reminiscences about the Reindeer Herders of China." *Cultural Survival Quarterly* 27, no. 1: 36–38.

———. 1991. "Jagd und Wanderviehwirtschaft in der Taiga Chinas: Zur Situation der Rentier-Ewenken im Großen Hinggan-Gebirge." In *Nomaden, Mobile Tierhaltung. Zur gegenwärtigen Lage von Nomaden und zu den Problemen und Chancen mobiler Tierhaltung*, ed. F. Scholz. Berlin: Verlag das Arabische Buch.

———. 1989. "Bericht von einer Exkursion zur Ewenkischen Gemeinde Aoluguya im Linken Ergun-Banner der Inneren Mongolei (VR China)." *Jahrbuch des Museums für Völkerkunde zu Leipzig* 38: 101–127.

Ohtsuka, Kazuyoshi. 1988. *Sogen to jukai no min* [The People of the Vast Taiga Forest]. Shinjuku Shobo.

Pöyry. 2008. Aoluguya Ethnic Reindeer Resort Master Plan. Beijing: Pöyry (Beijing) Consulting.

Qi Huijiun. 2006. *Xunlu ewenke ren shengtai yimin de minzuxue kaocha* [Ethnographic Survey of the Reindeer Ewenki People's Ecological Migration]. *Manyu Yanjiu* 1, no. 1: 98–105.

Qiu Pu. 1983. *The Oroqens: China's Nomadic Hunters*. Beijing: Foreign Language Press.

———. 1962. *Ewenke ren de yuanshi shehui xingtai* [The Primitive Social Organization of the Ewenki People]. Beijing: Zhonghua shuju [Zhonghua Book Company].

Shirokogoroff, Sergei Mikhailovich. 1935. *Psychomental Complex of the Tungus*. London: Kegan Paul, Trench, Trubner & Co.

———. 1929. *Social Organization of the Northern Tungus*. Oosterhout: Anthropological Publications.

Siqinfu. 2000. "Chugoku tonak aievuenki hito no shakai keizai henka 2" [Socioeconomic Change among the Reindeer Ewenki of China, 2], *Social and Environmental Research* 5: 173–186.

———. 1999. "Chugoku tonak aievuenki hito no shakai keizai henka 1" [Socioeconomic change among the Reindeer Ewenki of China, 1], *Social and Environmental Research* 4: 161–170.

Sirina, Anna Anatol'evna. 2006. *Katanga Evenkis in the 20th Century and the Ordering of their Lifeworld*. Edmonton: Canadian Circumpolar Institute Press.

Vitebsky, Piers. 2005. *Reindeer People: Living with Animals and Spirits in Siberia*. London: Harper Collins.

———. 1990. "Centralized Decentralization: The Ethnography of Remote Reindeer Herders under Perestroika." *Cahiers du monde russe et soviétique* 31, nos. 2–3: 345–358.

Wure'ertu. 1998. *Shushuo ewenke* [Ewenki Narratives]. Hohhot: Yuanfang chubanshe [Yuanfang Publishing House].

Xie Yuanyuan. 2010. *Shengtai yimin zhengce yu difang zhengfu shijian: yi aoluguya ewenke shengtai yimin weili* [The Ecological Migration Policy and Its Application by Local Authorities: A Case Study of the Aoluguya Ewenki Ecological Migration]. Beijing: Beijing daxue chubanshe [Peking University Press].

PART I

Encountering the Ewenki

1

FROM NOMADS TO SETTLERS

A History of the Aoluguya Ewenki (1965–1999)

Siqinfu

The unique culture and lifestyle of the Aoluguya Ewenki has caught the attention of many Chinese and overseas researchers. In 2003, the Aoluguya community's relocation from its settlement of nearly four decades (1965–2003) was featured on the national news and in several programs on China Central Television (CCTV). This generated a huge interest in the Aoluguya Ewenki, and concern for their fate. The attention is welcome, but if we aspire to a better future, we should listen to the people of Aoluguya and try to understand the essence of the "history" imposed on them since sedentarization and development policies were first initiated in the 1950s. The key pieces of their own stories are still missing. In order to recover and build their own stories, thereby locating themselves meaningfully within the larger history, their continuing role in that history needs to be reconsidered.

This chapter, based on research carried out between 1996 and 2000, focuses on the changes confronting the Aoluguya Ewenki between 1965 and 2000. It questions the driving forces behind these changes and describes how the Aoluguya Ewenki have responded. My research started in the summer of 1996, when I was studying environmental anthropology at Kanazawa University in Japan. I first encountered the Aoluguya Ewenki through the Ewenki author Wure'ertu. By that time, large-scale development of Daxing'anling, begun in the 1950s, had transformed the area's ecological features. Many Ewenki, Oroqen, and Daur had already left their homes in the Daxing'anling forest to work as farmers or live in the city. Daxing'anling, once so important to Chinese socialist construction, was still China's largest timber base. However, declining forest yields and growing overseas timber imports were bringing this role to an end. When I first visited Aoluguya, the Ewenki used the settlement as a base for hunting in the forests of the Mangui Forestry Bureau, where they also herded their reindeer. I first saw reindeer at Balajie's camp and was immediately captured by their grace. From then on I was also drawn to the Aoluguya Ewenki, who love their reindeer. I conducted fieldwork among the Aoluguya Ewenki five times between 1996 and 2000, for sixteen months altogether. On trips to the field I collected a wealth of unpublished government and private documents. Meanwhile, I lived with the Ewenki and conducted numerous interviews with people of various age groups, from young to old.

Since the Ewenki first moved to Aoluguya in the mid 1960s, they have experienced the turmoil of the Cultural Revolution and witnessed government policy change from a violent politics of ideological conflict to a market economy and culture of mass production and consumption spreading rapidly throughout Chinese society. China actively increased exchanges with other countries by developing communications, trade, tourism, and academic exchanges. The population increased its awareness, diversified its values, and became more mobile. People shifted their investments from government capital (fostering a "revolutionary identity" to succeed in political circles) to economic capital (pursuing other goals as they increase their wealth) and cultural capital (seeking academic qualifications). On the other hand, the atrophy of public space through the infiltration of the market economy and freedom of choice made it more difficult to sustain and preserve the languages, cultures, and lifestyles of ethnic minorities (Siqinfu 2004), even as massive urbanization and industrialization caused resource shortages. The plunder and exploitation of resources spread nationally, leading to an unprecedented expulsion of farmers and pastoralists (mainly ethnic minorities) from their land.

The year 2008 was historic for the Chinese government and people. Not only did China host the Olympics—the hundred-year dream—it was also the thirtieth anniversary of the introduction of the market economy, the Reform and Opening Up policy. Debate continues on how to evaluate this thirty-year history, but over these years China has undoubtedly developed a presence that the world cannot ignore. There is overwhelming agreement that the living standard of ordinary Chinese people has improved significantly. Yet China's economic growth and development has also wreaked considerable environmental damage, and the Chinese authorities are often criticized for endangering people's health and safety. Meanwhile, a strong focus on the story of the majority has suppressed the telling of "small stories" in many different languages, each of them colorful and unique, such as the story of the Aoluguya Ewenki.

Who are the Aoluguya Ewenki?

After asserting their claim to the name "Ewenki," the hunters of the E'erguna Banner were incorporated into the official Chinese ethnic classification as Ewenki in 1957 (Hahe'er 1991: 130–135). According to oral history, until about three hundred years ago the ancestors of the Aoluguya Ewenki lived in the Lena River basin, hunting, fishing, and keeping reindeer for transportation. After Russia invaded Siberia in the seventeenth century, the lifestyle changed over time in response to the forced payment of *yasak* (fur tribute), indirect Russian rule through the clan chiefs, the introduction of Russian Orthodox Christianity, and the growing importance of the fur trade. From the late eighteenth century, the Aoluguya Ewenki ancestors, feeling pressured by the Russians and other groups, moved farther and farther south seeking new hunting grounds. In the early nineteenth century, they crossed the Amur River and were "surprised by the abundant game" (as expressed in a poem by Njura, the last shaman). Thus they made the Daxing'anling area their new home (Siqinfu 1999).

Between the 1930s and the end of World War II, the forests of Daxing'anling were under Japanese colonial rule. Then, in the late 1940s the area was integrated into socialist China. In 1957, the government established an "ethnic township" in Qiqian—the old fur trading post where Ewenki hunters traded with Russian, and later Han Chinese, merchants. Qiqian was to be the hunters' settlement and the base for implementing the ethnic policy of the New China. After the alliance between the Soviet Union and China broke up in the early 1960s, the Ewenki hunters were forcibly moved away from the border. The Aoluguya Ewenki Ethnic Township was founded in 1965 as the hunters' new "home."

In the late 1960s, a hunters' production brigade was set up, the reindeer were declared government property, and their antlers were henceforth marketed under the socialist planned economy (Aoluguya Minzu Xiang Dang'an 1998: 88). Yet the income from antlers was of little importance to the Aoluguya Ewenki before the early 1980s. Their hunting lifestyle was not only their most important economic activity but a significant aspect of their social life, culture, and beliefs (Siqinfu 1999).

In the early 1980s, a wave of new development rushed over the region under China's Reform and Opening Up policy. By this time the transportation network, including a railway, highways, and numerous logging roads, reached deep into the forests. Economic growth had created a growing market for wild game and wildlife-based Chinese medicines, so poachers' illegal activities increased and much of the region's wildlife diminished or became extinct (Chen 1993). Meanwhile, loggers cut the virgin forests inhabited by the Ewenki—among the last in all of Daxing'anling. The forest resources were rapidly being depleted. During this period, government policies changed again and the brigade was dismantled. In 1984 the local government accordingly introduced the Reindeer Breeding Contract Responsibility System (Aoluguya Minzu Xiang Dang'an 1998: 114). After this, reindeer breeding became the key income source of the Aoluguya Ewenki.

The ethnic township

The old Aoluguya ethnic township was located in the very north of Genhe County, 17 km from the town of Mangui and the seat of Mangui Forestry Bureau, the northernmost production department of the Daxing'anling Forestry Company. The ethnic township covered an area of 1,096 m^2, mostly forested with Xingan larch, white birch, Mongolian pine, and other trees. Mangui is located at the railway's end station, and in the 1990s a single forestry road ran from the railway station through the middle of Mangui town and on to Aoluguya. West of the road were the ethnic township government building, a residential area, and the two township enterprises—a wood processing factory and a distillery. The hunters' housing area, the "ethnic school," and the Ewenki Hunting Cultural Museum were located on the east side. The post office and the bank were next to the museum, adjacent to the market. In the late 1980s, small shops and restaurants, run mostly by Han Chinese, sprang up around the settlement. In 1994, telephones were installed in the residential areas with national and local government assistance, and the residents also got television reception. The township was designated an Inner Mongolia Autonomous Region tourist area due to its unique "Aoluguya Ewenki culture" and beautiful nature.

According to the township's statistics, the population in 1999 was 569, and in ethnic terms, the Aoluguya Ewenki accounted for 167 people in 51 households. This population fell into three employment groups: 69 people in 19 households worked in the township, 62 people in 19 households were contract workers (i.e., herders and their families who depended on reindeer for income), and 36 people in 13 households were unemployed and lived on government assistance.

Citizens of the township spoke Chinese in everyday life. Lessons at the Ewenki ethnic school had in fact been taught in Chinese since its establishment in the 1950s. At the time of my fieldwork, approximately

80 percent of Aoluguya Ewenki youth under the age of twenty were unable to speak Ewenki. Most of those who spoke Ewenki as their everyday language were over the age of forty. This was due in part to changes in the ethnic composition of the township population, and to the language of teaching in the school.

In the late 1990s, the fiscal structure established in the 1950s under the Communist Party's ethnic policy was largely unchanged. The receipt of salaries, subsidies, and other government funding continued, and the two township enterprises still operated, though at a loss. However, in 1994 the central government introduced a policy of decentralization of taxation and service provision, in effect forcing local governments to cover their expenditures through local revenues. The amount of financial aid to the township thus dropped due to the financial problems of Hulun Bei'er League, which increased pressure on the township government to become financially independent.

Reindeer herding

In October 1998, nineteen reindeer-herding households renewed their Reindeer Breeding Contract with the township Hunting Office (Chinese: *Lieye ju*). However, not all Ewenki who entered into a contract were actually herding reindeer in the forest. In 1999, I counted 31 people who spent most of the year at one of four forest camps, herding a total of 585 of their own and relatives' reindeer

In principle, the Aoluguya Ewenki engage in free grazing, leaving the reindeer to freely forage for food year-round. However, in the 1990s a large number of reindeer were snared in traps for game, many of which were set by Forest Bureau employees. Another problem was poisoning deaths of reindeer from eating insecticides spread to prevent forest damage. Moreover, traffic accidents were on the rise, so herders had to keep constant watch over their reindeer. Herders adjust their activities to the annual cycle of nature and the changing needs of the reindeer. The following describes the seasonal cycle as observed in the 1990s.

In January and February, the coldest period, temperatures may drop to below -50°C, and the reindeer feed mainly on lichen. The herd does not roam far from the campsite, so the reindeer are easy to manage. The herders give the reindeer only salt—not only for nutrition, but as a way to control the reindeer, to persuade them to come to the herder. In late February, velvet antlers start growing on the bulls. In March, the reindeer hooves need to be checked frequently, as they are susceptible to injuries related to the snow surface on the sunny side of the mountain, which melts during the day and freezes at night. As April arrives, the herders move the herd to a location near water and abundant growth of lichen in preparation for the calving season, which starts later in the month. New-born calves require daily attention, as they are especially prone to attacks by wolves, bears, and other carnivores, and also risk falling into rivers and drowning. At this time the reindeer cows also start growing velvet antlers. In May the reindeer feed on grasses and tree shoots, such as willow and white birch, as well as lichen. At this time they begin shedding their winter fur and developing a lighter summer coat.

The cows can be milked as early as two weeks after giving birth, from May until October. Cows more than three years old are milked, usually every morning. The milk is high in fat content, but even at their peak production in July and August, the daily amount per cow is as little as 400–500 ml. Throughout the summer, the herders light bonfires near the campsite to protect the reindeer from mosquitoes, gnats, and other insects (Figure 1.1). Temperatures often rise to over 30°C, so the campsite is moved to a breezy, waterside location. The cutting of antlers lasts from late June until late July, a time when the reindeer are prone to illness and thus require regular checks. In mid August they can start feeding on their favorite food, mushrooms. At this time of year they roam over a wide area, so tending them is difficult.

Figure 1.1. Looking after the reindeer, July 2008, Alongshan. Photograph by Tashi Nyima.

As September arrives, mornings and nights start to get colder, and the reindeer mating season begins. The bulls form small herds and fight over the cows, and are most susceptible to injury during this period. The herders keep the cows in stockades during the day and let them out to graze in the evening. Bonfires are no longer necessary, and late in the month the reindeer begin shedding their summer fur as their winter fur comes in. The mating season ends in October. The reindeer return to eating mainly lichen, and milking is less frequent, so they require less care. Winter begins in November. The herders must now find a winter location, where they usually settle from late November or early December to March the following year. To decide such a location, they apply two main criteria: proximity to water, and abundant forage for the reindeer.

In earlier times, Ewenki society valued reindeer highly, using them as wedding gifts, in shamanistic ceremonies, and in funerals. As described by Shirokogoroff (1929: 63): "Reindeer play an extremely important role in religious ceremonies as the mediators between man and the gods. They are used to transport the souls of the dead to the next world. Special reindeer carried the objects representing the divine spirits and had no responsibility or work. The reindeer also performed an important role in Tungus folklore. It was forbidden to kill them with guns." Until the early 1980s, reindeer were used as pack animals when moving and also were ridden (mainly by the elderly, children, and sometimes women).[1] Reindeer were also essential for hunting. The main game, moose and red deer, are large animals weighing 250 to 300 kg, too heavy for the hunters to haul back to camp themselves. Therefore the Ewenki never left for a hunt without their reindeer. However, after development of the forest road network and introduction of ridge tents and iron stoves (both too heavy for reindeer to carry), the Ewenki turned to motorized vehicles for transportation.

In 1967, when the government declared the reindeer state property, it also set a fixed purchasing price for reindeer horn. This remained almost unchanged until 1982. The contract system was introduced in 1984, and by the 1990s antlers had become some herders' only source of income. Despite the reindeer's increasing economic significance in the 1980s and 1990s, their cultural and ideological value slowly eroded due to criticism of shamanism and other aspects of Ewenki traditional culture, the introduction of schooling, and cultural influences from mainstream society. As reindeer lost their cultural value and role as a mode of transportation, they were reduced to a mere source of cash income.

Antler production: The key cash income

In 1984, under the national government's Contract Responsibility System, the ethnic township government ended the Labor Distribution System, a labor point system that had been enforced for many years, and introduced the Reindeer Breeding Contract Responsibility System (hereafter the "contract system"). This system had two principles. First, it separated ownership rights from usage rights. The township government, representing what was then called the Hunting Industry Agency, managed ownership rights, while usage rights to the reindeer were contracted to the herders. Second, the contract system introduced "work performance distribution," a new distribution system that distributed profits according to the quality and volume of labor. According to these principles, the Hunting Industry Agency and the Ewenki "hunter"[2] who wanted to become a contracted herder would sign a contract under which each herder could graze thirty reindeer, and the herder and agency shared the profits at a ratio of 6:4. Further, the Hunting Industry Agency was to provide various services to the herders.

At the annual meeting of the Hunting Industry Agency in October 1993, the herders appealed to the ethnic township government to review the distribution system and improve camp services. In the spring of 1994, exactly ten years after the contract system was introduced, the government responded by renewing the existing contracts, including the following details:

a) The two principles established in 1984 remained unchanged and effective.

b) In principle, the number of contractors would not expand beyond the current number (partly because of insufficient reindeer), but adjusting the numbers within households was permitted (on condition that members were not employed in other jobs).

c) The Hunting Agency was renamed the Hunting Office. The Hunting Office would receive guidance from the ethnic township government, but would be an economically independent identity. In line with these organizational changes, the four officers who received salaries from the ethnic township were to become full-time employees of the Hunting Office, which would be staffed by eight full-time employees in total. The ¥50,000 in aid provided by the Forestry Bureau for the Aoluguya Ewenki would now help cover the Hunting Office's operating costs.

d) The antler income distribution was revised from 6:4 to 7:3; that is, the herders were to receive 70 percent of the income and the Hunting Office, 30 percent.

e) In principle, herders could not sell reindeer. However, since the income from antlers had become unstable, herders could sell reindeer to maintain their minimum standard of living if they applied by the "official procedures" (unspecified) and received permission from the ethnic township and the Hunting Office.

As for the selling of reindeer, at the time bulls fetched approximately ¥8,000, and cows approximately ¥5,000. The Hunting Office and the contractor would each receive half the proceeds from such a sale. Buyers were chiefly zoos, herbal medicine companies from Jilin Province, and local Han Chinese.

Every June and July, Hunting Office employees visited the camps to cut reindeer antlers, assisted by the camp's male herders. On average, each bull yielded 6 to 7 kg of antlers and each cow, 4 to 5 kg. The bull antlers were cut first. After a reindeer was caught, one person pulled on both rear legs to keep the reindeer from getting up from the ground. Another sat on the upper part of the reindeer's body, holding down its front legs and locking its neck, and a third sawed off its antlers. Until the early 1990s, the reindeer was restrained between two poles while its antlers were cut, but during my fieldwork this method was not used, despite it being extremely safe for the reindeer, because it was "too much trouble." The June temperatures in Daxing'anling are quite hot and disease spreads easily. To prevent various infections, the herders tied a thin cord around the antler base to avoid profuse bleeding and then applied ash to the wound. Weak reindeer were given an injection to prevent infections.

In September 1999, nineteen Aoluguya Ewenki households comprising sixty-two individuals were dependent on 585 reindeer for their livelihood. The Hunting Office was located in a two-story building with offices on the first floor and antler processing facilities on the second. All antlers collected at the camps were processed there. Until the 1980s, the processing was done by hand, but later a drying machine and other machinery were used.

As detailed below, it takes about two months to process raw antlers into products. First the antlers are sorted into large, medium and small (because the boiling time varies) and boiled for approximately three minutes. Then they are left to dry in a breezy room out of the sun for around a week, and after that, dried further in the drying machine.

This process is repeated six to eight times until the product is finished. About one and a half kilograms of raw antlers produces half a kilogram of dried reindeer horn. The antlers were once sold sliced (to fetch a higher price) but are now sold in their finished form in response to buyers' demands.

Until the late 1980s, the Hunting Office sold the antlers through the Foreign Trading Office in Genhe, which first bought the antlers in 1967, commercialized them, and as of 1984 marketed them. In the early 1990s, the Foreign Trading Office was in effect dissolved and the Hunting Office started selling the products directly. Ties with the Foreign Trading Office were severed, because it was maintained as part of the socialist planned economy.

Aoluguya had the only antler-producing facility in China, and until the mid 1990s, selling the antlers was extremely easy because buyers journeyed to the area. The main antler buyers at the time were individuals who sold them as herbal medicine ingredients in South Korea and China. However, heightened awareness of wildlife preservation around the world complicated exports of nutritional supplements made from antlers because the Washington Convention prohibited the trade of wildlife and wildlife products. Today these nutritional supplements are even harder to sell due both to constant development and introduction of new nutritional supplements in an expanding market, and to the entry of Siberian antlers on the Chinese market.

As mentioned, the Hunting Office was the party with whom the reindeer herders signed contracts. The contract stipulated that the office was in charge of production, processing, and sales of antlers, and was to provide contractors with vehicle transportation while herding. Each October, representatives of the ethnic township and related Genhe county organizations, the Hunting Office, the reindeer herding contractors, and their families assembled at an annual meeting where the conditions were assessed and contractors declared their income from antlers. The following is a summary of the meeting held on 3 October 1997:

a) The price per 500 g of antler dropped from ¥800–900 in 1996 to ¥400–450 in 1997, when Siberian Evenki antlers entered the Chinese market. The Hunting Office, which had not grasped the situation, had forecast a price ¥50 higher than the 1996 average of ¥850 per 500 g, so it had no buyers. The local government and the ethnic township government promised to allocate funds to compensate the contractors' losses at 30 percent. Some contractors proposed full independence from the Hunting Office, but most contractors disagreed with the motion.

b) Twelve reindeer were sold from a herd tended by four households, who divided the proceeds.
c) The herders and their families voiced dissatisfaction with cor-
ruption among the Hunting Office representatives and their failure to fulfill their contractual obligation to transport belongings
when camps moved and to transport foodstuffs from the ethnic
township to camps once a month.

These excerpts show that by the late 1990s, reindeer herding faced
problems, some of them structural or institutional, others stemming
from serious social issues within Aoluguya Ewenki society itself. As
described below, the problems included destruction of natural habitats and damage to herds caused by poachers. Moreover, due to the
increasing significance of market forces, the ethnic policy under which
the Aoluguya Ewenki contracted for the right to herd reindeer was rendered nonfunctional. The herders were up against the rapidly changing Chinese nutritional supplement market, where reliance on a single
product, reindeer horn, made them vulnerable.

Next I will explicate four main challenges to the future of reindeer
herding, drawn from my observations in the 1990s: the dramatic decline
in reindeer numbers, the lack of successors to herding, social problems
such as alcohol addiction, and problems concerning the environment
and poaching.

A declining reindeer population

During the 1990s, the number of reindeer fell from 924 in 1992 to 585 in
1999.[3] This can only be described as paradoxical, considering that the
herders made concerted efforts to keep numbers as high as possible
and improve their antler production.

Prior to the mid 1980s, the main reasons for reindeer population decline were infectious diseases; predators; human activity (e.g., poaching and the Forestry Bureau's use of pesticides); animal sales; natural
hazards; and human consumption. Natural hazards bear no direct relation to this chapter's principal theme, but it is relevant that ethnic
township and local government officials believed natural hazards to
be the chief cause of the reindeer's decline and viewed them as largely
due to the "primitive" herding methods of the Ewenki. However, the
government statistics construed traffic accidents and pesticides as "natural hazards." This type of error was not a technical mistake; rather, it
derived from an administrative framework that freed the Forestry Bu-

reau and ethnic township from responsibility for deaths due to natural hazards. According to the Ewenki, the number of reindeer lost to actual natural hazards changed little from the 1980s to the 1990s.

According to herders, each household needed at least thirty-five and as many as fifty reindeer to make a living from antlers alone in the market economy. Only a minority of the herders met this condition. As of September 1999, four of the nineteen herding households had income from sources other than reindeer, and the other fifteen did not. Moreover, nine of these fifteen households had debts (varying from ¥6,000 to ¥29,000) to the ethnic township, Hunting Office, and private individuals. Six of these households were also dependent on government aid. In fact, over 80 percent of poor households (whose members had neither reindeer nor jobs, and lived off government assistance) were former reindeer herders. The decline in living standards among reindeer herders was not due to reduced antler earnings alone, but also to diminished hunting income and their inability to provide meat for their own consumption. Although market economic development had triggered a five- to sixfold increase in the cost of living (including education and medical expenses) since the early 1980s, government assistance had actually decreased.

According to ethnic township statistics, from 1992 to 1999 income from reindeer sales made up about 28 percent of the total income from reindeer herding. Such numbers were unprecedented. Of the 118 reindeer sold during this time, 61 were sold at the request of the local government and the ethnic township (primarily for use in zoos and events like the Inner Mongolia Autonomous Region 50th anniversary and the Ewenki Autonomous Banner 40th anniversary). In 1996, the ethnic township imported 28 reindeer from Russia and procured 30 reindeer from the Aoluguya Ewenki to improve breeding. Reindeer herders also sold an additional 27 reindeer on their own. When selling reindeer, herders must notify the Hunting Office of their intent to sell and obtain permission. Although the provision of 30 reindeer was compulsory for "improving reindeer breeds for the sake of the Aoluguya Ewenki," 88 of the total 118 reindeer were sold by the herders' own volition (albeit partially in response to government requests).

The widespread phenomenon of selling reindeer relates directly to the "rationalism" pervading the younger generations. In their eyes, a reindeer that dies a natural death is a "wasted asset," so it is more economical to sell an old or barren reindeer. However, the root cause of increased reindeer sales was herders' lack of other options to provide for themselves. Rationalist herders were still few; middle-aged herders—the core herding labor force—saw reindeer as more than just economic assets. These women and men were deeply attached to their reindeer and did not believe in selling them. To be sure, the market economy had already affected middle-aged and older herders to some degree, but at the very least, reindeer herding held more significance for them than mere economic gain. But although rationalist thinking coexisted with consciousness of traditional values, the market economy was clearly eroding the latter.

Lack of successors to herding

During my fieldwork I found that although twenty-six Ewenki men and women aged 18–30 were unemployed, only five or six of them helped herd reindeer in the camps. In other words, the decline in herders discussed here is unrelated to the loss of hands to the workforce outside the township. Rather, the camps lacked workers despite the existence of a potential labor supply. I found that nine women aged 40–50 comprised the core work force of reindeer herding. Even though women and men in their twenties and thirties accounted for over half the campsite populations, they were not the main labor force. Herders over forty said, "If we left the reindeer to the younger generations, they'd all disappear within one year."

The results of the surveys I conducted in the camps over the four years from 1996 to 1999 show that three of the total twenty-three youth helping with reindeer herding left due to alcoholism, and another five became functioning alcoholics or lighter drinkers. Also, herders consumed as many as seven reindeer (flouting a tradition that reindeer are not for consumption, a code that herders over forty still observed). Moreover, the younger generations—unable to tolerate the monotonous, difficult camp life—tended to spend prolonged periods in the ethnic township. Sometimes they even returned to the settlement during busy seasons.

In 1965, the government built an ethnic school in the settlement. In the mid 1960s the population of Aoluguya comprised only the Ewenki and roughly twenty Communist Party officials. However, as logging bored into the heart of the Daxing'anling region, the number of Han Chinese migrants skyrocketed. By the late 1970s, 50 percent of the total population was Han Chinese. Over time, the culture and lifestyle in the ethnic township was increasingly sinicized due to demographic change as well as political and economic integration between the Party and the government. In addition, the newly introduced education system separated Aoluguya Ewenki children from their parents, keeping them at the boarding school in the ethnic township while their families roamed the forest herding reindeer and hunting. Children could visit the camps only during their summer and winter vacations, and had almost no opportunity to personally engage in reindeer herding and hunting. Moreover, because the national basic education policy dictated they must use standardized Chinese-language texts and be educated in "national culture," the children could not learn the history, culture, and language of their people. Influenced by culturally dominant national ideologies and mainstream society, the youth ultimately began to see reindeer herding and hunting—the work of their parents' generation—as "primitive" and "behind the times."

In 1997, I surveyed thirty Aoluguya Ewenki youth aged 12–25 (roughly 70 percent of the population). When asked, "Would you prefer to live in camps or in the ethnic township, and why?" twenty-two young people said they preferred living in the Ethnic Township, six preferred the camps, and two said they did not know. Those who preferred to live in the ethnic township for four reasons (roughly in order of prominence): (1) for the sake of their education, (2) because they could watch TV, (3) because life in the ethnic township was good (including a sense of convenience, comfort, and civilization), and (4) because it had places to go out and have fun (including a sense that they could be with friends). Those who favored life in the camps gave two reasons: (1) they could hunt, and (2) they were Ewenki. When asked, "What do you think of hunting and reindeer herding?" the youth replied that (1) they did not know, (2) hunting was a source of male pride, and (3) these were primitive systems of production. Asked "To what degree do you possess knowledge of the technical skills shaping these traditions?" the youth replied (1) they did not think it was very technical work, (2) they knew the techniques for hunting well, and (3) they did not know very much.

These data are inconclusive, but when considered in conjunction with findings from other surveys they indicate that despite reindeer herding being the sole livelihood of some Aoluguya Ewenki, the youth apparently have little interest in or knowledge of herding and tend to be averse to living in the camps, preferring instead to live in town.

Serious social issues

Between 1957 and 1998, as many as eighty-three Aoluguya Ewenki died prematurely of causes such as alcohol abuse, accidents (90 percent of them occurring while under the influence of alcohol), and suicide (Aoluguya Minzu Xiang 1998). Despite great concern about these trends since the 1970s, neither the county nor the township government was able to curb this unfortunate trend, though they took numerous measures, such as limiting Aoluguya Ewenki alcohol consumption, restricting alcohol sales (until 1982 the township's only shops were state-run enterprises known as "minority group shops"), and enforcing strict gun control.

Alcoholism within Aoluguya Ewenki society is primarily characterized by (1) rapid growth in the number of alcoholics since the mid 1960s (mandatory settlement was enacted in 1965) and an increasing tendency for women and younger generations to join their ranks since the late 1970s; (2) being a leading cause of premature death (in its relation to accidents and suicide); and (3) youths succumbing to alcoholism or suicide for no identifiable reason. These social phenomena have complex historical, political, social, and cultural causes. They have also profoundly affected reindeer herding. Considerable labor power has been lost to alcoholism and suicide, leading to a pronounced lack of successors to reindeer herding in particular.

The extent of the problem of alcohol abuse is illustrated by the fact that during my fieldwork in the 1990s, nearly all adults in their twenties and thirties had a problem with alcohol, whereas over half the women and men in their forties and fifties did not. As alcohol consumption grew more prevalent within Aoluguya Ewenki society as a whole, more than half of all households became single-parent homes with an absentee father. Seventeen children were orphans. Also, 85 percent of men of marriageable age were unable to marry due to problems with alcohol addiction, mental health, and physiological issues. These problems hampered the intergenerational transfer of cultural traditions and education within the community. They also led to a breakdown in parent-child communication, producing an overall loss of hope for the future and deterioration of the social meaning of reindeer herding.

Once, the Aoluguya Ewenki lived from herding and hunting—not only economically but also culturally. In other words, herding and hunting was their economic and ideological foundation. Now, however, the Aoluguya Ewenki are losing their culture, largely through their integration into Chinese politics, economy and culture.

Environmental issues and poaching

Following the start of efforts to "develop" Daxing'anling in the 1950s, and particularly after China implemented its policy of Reform and Opening Up, the natural environment underwent huge transformations, for several reasons. First, the "responsibility system" that the Forestry Bureau implemented in its production divisions spurred each division to pursue profit, ignoring environmental and social costs along the way. Meanwhile, local residents cleared timber to use as fuel and also engaged in illegal logging and illicit tree sales, with significant impact. Also, timber processing and paper manufacturing industries released untreated runoff into rivers, even as illegal alluvial gold mining operations throughout Daxing'anling polluted rivers too. Thus the Aoluguya Ewenki, who depended on the land for hunting and herding, suffered the following problems.

First, hunting grounds and herding areas decreased. According to Genhe Forestry Bureau materials, hunting areas covered a total of 8 million hectares prior to 1950. By the 1980s, this had diminished to a mere 2.5–3 million ha. By the 1990s, this had further receded to between 500,000 and 700,000 ha (although some estimates are lower, from 300,000 to 500,000 ha). The Aoluguya Ewenki attributed these changes to excessive growth in "human developments"—towns, infrastructure, cropland—and to their own inability to travel very far, owing to the overall shift to sedentary life. Logging by the Forestry Bureau also played a role by causing a sharp reduction in the area of virgin forest. Although large forested areas remained, not all the land was good for grazing, for the land was no longer usable when the lichen—the reindeer's staple food—was destroyed.

Another problem was the destruction of the forest ecosystem. For example, the Forestry Bureau cut small trees and shrubs around larger trees to hasten the growth of trees for timber. They also used pesticides on the land. These actions had a profound impact on the forest ecosystem, extending to the reindeer's food supply. In a series of incidents, reindeer died from eating pesticide-laden branches or lichen. Moreover, mechanized logging directly damaged forest lichen and other low-growing plants. The Aoluguya Ewenki pointed out that lichen has low restorative capacity and grows very slowly. Even in the remaining habitats where lichen could grow, recovery would take five to seven years. In recent years, growing numbers of reindeer have perished in winter due to inadequate nutrition in autumn. As a female herder in her fifties observed, these things never happened in the past and thus are clearly related to ecological changes.

The developing market economy brought abundance to dinner tables throughout the region, but at the same time it led to increased consumption of game animals. According to data from the Genhe Supply and Marketing Cooperative data and my 1997 survey of the locality, one moose (including meat and skin) sold for ¥200–300 in the 1980s. But since 1990, a single moose muzzle—considered a delicacy in China— has sold for ¥5,000–7,000. A moose caught in autumn could sell for as much as ¥30,000. A Han Chinese poacher who had operated for fifteen years said that not only local restaurants and inns but also people from as far as Guangzhou, Wenzhou, and Qingdao came to buy game caught by poachers. The tradition of treating wild game as a delicacy has deep roots in China. Local fauna and flora such as ginseng and *reishi* mushrooms are very highly prized as gifts for relatives, employers, and friends. They are also an indispensable element of meals served to visiting guests, or big celebrations such as the Chinese New Year. However, this demand has affected not only the wild fauna and flora, but also reindeer herds.

From 1992 to 1999, a total of 180 reindeer were lost to traps set by poachers (including Forestry Bureau employees and town residents); poisons used to kill wild animals; theft; traffic accidents; and pesticides spread by the Forestry Bureau. These deaths accounted for 53 percent of the overall drop in reindeer numbers over the seven year period. The value of these reindeer was equivalent to the total income from reindeer herding over the same seven years. In addition to the economic loss, these problems also incurred labor costs, as whenever the herders move to a new campsite they must expend considerable time and effort "cleansing" the area of traps and pesticide deposits.

The convergence of a culture of mass consumption, Chinese medicine, and traditional food customs—triggered by the market economy—has not only damaged ecologies and threatened the existence of numerous animal and plant species but also subjected the reindeer of the Aoluguya Ewenki to both direct and indirect damage.

Conclusion

The Aoluguya Ewenki once survived by hunting and reindeer herding. Their social organization, customs and beliefs (including shamanism), and culture—that is, their "superstructure"—was based on this economic adaptation. In other words, their economic activities also held cultural significance. Their year followed a "reindeer calendar" and a shorter cycle defined by hunting. Everything—their beliefs, ceremonies, folklore, oral traditions—was linked closely to their practices of hunting and reindeer herding. Transhumance was their basic lifestyle. The Aoluguya Ewenki lived in rhythm with nature, fauna, and flora. Their material "poverty" or simplicity, their mobility, and a spirit of mutual assistance and egalitarianism were key features of their society. Their self-asserted identity as Ewenki was also a part of their psyche. Under policies of national integration, however, their social system collapsed. Their livelihood too was incorporated into the socialist economic system, and regional government plans and orders controlled their movement. Their traditional culture was considered "something to be eliminated," so schooling was introduced, the Ewenki were subjected to the influence of national ideology, and Han Chinese immigration surged, changing the demography. The resulting fragmentation within Aoluguya Ewenki society and the confrontation between the ethnic township and the camps impeded the succession of their traditional culture, creating a generational gap and mental confusion.

Behind the various problems facing the Aoluguya Ewenki is the remarkable change wrought in their society by its integration with the state. The problems of reindeer herding related directly to the destruction of the old lifestyle via its accommodation to national politics, economy, and society. The ethnic policy, which simultaneously promoted integration and preservation, was slow to respond to the new phase of market economy and lost its functionality. The order maintained through government power also deteriorated. The development of the market economy created a new paradox, failing to resolve old problems and actually heightening them.

The Ewenki, the Oroqen, and other ethnic minorities had a long history of economic adaptation to their environment, but the state, taking the viewpoint of the Marxist theory of history, saw them only as "backward." Introducing these societies to "settlement" and "agriculture" was seen as a significant historical advancement. The unique cultures of the Ewenki, the Oroqen, and other ethnic groups known as "forest people" in China originated in their lifestyle experiences over time and were well adapted to the forest ecology. But the state never appreciated this aspect of their cultures. From the outset of national integration of the regions these minorities inhabited in the late 1940s, they were labeled "primitive societies" and given no space to advocate their lifestyle, history, and culture.

The Hulun Bei'er League faced various developmental problems. The Mongols, Ewenki (southern), Daur, and other herding ethnic groups had their *nutugh* (Mongolian for homeland, pasture, and land), and the Han Chinese farmers had "cropland" and "forest land" that could be leased under new legislation such as the Land Law and the Rangeland Law. The Aoluguya Ewenki had no such landholdings, although it cannot be said that they lacked the concept of homeland. The approximately six to eight million ha from the south bank of the Amur

River to the edges of Daxing'anling was once their habitat, hunting grounds, and reindeer pastures. They had no sense of land ownership, but each camp had a strong awareness of the hunting grounds each group occupied (Siqinfu 2000). Moreover, the forests held many sacred sites—rock paintings (two or three locations), mountains, large trees, bizarrely shaped rocks, streams—connected to their beliefs, customs, and lifestyle. In sum, the Aoluguya Ewenki felt a strong bond with the forests.

In the late 1940s, this region was integrated into China. "Development" of Daxing'anling began in the 1950s, and the Aoluguya Ewenki lost their homelands due to the nationalization of the forests. Since their resettlements, they have continued to demand their reindeer pastures from the Forestry Bureau, but they have yet to receive permission. The ethnic township established under the national ethnic policy in 1965 gave the Aoluguya Ewenki an autonomous zone where they should have enjoyed the right to self-government, under which they could develop their culture, customs, and economy. But this autonomy is in name only.

Aoluguya Ewenki society has been offered only one path to the future—assimilation into mainstream society. The Aoluguya Ewenki never received national education in their own language. Shamanism was also forbidden, as the Chinese government did not recognize it as a religion. The government recognized agriculture, livestock breeding, and handicrafts under their occupational specialization concept, but not hunting and reindeer herding. Since the 1950s the government and mainstream society have called the Aoluguya Ewenki a "hunting people," but hunters, farmers, and pastoralists are fundamentally different categories. In the "modern" agriculture, livestock breeding, and other industries since the period of Reform and Opening Up, farmers and pastoralists have found their place within the rapidly evolving market economy of China. However, there is no such thing as "modern hunting." In fact, this is strategically emphasized. Livestock breeding and especially agriculture are held up as development models to which hunters and reindeer herders should aspire. The government once explained this way of thinking as the "theory of historical evolution" but has since incorporated the new view of "environmental protection" to make its discourse more persuasive.

The Chinese word "development" is a concept synthesizing politics, economy, history, culture, society, and the natural world. Imported via the Marxist Soviet Union, this concept was not only the dominant discourse linked to authority but also a fundamental tenet in the body of knowledge embraced as the "truth." The Chinese Communist Party and government used development to justify their aim of developing each ethnic group into a *Zhonghua minzu* (Chinese nation). Meanwhile, they considered ethnic minorities' indigenous cultures and identities an impediment to growth. The government deemed it necessary to introduce advanced culture and relentlessly "modernize" all lesser elements. More recently, introduction of a policy of sustainable development has stopped some development plans. However, the authorities are mainly concerned with benefiting the nation, without seriously considering the benefit to local people. Thus they steadfastly uphold the old concept of development.

Notes

1. Before the 1980s, the packs contained food supplies, simple eating utensils (often handmade from birch bark), and clothing. They left tent poles, hides, and birch bark tent coverings at the campsite to be used by other people or by themselves when they someday returned. Each tent needed twenty-five reindeer to carry household goods and people.
2. Anyone, regardless of gender, can obtain the right to graze reindeer in the mountain forests. However, the contract holder must be a "hunter," i.e., an Ewenki who does not fit into the categories of management or full-time employee. See Siqinfu (2000) for more details. See also Xie, this volume.
3. Figures for 1992 are drawn from township statistics; 1999 figures are based on a survey I conducted the same year.

References

Aoluguya Ewenke Minzu Xiang [Aoluguya Ewenki Ethnic Township]. 1998. *Minzu xiang ziliao* [Ethnic Township Data]. Aoluguya: Aoluguya ewenke minzu xiang zhengfu [Aoluguya Ewenki Ethnic Township Government].

Aoluguya Ewenke Minzu Xiang Dang'an [Aoluguya Ewenki Ethnic Township Archives]. 1998. *Minzu shehui wenti duici baogao shu* [Report on Measures to Address Ethnic Social Problems]. Aoluguya: Aoluguya ewenke minzu xiang zhengfu [Aoluguya Ewenki Ethnic Township Government].

Chen Zhaojing. 1993. *Xunlu qun de xianzhuang diaocha* [Survey of the Status of the Reindeer]. Genhe: Genhe shi linye ju [Genhe Forestry Bureau].

Hahe'er. 1991. "Tongyi ewenke minzu zu cheng zuotan hui jishi" [Records of Ewenki Clan Names]. In *Ewenkezu yanjiu wenji* [Ewenki Study Series], ed. Ewenki Research Association. Aoluguya: Ewenki Research Association.

Shirokogoroff, Sergei Mikhailovich. 1929. *Social Organization of the Northern Tungus*. Oosterhout: Anthropological Publications.

Siqinfu. 2004. "Kura nama" [Pure Mongols]. In *Chugoku 21* [21st-Century China], ed. International Center for Chinese Studies, Aichi University. Nagoya: Aichi University.

———. 2000. "Chugoku tonak aievuenki hito no shakai keizai henka 2" [Socioeconomic Change among the Reindeer Ewenki of China, Part 2], Graduate School of Social and Environmental Sciences, Kanazawa University, *Social and Environmental Research* 5: 173–186.

———. 1999. "Chugoku tonak aievuenki hito no shakai keizai henka 1" [Socioeconomic Change among the Reindeer Ewenki of China, Part 1"], Graduate School of Social and Environmental Sciences, Kanazawa University, *Social and Environmental Research* 4: 161–170.

PART II

MIGRATIONS
Reindeer Herding in Flux

🕊 2

IN THE FOREST PASTURES OF THE REINDEER

Tang Ge

In 1953, China carried out its first nationwide census, following the principle of self-reporting of ethnic identity. By the end of 1953, over four hundred ethnic identities had thus been reported and presented to the State Council. Among them were the Solon, Tungus, and Yakut. The term Yakut was introduced by the Russians, whereas in academic circles this group is known as the reindeer-using Ewenki or Reindeer Ewenki. In 1957, the Ewenki nationality was recognized as one of the fifty-six nationalities of China, combining all three aforementioned groups. For the sake of convenience, I use the term Ewenki hereafter to refer to the Yakut or Reindeer Ewenki. According to statistics, their population today is only 250 people, living in 62 households. For administrative purposes they are inhabitants of Aoluguya Ewenki Ethnic Township, located in the southern part of Genhe County in Inner Mongolia. However, because they need pastures for grazing their reindeer, their activity sphere covers large parts of Genhe and sometimes even neighboring counties in Heilongjiang province.

A key concept in the life and social organization of the Ewenki is that of the *urilen,* which might best be translated as "camp," for lack of a better English word. The *urilen* comprises a relatively stable group of people, usually members of several families, living and working together in the forest. The Chinese word for such a camp—*liemindian,* literally "hunting field" or "hunters' field"—originated at a time when hunting was the key livelihood of the Ewenki. The term *liemindian* has both geographical and social dimensions. The first characters of the term, *liemin,* denote the group of hunters, while the last character, *dian* (or *dian'er*) can be combined with other characters to describe several kinds of fields, such as pasture fields (including cattle fields, sheep fields, etc.), forest fields, agricultural fields (including wheat fields), and in the case of the Ewenki, hunting fields. Generally, *dian* denotes a relatively stable, small area used for a specific type of production. The term *liemindian* takes attention away from the social dimension of the camp and redirects it to the geographical dimension, which is moreover represented poorly. Therefore, I will use the Ewenki word *urilen* in this chapter.

I conducted research on the Ewenki from August 1991 until August 2008, carrying out fieldwork in three *urilen*. I visited their forest campsites six times in total, including three periods of participant observation in two different *urilen*: 30 July–18 August 1995, 21 July–7 August 2000, and 16–24 August 2008. The other three, shorter visits took place in August 1991, April 2005, and August 2007. In 2009, the Chinese Social Science Foundation funded my project "A Comparative Study of Cultural Change among the Reindeer Ewenki." I was thereby able to return to Tamara's *urilen* and the people I had previously visited for participant observation in 1995 and 2008. In addition, over a period of nearly a year from April 2010 to February 2011, I conducted five periods of participant observation in this *urilen*, covering all the major seasons of the reindeer herding year, as shown in the table below.

Table 2.1. Fieldwork

Period of fieldwork	Season
26 April–5 May 2010	Reindeer calving season
9–19 June 2010	Antler cutting season
22 July–12 August 2010	Summer season
4–11 October 2010	Reindeer mating season
14–26 February 2011	Winter season

Though I have consulted the work of other ethnographers and anthropologists, this chapter is based largely on the primary data I collected during fieldwork in Aoluguya, especially the extensive participant observation from April 2010 to February 2011 in Tamara's *urilen*.[1] Having found that the Ewenki have changed their source of livelihood and some aspects of their way of life from traditional forest hunting to reindeer herding, I now focus on what this change represents.

The role of the reindeer in Ewenki society

Worldwide, there are altogether three categories of "reindeer-using people": hunters of wild reindeer, who can be found in North America and some Arctic areas of Asia; reindeer herders whose herds graze on tundra vegetation, who live in northern Europe as well as the Asian Arctic; and finally, reindeer herders of the Asian taiga south of the Arctic tundra, whose reindeer graze in dense forest pastures made up of coniferous broad-leaved and soft-wooded trees and bushes. These taiga woodlands are the forest pastures of the Reindeer Ewenki of China. Unlike other reindeer users, the people of the taiga do not consume reindeer as food but keep them as a means of transportation. Reindeer harnessed to sleighs are a means of transportation in the culture of the tundra herders, but to the south of the tundra, the forest is so dense that the reindeer itself replaces the sleigh. To ride reindeer, the Ewenki use a kind of saddle evidently borrowed from pastoralists in grassland regions to the south and west. A reindeer's back is flatter than that of a horse, so a reindeer saddle differs in shape from a horse saddle. Because reindeer are smaller than horses and cannot carry as much weight, only women and children can ride them. Men move around by foot.

The Ewenki have used reindeer as a means of transportation to move between campsites, to carry game back to camp, and to carry trade goods. In the mid nineteenth century, the Ewenki developed stable trade relations with Russian merchants. In winter, the merchants traveled to the forests with their goods to trade with the Ewenki. In summer Ewenki people traveled to Russian villages with reindeer bearing exchange trade goods, usually tied to a saddle so that a load hung on each side of the reindeer's back. They transported food supplies, especially flour, in reversely trapezoidal panniers padded with birch bark, covered with animal hides, and connected in pairs by a leather belt across the back of a reindeer, again hanging the load on both sides.

Although the Ewenki do not eat reindeer meat, they drink reindeer milk, preferably using it to make milk tea. Traditionally, their main source of food was the wildlife they hunted in the forest, including the meat and internal organs of the game. Labor was divided by gender. Males were mainly in charge of the hunting, while females were responsible for looking after the reindeer. Unlike the domestic animals of pastoralists in the grasslands, the reindeer are semi-wild. They find their own food in the deep forests and receive care only after they return to the campsite. Ewenki women take care of the reindeer by lighting smoky fires to keep mosquitoes away from them, feeding salt to them, milking them, treating their injuries and diseases, and caring for their calves.

The shift to reindeer herding

The shift from hunting to reindeer herding has two components: a change from hunting produce to reindeer antlers as a chief commodity, and a shift from using reindeer for transportation to using them for antler production. These changes took place over time, starting in 1961 with the first trial cutting of reindeer antlers.

Having bartered their hunting produce regularly with Russian traders for several decades, by the early twentieth century the Ewenki were supplying the global market, particularly Russian and European buyers, with the furs of wild animals, especially squirrel (Lu 1986: 534). In the 1860s, people from Chinese provinces south of the Great Wall's Shanhai Pass had begun to migrate into the northeastern region. In the 1880s, the migration wave reached the eastern bank of the Argun River. Initially bartering with Russians only, after 1918 they began to trade with Han Chinese migrants as well. Like the Russians, the Han Chinese traders purchased furs for the Russian and European markets, but they also launched a trade in raw materials for the production of Chinese medicine, including antlers, deer placenta, deer's heart blood, bear gall, and so forth. By the nineteenth century's end, reindeer antlers had become a high-value trade good (Lu 1986: 173). Interestingly, traditional Chinese medical books make no mention of reindeer horn; reindeer antlers first entered the Chinese medicine market as a substitute for the antlers of the wild red deer. This was because reindeer crossed the present-day border between China and Russia only some 350 years ago, and before the late nineteenth century the Ewenki had hardly any contact with Han Chinese. Once reindeer horn was introduced into Chinese medicine, however, the recentness of its discovery did not impede exploration of its medicinal value.

The Ewenki were drawn closer into the Han cultural circle as of the mid 1950s, when the Russians living in the border regions left the "New China." The local government first tested the cutting of reindeer antlers in 1961, announcing it a success. Antlers were thereafter purchased by the state, though with a break from 1963 to 1967. After regular production was started, antler sales became increasingly important to the livelihood of the Ewenki, bringing in about a third of their annual income on average. In the 1980s the price of reindeer horn rose, and the economic importance of proceeds from antler sales increased year by year, making up as much as 82.46 percent of the average Ewenki income in 1992. The growing economic importance of antlers was due not only to rising antler prices but also to wildlife depletion and the decline of hunting. The increasing exploitation of timber and other forest resources in the Daxing'anling Mountains reduced the forested area and wildlife habitat, leading to a steady decrease in wildlife populations. By the 1980s, the Ewenki found hunting increasingly difficult, so they began to shift attention from hunting to antler production and reindeer herding.

As mentioned above, the use of reindeer for transportation was an important feature of the Ewenki hunting lifestyle. The government's 1995 introduction of the use of trucks to replace reindeer for transportation dramatically altered the circumstances. Previously Ewenki hunters had used reindeer to carry game back to camp. Trucks, however, cannot negotiate the dense coniferous forest, so the shift to trucks therefore marked the end or near end of hunting.

A third landmark event in the shift from hunting to reindeer herding took place in August 2003, when the government carried out its plan to resettle the Aoluguya Ewenki community, conducted in two main phases. First, the public security bureau of Genhe county and the local police of Aoluguya ethnic township took possession of all the hunting guns. Second, the Ewenki and their reindeer were moved from the mountains to a new settlement constructed by the township government. Before a week had passed, the herders had returned to the forests with their reindeer. Despite the loss of their hunting guns, the Ewenki succeeded in changing their identity, both systemically and legally, from hunter to reindeer herder.

Reindeer antlers are now the major income source of the Ewenki. In 2007, their total antler production was 500–600 kg (300–400 kg after drying), worth more than ¥100,000. A single family of reindeer herders was able to bring in ¥18,000 in one year alone. In addition to reindeer antlers, the Ewenki have actively developed new reindeer products to create further income, opening up stores for reindeer products and souvenirs, and engaging in reindeer-related tourism. Nevertheless, hunting has not vanished completely from the Ewenki economy and way of life.

After hunting was banned in 2003, the government allowed each *uri-len* to keep a rifle, though they were only allowed to hunt grouse and some other birds. Despite the ban, people continue to lay snares, set coil-spring traps, and use other methods to catch squirrel, sable, roe deer, and sometimes even bigger game such as red deer and moose (Figure 2.1). One hunter even shot a bear with a gun borrowed from the public security bureau in Genhe. It is primarily young men who engage in trapping and hunting today. They are busy herding reindeer from spring to autumn but turn to hunting in winter, when they have spare time.

In a sense, the shift from hunting to reindeer herding is a result of continuous negotiation between the Ewenki and the government. The government's goal was to transform the Ewenki from nomadic forest hunters to sedentary reindeer ranchers. From the 1960s until 2003, the government conducted several experiments on keeping reindeer in

Figure 2.1. Meat and hides drying, August 2004, Alongshan. Photograph by Xie Yuanyuan.

pens, while also making efforts to sedentarize the Ewenki. However, the introduction of antler cropping gave reindeer a new economic importance that also inspired new forms of mobility. The Ewenki wanted to maintain their traditional way of life but had to make concessions to the powerful guidance of the government. Rather than completely reject this guidance, they usually took an attitude of compromise, accepting the government's measures for change to a certain degree while also trying to blend them in with their traditional ways.

By returning to the forest after the resettlement, the herders have managed to restore key aspects of their traditional culture. They still make their living in the forest, move about with the reindeer wherever forage can be found, herd the reindeer, live in tents, and retain their traditional form of social organization.

The Ewenki see reindeer herding as a livelihood essentially based on antler, a key commodity that can be traded for other products with the Han Chinese. Like hunting, reindeer herding is not just an economic activity but a way of life. As a way of life in the forest, reindeer herding is the only means, but as a source of income, herding is not the only livelihood. Today's Ewenki herders alternate between moving about in the forest and staying in the village of Aoluguya. Certain binary characteristics of their lifestyle reflect the special conditions in Daxing'anling, China, which is at once the southernmost location of taiga and reindeer, and the northernmost area dominated by Han culture.

The *urilen*

Soon after the founding of the People's Republic, ethnologists defined the *urilen* as patriarchal. This conclusion was drawn from data on a single case, that of the Yageluqiqian camp. However, other *urilen* may have been very different. Tamara's story shows how diverse and flexible the composition of the *urilen* might be. Until 1952, when her father died, Tamara's household or "tent" (Ewenki: *djiu*) belonged to an *urilen* made up of five households in total. In addition to her own, the *urilen* included the households of Tamara's paternal aunt, great-aunt, and two others in which the men were brothers. The son of Tamara's great-aunt—that is, Tamara's uncle—was the chief of this *urilen*, known as *shinmamalen* in the Ewenki language. After Tamara's father passed away, her brother was still too young to be the household's breadwinner, so their maternal uncle came from the eastern bank of the Argun River to take them away from the Genhe area and absorb them into the *urilen* of Tamara's maternal grandfather Pjotr, who was the *shinmamalen*. The other households in this *urilen* were all headed by Pjotr's children. The composition of this *urilen* was recorded by the ethnologists Guo Buku and Mandu'ertu in 1960 (Lu 1986: 523).

After Pjotr died, his second daughter, Pasha, took over as the *shinmamalen* of Pjotr's *urilen*. The position later passed to Tamara when Pasha grew old. Over the years, Tamara's *urilen* has been divided and reunited several times. In 1995, it held a total of seven households: that of Tamara herself, and those of Tamara's sister Nihao with her daughter Qibie; Tamara's second aunt Pasha and her younger brother, Gelisike; Tamara's youngest aunt, Anta; Tamara's uncle with his child, Dongxia; the household of Tashi Sologon and his brother Yariman; and the household of Li Changshun, of mixed Chinese and Russian descent.

The members of an *urilen* herd their reindeer together and jointly carry out important activities such as searching for reindeer and lighting fires against mosquitoes. Different households in an *urilen* may also share their possessions during herding activities. After the resettlement in 2003, there were a total of five Ewenki *urilen*. Later on, one of them was divided into three, so in 2008 there were seven *urilen*.[2] When I returned to Tamara's *urilen* for the second time in 2008, it seemed that only two households were left—Tamara's own household and her sister

Nihao's. However, the younger generation had grown up, and judging from their possessions, there were actually four households in Tamara's *urilen*. Along with the households of Tamara herself with her adult son Botao, and Tamara's sister Nihao with her married grandson Pangpang, there were also the households of Nihao's daughter Qibie and Tamara's daughter Xuefeng. Yet in terms of consumption, the *urilen* had only two units—Tamara's and her daughter Xuefeng's households, and Nihao's and her daughter Qibie's households. Most of the time, Nihao lived alone at the campsite, and the two consumption units would unite temporarily.

To conclude, even though the *urilen* originated in the era of hunting, it remains the key social unit of the Ewenki, regardless of frequent divisions and reunions. The scope, structure, and characteristics of the *urilen* are now defined by the requirements of reindeer herding rather than hunting. Nevertheless, the Ewenki still depend on the *urilen* to organize their forest-based production and livelihood. The *urilen* comprises at most about ten households (especially in summer) and at least two households. Labor requirements define this lower limit. The upper limit, previously defined by the number of wild animals that could be hunted in the area, is now defined by the carrying capacity of accessible grazing areas.

Labor division between the genders

As the livelihood of the Ewenki changed from hunting to herding, the division of labor between genders and the labor role of Ewenki men changed as well. Earlier, when hunting was Ewenki men's main occupation, Ewenki women took care of the reindeer. Today, both men and women are occupied with the reindeer. The main difference is that men look after the reindeer when they graze in distant areas, whereas women tend them in the vicinity of the campsite. Back when Ewenki depended on their reindeer for transportation, the reindeer were highly domesticated. When used as pack animals they could not graze freely during migration, but movement was frequent, so forage could usually be found near the campsite. The reindeer did not wander far to graze, so there was no need to go searching for them in remote areas. Today, the situation is very different. When I lived in Tamara's *urilen* in 1995, the Ewenki had already started to use trucks rather than reindeer to move to new campsites. No longer used for transportation, the reindeer had become semi-wild, and managing them was harder than before. At present, the move to a new campsite has to be made in two steps. First, equipment, materials, and supplies are moved to the new site to set up the camp; second, the reindeer are brought to the new site. In the following days, the herd is unfamiliar with the new site and must be watched closely to keep the reindeer from returning to the old one.

At present, considerable work goes into keeping track of the reindeer, which requires the labor of adult men. In late summer and early autumn, when mushrooms abound, the reindeer often wander long distances for grazing. In this season, finding the reindeer is more troublesome and requires more work. Another, increasing problem is the loss of reindeer to poachers. When reindeer cannot be found for several days, a more thorough search is undertaken. In addition to the everyday herding, men are also responsible for work related to the cutting of antlers. A team of workers from the township government visits all the *urilen* in late spring or early summer to cut antlers. Several young men are needed to overpower a reindeer for antler cutting. In autumn, when the reindeer mate, two pens must be built to allow sufficient space for two fully grown reindeer to mate. As each pen has to be big enough to contain all the adult cows in the herd, the job involves a considerable amount of work, for which adult men are needed. Managing the reindeer within the pens is the women's responsibility.

Every day, the herders must calculate the number of reindeer in their herd. The women are responsible for the counting, for which they depend on their amazing ability to memorize and recognize individual reindeer. To any other person the reindeer may look the same, but in the eyes of Ewenki women they are all distinct. The women can even distinguish differences in the reindeer's braying sounds. In summer the reindeer leave the campsite for grazing late in the afternoon and return in the morning, whereupon the women begin their count. They always carry a small bag of salt, which reindeer love to eat. The women hold salt out on their hands, and the reindeer approach them to lick it.

The reindeer calving season is in April. Normally, a cow gives birth in the forest and brings her newborn calf back to camp with her. Sometimes cows refuse to let their calf suckle, so the women tie the cows up next to the campsite so that the calf can feed and the cow can learn to recognize the calf. The women also milk reindeer cows as long as they continue to produce milk. They usually milk only the cows that belong to their own household. In summer, the forest is full of mosquitoes and other biting insects that cause disease and discomfort to the reindeer. To keep the insects away, the women light smoky fires—one for every thirty to forty reindeer. To heal sick reindeer, the herders buy veterinary medicines from drugstores and sometimes administer them with the help of the township veterinarian. The herders also make their own traditional herbal medicines that are mainly applied by women.

Patterns of mobility

When the Ewenki still subsisted mainly on hunting, they were highly mobile. In winter, the busiest season for hunting, they moved camp every few days or even daily. But the gradual transition from hunting to herding has significantly reduced their mobility. They practice three kinds of migration, moving over long, medium, and short distances. The long-distance migration is movement between valleys, which takes place at intervals of several years. In these valleys, where they once used to hunt, the herders set up campsites close to the road on the shady slope, where the lichen grows better and thus provides more food for the reindeer. In 2003, after the ecological resettlement, Tamara's *urilen* moved to a valley north of the Jinlin railroad after a year of living in the Wufeng area. They settled in the new area for four years, followed by two more long-distance movements, first to the south of the Jinlin railroad in March 2008, and then to the Dalai Valley in November 2009.

Medium-distance movement concerns the more frequent moves between two ranges within a valley. The reindeer's diet is varied, but their main food source is the gray-green "reindeer lichen" (*Cladonia rangiferina*), which is especially important in winter. As one of the coldest areas in China, Daxing'anling is famous for its dense cover of lichen, which creates a good environment for reindeer. The range includes the areas around the campsite where the reindeer go to graze. Reindeer usually graze while walking or running, often moving very fast. Because of their fast pace, the scope of their range can be considerable. The distance from the camp to the edge of the grazing area is usually 17–19 km. Taking the median value of 18 km as a radius, the range will measure about 1017.36 km², and the distance of their movement is on average about 36 km. The herders can stay in such a range for several months before the vegetation is depleted.

At present, medium-distance movement between campsites normally occurs three or four times a year. The herders tend to stay relatively longer in their winter camp, usually from September or October to March, when they make their first move of the year. Another move follows in July, and some also move again in August before moving to the winter camp in October.

Short-distance movements cover a distance of a few kilometers, and their frequency depends mainly on two factors. The first is the size of the herd. As noted, the reindeer usually gather around a smoky fire at the camp in summer. However, reindeer are tidy and will not come to a fire with too much feces around it, so the fire has to be moved every few days. If the campsite is covered with reindeer feces and no clean place can be found, the herders must move. The second factor is the availability of standing dead trees and peat moss near the camp. The preferred tree species for firewood is the Dahurian larch, which is used for heating and cooking. When such trees fall, they decay and thus cannot burn—nor can newly cut trees, which are too wet. The Ewenki use mostly peat moss to make the smoky fires that repel mosquitoes. In most cases, the herders move when they have used up the dead standing trees and peat moss near the camp. Generally, water is not a deciding factor in short-distance movement. Even without a river nearby, herders can find other sources of water near their camps.

During 2010 and 2011, Tamara's *urilen* moved camp over short distances three times. On 7 April, they moved from the winter camp to the spring campsite. The shady slope still held a lot of snow, so they temporarily stored the tents near the road, erecting only one of them. By 1 May all the snow had melted, and they set up their spring camp in the desired place. On 21 July, the *urilen* moved again, covering only a few kilometers. When the mating was over, they returned to a site only 50 m from their spring camp and set up their winter camp there.

Usually the herders integrate short-distance movement with medium-distance movement, so that only medium-distance movement occurs. The frequency of movement between campsites depends mainly on the supply of lichen and other forage plants, and the number of reindeer in the herd. When the supply of lichen decreases, the herders move to another range to let the lichen in the old range regenerate. They may return to the old range when it can again provide several months of fodder for the herd. Such regeneration may take seven to eight years. Similarly, once grazing has depleted the lichen in an entire valley, the herders must undertake another long-distance migration.

The four seasons of Ewenki reindeer herding

Daxing'anling is located on the southern frontier of the taiga, which covers arctic and subarctic areas. The climate displays great annual variations over four distinct seasons. Climatic variations affect the annual growth of plants and stimulate recurring physiological changes in the reindeer. Accordingly, the work of the herders varies from season to season.

Early spring: The time of reindeer procreation

The reindeer calving season is usually in April, when the snow is melting. The herders move from the winter camp to the spring camp before calving begins. Vegetation is still sparse during this period, so the reindeer rely mainly on lichen. However, the snow is melting and the reindeer do not need to dig through it to graze; nor are they bothered by mosquitoes. Therefore they are reluctant to return to the campsite. Finding the reindeer is one of the most time-consuming jobs in this period, especially because the calving usually happens deep in the forest, far from the camp. At birth, calves are weak and vulnerable to attacks by predators. To protect the newborn calves, the herders must bring the reindeer back to the campsite regularly, making sure that the calves are not lost on the way.

Spring and early summer: The antler cutting season

Vegetation grows rapidly in spring and early summer, so the reindeer's fodder changes from lichen to fresh leaves and grass, including their favorite leaves of white birch and other *Betulae*. At this time of year, the reindeer grow velvet antlers. Once this season has passed, the antlers turn tough as armor and lose their value, so it is crucial to cut them at the right time. Cows start growing velvet antlers only after calving, but bulls start earlier. Bull antlers can therefore be cut earlier than the antlers of cows and two-year-old calves.

The summer season

Mosquitoes and insects plague the reindeer from spring throughout the summer season and into the autumn. The women light smoky fires against the mosquitoes in the open area around the campsite. During the day, the reindeer prefer to avoid insects by staying near the fires. At night the insects rest, and the reindeer leave the campsite to graze.

Late summer and early autumn: Foraging on mushrooms

Plentiful rain in late summer and early autumn means abundant mushrooms, which grow rapidly after rainfall. Reindeer love mushrooms and will even leave the campsite to graze during the day at this time, ignoring the swarms of mosquitoes and other insects. Furthermore, when foraging for mushrooms the reindeer do not stay together, but scatter across the range in a large radius. Their dispersion makes herding them even tougher, as the men have to walk long distances to find all the reindeer and bring them back to camp. After feeding on mushrooms, cows produce more and richer milk. Since the calves are no longer suckling, the reindeer milk can be used for human consumption.

Late autumn: The mating season

In late fall, the reindeer try to form harems consisting of a bull and several cows (Chinese: *qiqun*). To keep bulls from fighting and cows from being harmed, the herders keep the cows in a pen. They build at least two pens, using them alternately so as to keep the space clean and dry. Reindeer calves are always kept together with their mother. After mating is done, the harems disperse and the reindeer again form a single herd.

The winter season

Lasting from the first snowfall in mid October until the snow finally melts in April, winter can be as long as five months. Less labor is required in this season, so only two or three people are needed in the herding camp. Relieved of biting insects, the reindeer wander freely in the forest until the herders find them and return them to the camp. The reindeer may also return to the camp on their own, especially if they are fed with salt and bean cakes or bean dregs at the campsite. Reindeer that do not return to be fed can safely remain in the forest for as long as two weeks at a time.

Challenges to the future of reindeer herding

Reindeer were first introduced to Daxing'anling some 350 years ago, but reindeer herding has been practiced as a livelihood for only a relatively short period of time. My research offers little reason for optimism about its future. The reindeer population has stagnated or declined. Available historical records show that the reindeer numbered 853 in 1938 (Nagata 1985), 552 in 1952 (Lu 1986), 815 in 1964 (Ma and Chen 1980), and 924 in 1992 (as reported in an unpublished government document). In August 2008, I did a survey of reindeer counts in all the five *urilen* and those kept in the tourist park. The data showed there were about 300 reindeer in the herd of Maria Sologon, 120 in Tamara's herd, 60 in Dongxia's, 58 in Dawa's, 30 in Marusja's, and another 7 in the tourist park, for a total of 650 reindeer at most. This count reveals considerable decline since 1992 in China's only reindeer population.

The resettlement in August 2003 was a major setback for the herders. The government's various preparations before the move included the construction of new houses, and of reindeer pens equipped with taps to supply drinking water. However, the government failed to provide sufficient fodder for the reindeer in the form of lichen rather than grasses. After the move, the government tried to call in groups of officers to collect willow leaves for the reindeer, but this supply lasted just a few days. Moreover, the reindeer refused to drink the tap water because it contained rust from the public water system. Therefore the Genhe government had to fetch mineral water for them. It was rumored that the reindeer would only accept a certain brand. The herders had to watch their reindeer fall ill or die. Some took the reindeer back to the forest after only three days. Tamara's *urilen* took its herd back to the mountain after seven days, losing more than ten reindeer in the process. Some died in the pen, and some on the truck going back to the forest; meanwhile, some were lost during the unloading due to lack of attention.

Although the government compensated herders for reindeer losses during the resettlement, the money failed to spur an increase in the reindeer population. At the time of writing, a decade has elapsed since the resettlement. Reindeer cannot breed until their third year, whereupon they become able to procreate every year for at least ten years. Since the reindeer are not slaughtered, these natural facts suggest that the reindeer population should be increasing rapidly; on the contrary, however, it is declining. My careful investigation found that this state of affairs has two causes, one direct and one indirect. The direct cause is the high death toll among the reindeer for reasons such as disease, traffic accidents (car and train collisions), attacks by predators (bears, wolves, and lynx), and poaching. Among these, the greatest threats are predators and poachers.

Illegal hunting has a long history in Daxing'anling. In the past, almost every household had a hunting gun, and there were several professional hunters. In 1996, hunting was banned to protect the wildlife of the Inner Mongolia Autonomous Region, and private guns were forcibly confiscated. This was effective in the short run, but even without guns, poachers soon returned to their activities by setting traps. So many reindeer are inadvertently caught and killed in these traps that trapping has proved more harmful to reindeer populations than hunting with guns. A related problem is the theft of stray animals. For instance, in late 2005 all the reindeer of Anta's family went missing, and seven of them wandered into the territory of the forestry bureau of Ganhe in the Oroqen Autonomous Banner, where an enterprise caught and penned them. The township government made repeated efforts to recover the reindeer, after six of them were found alive. However, the enterprise demanded ¥20,000 to cover the cost of keeping the reindeer, which Anta's family refused to pay. After another year had passed, they returned to Ganhe but could no longer find their reindeer. The enterprise announced that they were all dead. The family wanted to sue the enterprise but had to give up due to lack of evidence.

The indirect cause of reindeer loss is the lack of male labor for herding. Herders frequently find trapped reindeer that have been dead for days, so the rate of reindeer loss would clearly be lower if trapped and injured reindeer were rescued and treated in a timely manner. The herders' most important responsibility is to find the reindeer and regularly return them to the campsite. This labor-intensive task is mainly carried out by grown men. However, many Ewenki are fond of alcohol, and quite a few have died prematurely due to alcohol-related diseases or accidents. Most such deaths occur among adult males. Consequently, every *urilen* now suffers from a shortage of manpower. Moreover, many younger men find it hard to adapt to life in the forest and prefer to stay in the settlement. Today there are only three men in Tamara's *urilen,* and only one of them stays frequently in the forest, as compared to five in 1995.

Although the government's efforts to sedentarize the Ewenki have not succeeded in ending their forest lifestyle, they have certainly had an impact, especially among the youth. Meanwhile, as all the *urilen* face a desperate lack of male labor, some Han Chinese men have married Ewenki women and become herders. The Ewenki language is vanishing, so the future reindeer herders of Aoluguya will likely speak Chinese. The herders are also taking full advantage of the numerous logging roads that now twine through the forests of Daxing'anling. Today's herding lifestyle involves frequent movement, not only between shifting forest campsites but also back and forth between the campsite and the settlement. The Ewenki have experienced tremendous changes, but as long as reindeer herding continues, the *urilen* will remain.

Notes

1. This chapter is a result of the project "A Comparative Study of Cultural Change among the Reindeer Ewenki" funded by the Chinese Social Science Foundation (Grant No. 09BMZ024) and a pilot project in the social sciences funded by Heilongjiang Province entitled 'A Study of Cultural Change among the Reindeer Ewenki' (Grant No. 08D060). After this project ended, I also returned for another period of participant observation from 27 June–7 July 2011.

2. In the autumn of 2010, two of the camps were reunited, bringing the total to six.

References

Lu Guangtian. 1986. *Ewenkezu shehui lishhi diaocha* [Social and Historical Investigation of the Ewenki]. Hohhot: Neimenggu renmin chubanshe [Inner Mongolia People's Press].

Ma Yiqing and Chen Zhaojing. 1980. *Xunlu diaocha baogao* [Investigation Report on the Reindeer]. Genhe: E'erguna linye ju [E'erguna Forestry Bureau].

Nagata, Haruka. 1985. *Xunlu Elunchunzu* [The Reindeer Oroqen]. Aoluguya: Aoluguya xiang zhengfu [Aoluguya Township Government].

⟫ 3

AMBIGUITIES OF THE AOLUGUYA EWENKI

Åshild Kolås

The Ewenki of Aoluguya used to be hunters. Their ancestors moved back and forth across a region alternately controlled by Russian and Manchu administrations. The settlement of Aoluguya was built for them in the early 1960s, when they were relocated from the banks of the Amur River due to deteriorating relations between the People's Republic of China and the Soviet Union. This chapter outlines subsequent efforts to integrate the Aoluguya Ewenki into the Chinese state, describing the evolution of policy and its application to reindeer herding over time, as well as the reindeer herders' maneuvers in the changing, often ambiguous policy landscape. As described in the following pages, the Aoluguya Ewenki's unique adaptation as hunter-herders and the difficulties of fitting their particular forms of livelihood into national policy frameworks and official categories have often led authorities to make exceptions for them. At times their exceptionality or uniqueness has provided advantages; at others, it has left the reindeer herders in an ambiguous, potentially problematic legal or political space.

Soon after the relocation to the settlement of Aoluguya, the state collectivized the reindeer. In the days of the communes the reindeer were thus collective property, and hunting was the main activity of the newly founded hunting production brigade (Chinese: *lieye shengchandui*). The brigade also introduced the new economic activity of cutting reindeer antlers for the production of Chinese medicine. By the late 1970s, reindeer horn had become a key product (Kong 1994: 228–230), and when the brigade was dismantled in 1980, a hunting cooperative (*lieye lianshe*) and later a hunting enterprise (*lieye gongsi*) took over the marketing of meat, furs, and reindeer horn. In 2003, hunting was brought to an end when the government confiscated the guns, banned all hunting, and moved the community as "ecological migrants" to a new settlement 250 km to the south.

After Deng Xiaoping introduced "Economic Reforms" (*Gaige kaifang*) in 1979, the Aoluguya Ewenki were subjected to a series of policies and programs intended to privatize and marketize reindeer herding through household contract herding, with reindeer horn as the key product. However, as Beijing introduced its brave new modernization policies, local authorities repeatedly excepted themselves from market-driven rationalities, resulting in a range of ambiguities and contradictions pertaining to reindeer herders' rights and obligations as well as the management of reindeer husbandry. For instance, although the hunting ban and resettlement plans were explicitly intended to protect the environment and modernize the Ewenki, the plans were introduced with a promise from the government that the Ewenki would no longer need to hunt after moving to the new settlement, because they and their reindeer would be provided for.

While the inhabitants of Aoluguya were being relocated to their new, relatively comfortable homes in August 2003, several hundred reindeer were moved by truck from the taiga to enclosures where they were supposed to be hand-fed. The move itself was carried out quite efficiently, and few of the reindeer were lost in the process. However, only days after their relocation the reindeer started to fall ill, and some of them soon perished. Anger and desperation spread among the herders as they watched the animals suffer, gradually realizing that the government was incapable of restoring their health. Finally they took action, letting the reindeer out of their enclosures and returning them to the taiga. At this point the flaws in the government's reindeer ranching scheme were plainly evident. The government effort to modernize reindeer husbandry was a failure, and the herders were left with no other viable option than to return to the taiga areas where the reindeer could find food. Although the failed "sedentarization" scheme resulted in a hazardous situation, it also gave the herders the opportunity not only to return to the forest, but also to renegotiate their rights as reindeer herders.

Since the resettlement, reindeer herding has become the only livelihood by which the Aoluguya Ewenki can continue their seminomadic lifestyle. As of today there are six or seven "hunters' camps" (*liemin dian*) in the Daxing'anling Forest. The largest herds belong to the camp of Maria Suo (Maria Sologon in Ewenki) in the Alongshan Mountains (Figure 3.1), and at least four smaller camps are located to the south of Alongshan. Except for regular milking and occasional slaughter of ailing animals, the reindeer are not kept for subsistence or transportation, but mainly for the annual cropping (or cutting) of antlers. Chinese medicine creates a demand for dried reindeer placenta, penis, and "reindeer heart blood" (*luxin xue*) as well as reindeer horn. The township production unit is in charge of cutting, drying, and marketing the reindeer antlers, but the herders harvest other reindeer products them-

Figure 3.1. Andao and his dog, July 2008, Alongshan. Photograph by Tashi Nyima.

selves. Beach (2003: 33) calls this a "dual ownership system" based on milk and antlers, in which the "subsistence aspect" (milk) accrues to the herding families while the state owns the antler crop.

After the resettlement, the Bureau of Civil Affairs (*Minzheng ju*) has provided residents of Aoluguya with a monthly welfare payment of about ¥200 Chinese (US$30). Tourism is being developed as an alternative source of income and employment for inhabitants of the new town. With the help of the Finnish consultancy firm Pöyry, the settlement is being transformed into the Aoluguya Ethnic Reindeer Resort (Pöyry 2008), adding to reindeer herding's significance in the local economy. In 2009, the community of Aoluguya numbered sixty-two households, of which about twenty had income from government employment and another three or four lived on earnings from migrant labor outside the municipality, in the factories of large companies such as Haier. About twenty-five households had income from herding, although not all members of these households stayed regularly in the forest to tend the reindeer.[1]

In Aoluguya both the state (government agents) and its subjects (reindeer herders) draw variously on competing environmental and economic rationalities, and neoliberal and socialist values, to stake their claims and counterclaims. Although neoliberalism is officially rejected in China, neoliberal logics have in many ways shaped the contemporary Chinese economy (Ong and Zhang 2006). Thus, "privatizing norms and practices proliferate in symbiosis with the maintenance of authoritarian rule" (Ong and Zhang 2006: 4; see also Yeh and Gaerrang 2010). The creation of Special Economic Zones (SEZs) exemplifies neoliberalism as exception (Harvey 2005; Ong 2006), whereas exceptions to neoliberal rationality are also invoked "to exclude populations and places from neoliberal calculations and choices" (Ong 2006: 4). In contemporary China these contradictions and ambiguities have opened up new possibilities for contesting moral claims as well as economic and environmental rationalities. In Aoluguya, new contradictions in the nexus between neoliberalization, socialism, and environmentality mix with preexisting contradictions born of the difficulty of fitting nationwide policies to unique adaptations, producing a range of ambiguities that I will try to disentangle in what follows.

Ambiguities of ownership and use rights

One ambiguity involves grazing rights and the reindeer herders' exemption from key facets of the Household Contract Responsibility System (*Jiating chenbao zerenzhi*). As explained previously, animal husbandry and household farming were both decollectivized after the onset of Economic Reforms. The Household Contract Responsibility System, introduced in the early 1980s as communes and production brigades were dismantled, was a means to distribute use rights to agricultural land to individual farming households. In pastoral areas, livestock was distributed to individual herding households. After the introduction of the 1985 Grassland Law, each household received extended use rights to pastures under contract (e.g., Banks 2003; Banks et al. 2003; Wilkes 2006). The Thirty-Year Use Right policy, enacted by the 1998 Land Management Law, was implemented by the early 1990s.

The policy of dual rights to animals and pastures was supposed to be nationwide, but the Ewenki reindeer herders were never offered pasture contracts. The problem was that reindeer herding took place in state-owned forests rather than areas designated as grasslands or "pastoral" areas. These forests are managed by national forestry authorities, not by local authorities who would normally be charged with the management of grasslands. In effect, the reindeer herders were left without contractual use rights to grazing land.

The decollectivization of the Ewenki hunter-herders was implemented by the hunting cooperative (*lieye lianshe*). In 1984, every Ewenki household head not employed by the state was offered a contract (*het-ong*) conferring formal status as a reindeer herder. Twenty-five herders undertook contractual responsibility for thirty reindeer each, for a total distribution of 755 reindeer (for statistics on reindeer populations from 1950 to 1994, with annual figures provided for the 1971–94 period, see Kong 1994: 225). The contracts did not transfer property rights to the reindeer, nor did they specify any pasture use rights or designated grazing areas for herding. Rather, they set a target (and promised a prize) for increasing the size of each herd from thirty to forty animals in the course of a year. About half the contractors met the target, but the contracts were not renewed after the initial year, and the authorities did not set further targets for increasing herd size. Statistical records confirm the increase in the number of reindeer between 1984 and 1985 (from 755 to 883 animals), followed by a decline in subsequent years (see Kong 1994: 225).

Though the year-long contracts issued in 1984 were supposed to be renewed annually (Beach 2003: 34), they were signed only once. Thus the formal ownership of the reindeer, like the rights to grazing land, remained indeterminate. According to the former head of the hunting enterprise, the reindeer actually remained collective property despite the issuance of herding contracts. Today, though government representatives continue to insist that they encourage herding, the herders still lack the security that comes with a legal contract stipulating use rights to grazing land or clarifying rights of ownership to the reindeer. The herders are arguably left in a "liminal space of law" (Humphreys 2006), or even a "zone of indifference" (Agamben 2005).

Resettlement and ambiguities of environmental protection

In 2003, the Aoluguya community was relocated with central government funding earmarked for ecological migrants in a scheme for resettling herders away from pastoral areas where grasslands are severely degraded. In western China, large-scale programs launched to "restore grasslands" (*caoyuan huifu, tuimu huancao*) have also addressed rangeland degradation, which policy makers see as a problem of overgrazing or overstocking by pastoralists (for counterarguments, see Banks 2001; Clarke 1987; Harris 2010; Longworth and Williamson 1993; Taylor 2006; Williams 1996; Yeh 2009; Zhang 1988). These programs include measures to fence pastures and move herders out of the grasslands (*weifeng zhuanyi*), as well as schemes to limit grazing such as the Grass for Green (*Caoyuan lüse*) program.

In many parts of Inner Mongolia and the Qinghai-Tibetan Plateau, environmental protection programs have relocated or sedentarized previously self-reliant pastoralists. After their resettlement at sites built specifically to accommodate ecological migrants, failed employment schemes have often resulted in dependency on government welfare. In Aoluguya, however, employment is actively generated through the development of "reindeer tourism." Drawing on the uniqueness of the "reindeer culture," reindeer herding has thus become important as both a cultural marker and a resource for tourism, where cultural uniqueness or exceptionalism obviously lends a competitive advantage.

The policy of ecological migration is founded on the claim that China's pastoralists represent a major threat to the environment, having overgrazed grasslands, overstocked herds, or in the case of the Ewenki, overhunted wildlife. In some cases, the sedentarization or resettlement of herders is seen as the only viable means to "save the environment" from detrimental human activity (Kolås 2014). Policy makers arguing for large-scale interventions have posited a connection between ecological degradation in western China and the "security" of downstream areas (Yeh 2009: 888). With the "ecological security of the country" at stake (Yeh 2009: 892), the wholesale removal of people from "degraded" (*tuihua*) environments has become crucial to the government's environmental management strategy.

According to the government, wildlife protection was the primary reason for resettling the community of Aoluguya and imposing a hunting ban. In its funding proposal to the central government, the municipal government named wildlife depletion due to overhunting by Ewenki hunters as the key grounds for the resettlement. However, the proposal did not cite any wildlife population studies as evidence supporting this claim. Indeed, scientific studies of local wildlife populations apparently were never carried out, either before or after the resettlement.

When I interviewed former hunters about the extent and causes of wildlife depletion in the Daxing'anling Forest, they dismissed the government's claims. According to them, the wildlife in their old hunting grounds had admittedly decreased over the past decades, but this trend had not ended with the 2003 hunting ban, since "outsiders" (*waidi ren*) continued to hunt regardless of the season. The illegal hunting, they argued, continued to deplete many species of wildlife after the ban was imposed. Rejecting the need for the hunting ban, former hunters gave me details of the traditional Ewenki hunting restrictions protecting wildlife from depletion, for example, prohibition against hunting female deer in autumn and spring, especially in the calving season, and against hunting birds during the nesting season. Some former hunters were highly critical of the hunting ban, describing the new policy as an eradication of their centuries-old hunting way of life, and of their very culture and identity. In the words of one elderly man: "What are we, if we are not allowed to hunt on our own land?"

Local authorities conceded that despite the threat of heavy fines, prison sentences, and local forest guard patrols, poachers still managed to get into the forest to hunt illegally with traps and even guns. The herders maintained that hunters (again described as "outsiders") were killing many of their reindeer as well. In several encampments I heard of cases of reindeer found killed or wounded by bullets, or caught in illegal traps set for big game. I was also told that reindeer sometimes just disappeared without a trace. These problems were widespread, except in the one camp that was inaccessible by logging roads. According to the herders, the authorities were making serious efforts to address the problem of illegal hunting but were incapable of stopping it. The herders also complained that reindeer died after eating thin plastic bags left in the forest by people picking wild foods like mushrooms and berries. Attacks by predators—wolves, bears, and especially lynx—were another major cause of reindeer casualties. Each camp of herders was allowed to keep one gun for protection against predators, but they were not allowed to hunt any of these predators, not even those known to have preyed on reindeer.

As chief custodians of the environment, various government entities have established nature preserves (*ziran baohuqu*) to protect forest environments and wildlife in the Daxing'anling region. One such preserve, Mangui Alu, is located to the north of the old Aoluguya settlement. About half of this reserve, covering 64,386 hectares, lies in Heilongjiang Province. Another preserve, called Hanma, lies to the east of Alongshan and also borders Heilongjiang. The state-level Hanma nature preserve covers 107,348 hectares. Chaocha, a municipal-level preserve located to the north of Genhe has an area of 11,791 hectares (Genhe Bureau of Environmental Protection 2009). In principle, these large forest areas are off-limits to reindeer herding because herding is prohibited in all nature preserves, as is the picking of wild foods and cutting of timber.

Notwithstanding the regulations, reindeer herders have received special permission—granted as yet another exception—to cut a limited amount of timber for the supports for their ridge tents. They are also allowed to collect firewood, though only outside of nature preserves. In 2009, a herding camp was based in the northern part of the Chaocha nature preserve. The herders there did not relate any problems in this regard, although they were planning to set up their next camp outside the boundaries of the preserve. However, one Alongshan camp had requested the local forestry station's permission to move into the Hanma preserve and was denied. Exceptions are evidently case-by-case and constantly open to reinterpretation. Because they leave herders vulnerable to the interpretations of state agencies, ambiguities are often sources of insecurity.

Ambiguities of tourism

After the resettlement, the government promoted tourism as a more economically viable alternative to hunting. According to a "master plan" for tourism formulated by the Finnish consultancy firm Pöyry, hunting and reindeer herding are important cultural resources for tourism development in Aoluguya. Pöyry (2008) therefore proposed to establish a "hunting park" and develop hunting trips as a tourist "product." As described in the master plan, the hunting guide should be from Aoluguya, "using his knowledge about animals" (Pöyry 2008: 76). As explained by the head of the municipal Bureau of Tourism (*Lüyou ju*), the master plan was well received and the bureau planned to implement many of the proposed activities, although there was no follow-up on the "hunting park." Since the main rationale for imposing a hunting ban on the Ewenki hunters was the protection of wildlife, local authorities were having trouble justifying a new "hunting park" where tourists would hunt the very wildlife that was supposed to be protected by the resettlement.

The relocation of Aoluguya was officially described as "ecological migration," which was also how the case was framed in the state-sponsored media. However, protection of wildlife was not the only argument for relocating Aoluguya. Other factors, brought up in interviews and government reports, centered on the need for development and modernization, especially of infrastructure such as electricity supply, housing and transportation, and also employment opportunities. Before the resettlement, most of the buildings in old Aoluguya needed renovation. Also, the old settlement, located 17 km north of the nearest town and railway connection at Mangui, was deemed "remote" by the authorities in charge of the resettlement. Mangui is on the same railway line that runs through the county capital of Genhe. Located less than 5 km from the center of Genhe, the new Aoluguya settlement is thus closer to a railway station, providing better access for tourists and other visitors.

   Proponents of the relocation argue that the new settlement provides easier access to markets as well as improved facilities and infrastructure. Another problem with the old settlement may have weighed heavier for the Genhe authorities. This was the repeated flooding of the local river, caused by siltation and accumulation of debris at a fork in the river just downstream from the old settlement. When the resettlement plan was first introduced, the Genhe authorities claimed that flood prevention would require rerouting the river at a cost of millions of yuan. Accessing the funds needed to carry out a river diversion project would be simply impossible, they argued. However, central government funding was readily available for construction of new settlements for "ecological migrants," and from a special fund for small ethnic groups. Resettlement was therefore presented as the only economically viable alternative.

   Not long after the move, when the old Aoluguya settlement was left abandoned, municipal authorities signed an agreement with Daqing Oil Company to take over the entire settlement, complete with land and buildings, for the sum of ¥150 million (US$22 million). The old Aoluguya settlement, with its exceptionally beautiful location, was privatized and marketized by its transformation into a tourist resort, perfectly exemplifying Chinese neoliberalization at work. At the time of my visit in July 2009, most of the buildings were still standing and were being re-clad with new wooden panels. The school had been made into a hotel, and people's houses had been converted into cabins for guests, already fully equipped with high-quality bathrooms, telephones, modern wooden furniture, and brand-new wood-burning stoves. Only one or two buildings had been demolished. The old TV station was being rebuilt to accommodate the tourist resort, as were the hospital, township government buildings, post office, bank, store, museum, and old people's home. Interestingly, no flood prevention measures had been undertaken, although the cabins and hotels were nearly completed.

   Tourism is also being introduced as a major force for modernization and marketization in the new settlement, where the consultancy firm Pöyry has drawn up plans for the Aoluguya Ethnic Reindeer Resort. Once it is finished, the resort intends to provide locals with employment opportunities, including hotel jobs, souvenir production, and jobs in services such as "Ewenki homestays." The plans for the resort even include a reindeer research centre with twenty to thirty reindeer. The idea behind it all is "to preserve the Aoluguya cultural heritage and old livelihoods by turning the old skills and unique lifestyle into a tourism product" (Pöyry 2008: 7).

In this settlement reconstructed as a resort, the town houses have been completely refurbished in Finnish design, with modern amenities such as central heating and cable TV. There is a hotel (formerly the school), and a new, state-of-the-art museum has been built. In a forested theme park across the road, tourists can sit in a birch bark tent, sip tea from bark cups, and feed the half-dozen reindeer kept there while tour guides dressed up in so-called traditional Ewenki costume tell stories about the Ewenki and their shamans. The Ethnic Reindeer Resort hopes to stand out from other resorts thanks to its "unique cultural products" (Pöyry 2008: 2). The question is how viable these products will be, if what is marketed as "the Ewenki reindeer herding and hunting culture" is sustained only within the parameters of the resort.

Neoliberalizing reindeer herding

Following the nationwide policy of decollectivization, the hunting production brigade (*lieye shengchandui*) was transformed into a hunting cooperative (*lieye lianshe*) in 1980. In yet another modernization effort, the cooperative provided ridge tents for the herders. By the mid 1980s, most herders had discarded their traditional birch bark tents and started to furnish the ridge tents with heavy cast iron wood-burning stoves. From then on the herders moved less often, and tended to use the cooperative's vehicle for moving, setting up their camps along the ever-expanding network of logging roads that now cut through the forest. In 1988 the hunting cooperative bought its own truck with proceeds from the sale of thirty-one reindeer at ¥5,000 per head (US$735 at today's rate). The cooperative kept 30 percent of the income from the sales, and the individual herders received the remaining 70 percent.

In 2001, the cooperative was transformed into a hunting enterprise (*lieye gongsi*). Whereas the cooperative had taken 30 percent of income from sales of products, the enterprise charged only 20 percent—an important change, from the herder's perspective. The cooperative, and later the enterprise, held annual meetings to explain to the herders what its share had gone toward, such as maintaining the antler-drying factory and paying the workers who cut the antlers.

Since the founding of the hunting enterprise, individual herders have been allowed to keep all proceeds from the sale of reindeer, although the production unit continues to charge a fee (*fei*) of 20 percent of proceeds to cover the cutting and marketing of reindeer horn. The herders hence regard the reindeer as the property of individual households responsible for deciding whether to sell or slaughter animals if necessary. The reindeer are still collectively herded and looked after within the camp, and all related activities, such as moving between campsites, veterinary care like administering medicines, and antler cutting is also carried out collectively by the people of each camp.

The fee charged by the production unit is a bone of contention for many herders, who would rather keep all the income from antler production to themselves. Herders are also discontent with the price offered for the reindeer horn and the time it takes to receive payment. After cutting the antlers, the workers from the production unit give the herders a receipt. Only when their produce has been sold, up to a year later, can the herders collect their money. Some of the reindeer horn is sold while it is still wet (for use in alcohol infusions), but most of it is machine dried. The delay in payments reflects the time it takes to sell the reindeer horn. Aoluguya has the only reindeer-horn processing plant in China, and according to the head of the production unit, it is well known for top-quality produce. The marketing problem is mainly due to the smuggling of large quantities of reindeer horn into China from Russia, which affects the market price and demand for reindeer horn from Aoluguya. With the gradual shift toward privatized reindeer herding, herders have become more vulnerable to competition and price fluctuations. At the same time they continue to depend on the township production unit, not only to cut and market reindeer horn, but also to provide veterinary services, emergency supplies in bad weather, and assistance when moving camp.

The contemporary structure of governance and planning catches reindeer herders up in other contradictions as well. Every authority seems to perceive them as somehow ambiguous or outside the parameters of their particular mandate or purview. Hunting is banned, so they are no longer "the last hunting tribe" (Dong 2007), nor are they seen as true pastoralists (*shoulie buluo; mumin*). A common term for them now is *yangluren,* or "breeders of [rein]deer," which underscores the paradox of "cultivating" (*yangzhi*) an animal that usually is not domesticated (the deer). Apart from the conceptualization of the herders, such a contradiction in terms is also evident in the inconsistent classification of the reindeer. Local government officials, claiming the reindeer are second-level protected animals on China's list of endangered species, want to create a nature preserve specifically to protect reindeer. Meanwhile, the central government's wildlife protection unit under the Ministry of Forestry understands the reindeer as domesticated animals and has adopted the International Union for Conservation of Nature standard by including only wild animals on their Red List of endangered species. Staff of the municipal Bureau of Environmental Protection

(*Huanbao ju*) also told me that because reindeer are domestic animals, herders are prohibited from keeping them in nature preserves and national parks. But whereas the reindeer are "domestic" (*xunhua*) for the purpose of wildlife protection, they are "wild" (*yesheng*) for management purposes, according to officials in the Bureau of Agriculture, Pastoralism and Water Management (*Nongmushuili ju*), a department that takes no responsibility for planning or management of reindeer herding because reindeer are "wild animals" and their herders are not pastoralists.

The reindeer herders keep their herds in state-owned forests. Many bureaucrats regard the reindeer as wild animals, but this does not mean herders can move freely around the forest. They must report their camps' whereabouts to the local forest station (*linchang*) and are expected to stay within the jurisdiction of the forest station they report to. Officials in other government departments claim that their colleagues in the Bureau of Forestry (*Linye ju*) are responsible for the reindeer because they graze in the forest. However, Forestry Bureau officials argue that the reindeer are the responsibility of the township government (*xiang zhengfu*), despite the lack of ranges for reindeer within the boundaries of either the abandoned old Aoluguya township or new Aoluguya, where the herders officially reside.

The Aoluguya township government is formally in charge of the management of reindeer herding and employment of the township's inhabitants. The township leader explained that whereas reindeer herding is still an important occupation, forage vegetation is scarce; therefore the reindeer population needs careful management (*guanli*). Citing a survey conducted by Finnish consultants hired by Pöyry, he reported that the present herding areas had a carrying capacity (*zaichuliang*) of 3,000 reindeer, and that reindeer currently numbered about 1,200. As a good custodian of the government policy line, the township leader reiterated concerns for environmental protection as well as the economic viability of reindeer herding.

The township production unit compiles statistical data on the reindeer population to support the township government's efforts to manage the reindeer population. The workers collect the data every year when they cut antlers, counting adult reindeer and asking the herders for the number of calves. Of course this procedure is problematic, as herders have incentives to underreport the number of reindeer. If the government finds out they are selling reindeer, it may try to tax the sales. The herders themselves also explained that they fear the government will start limiting the number of reindeer to prevent overgrazing. On the other hand, incentives to report higher figures include a policy of providing financial assistance to herders based on the size of their herds. In 2007, the central government allocated financial support of an annual ¥300 (US$44) per reindeer to herders, although in 2009 the municipal government was withholding these funds from the herders on the pretext that the numbers of reindeer were unclear. The township government's simple need to succeed is also an incentive to over-report reindeer numbers, especially since the resettlement. As a government official admitted, "as long as the numbers are going up, everything is fine." Not surprisingly, the reported numbers are in fact increasing.

At the new Aoluguya settlement, the township government has kept records of the reindeer population since the move in 2003. They indicate steady growth in the reindeer population every year, from 706 in 2003 to 1,204 in 2008. The preliminary figure for 2009 was as high as 1,497 head as of that July. However, the Finnish consultants reported a much lower figure of 595 animals, based on their own data collected in March 2008. Although their survey was done before the calving season, the number of calves was relatively low, mainly because of the high ratio of males, whose larger antlers are preferred for antler production. Furthermore, losses are also quite high. According to my own estimates, the reindeer population remained stable at around 650 reindeer as of July 2008 and 2009. This represented a decline from the number in 2003, when the reindeer were moved to the new settlement. Whatever the reasons for the apparent stagnation, it is clearly easier for government cadres to repeat the mantras of economic progress and environmental sustainability than to admit to difficulties and call for resources to remedy the situation.

Concluding remarks

China's transition into a "socialist market economy" eventually put the central government face-to-face with the effects of its own free-market rationalities and emphasis on entrepreneurial efficiency, which for decades contributed to increasing pressure on China's grassland and forest resources. The government responded by introducing ecological migration, an extraordinary departure from marketization policy that was justified by environmental degradation so severe as to threaten the ecological security of the country itself. Previously criticized for their lack of market orientation, the herders were now held responsible for destroying the environment, while the government upheld its role as custodian and protector of the country's ecology and resource base.

When municipal authorities planned the relocation of Aoluguya, they trotted out the central government's discourse of environmental disaster to justify the hunting ban and the building of a new settlement for the Ewenki. Their scheme to keep the reindeer in enclosures on a reindeer ranch was inspired by the discourse of marketization and nationwide programs to transform herders into ranchers. The failure of the ranching scheme was all too clear after the move, opening a space for the herders to contest the local government and return the reindeer to the taiga. Realizing the urgency of the situation, the authorities agreed to help the herders move the reindeer back to the forests where they could graze. Although the reestablishment of forest herding camps is a constant reminder of the government scheme's failure, the authorities were hard pressed to find a solution better than letting the reindeer and their herders return to the forest.

Even after their return, the reindeer herders are still dependent on the township production unit. Individual herders respond differently to this dependency. Some make their own market-driven calculations, aiming to increase their self-reliance and supplement their income by receiving tourists at their camps. Others seize on fresh opportunities of the neoliberalizing economy, moving away from antler cropping toward meat production and the sale of live animals. Key to pursuing this strategy is gradual modification of herd composition, favoring females to increase herd growth. This strategy has its own set of risks and dependencies, such as the market for reindeer meat, which has so far not been developed, and the tourism industry's demand for live reindeer.

It is difficult to predict the future of reindeer herding in the Amur River bend. Whatever is held in store for the herders, they will no doubt need the freedom to respond pragmatically and flexibly to the challenges ahead. In this sense, ambiguity may not be the worst of circumstances.

Notes

This chapter revised and reproduced by permission of the Society for Applied Anthropology from Human Organization, volume 70, number 4.
1. A few herders stay in the forest more or less permanently, but many move back and forth between settlement and camp. On the reindeer herders' mobility, see the chapter by Dumont in this volume.

References

Agamben, Giorgio. 2005. *State of Exception*. Chicago: University of Chicago Press.
Banks, Tony. 2003. "Property Rights Reform in Rangeland China: Dilemmas on the Road to the Household Ranch." *World Development* 31, no. 12: 2129–2142.

————. 2001. "Property Rights and the Environment in Pastoral China: Evidence from the Field." *Development and Change* 32, no. 4: 717–740.

Banks, Tony, Camille Richard, Li Ping, and Yan Zhaoli. 2003. "Community-Based Grassland Management in Western China: Rationale, Pilot Project Experience, and Policy Implications." *Mountain Research and Development* 23, no. 2: 132–140.

Beach, Hugh. 2003. "Chinese Dual-Ownership System Remains a Hopeful Model Despite Evenkis' Forced Relocation from Ôlguya." *Cultural Survival Quarterly* 27, no. 1: 33–35.

Clarke, Graham. 1987. "China's Reforms of Tibet, and their Effects on Pastoralism." IDS Discussion Paper no. 237. Brighton: Institute of Development Studies.

Dong Liansheng. 2007. *Zhongguo zuihou de shoulie buluo* [The Last Hunting Tribe of China]. Hohhot: Neimenggu renmin chubanshe [Inner Mongolia People's Publishing House].

Genhe Bureau of Environmental Protection [*Genhe shi huanbao ju*]. 2009. Genhe shi huanbao ju [Genhe Bureau of Environmental Protection]. Accessed 1 November 2009 at www.ghshbj.com/list.asp?id=375

Harris, Richard B. 2010. "Rangeland Degradation on the Qinghai-Tibetan Plateau: A Review of the Evidence of its Magnitude and Causes." *Journal of Arid Environments* 74: 1–12.

Harvey, David. 2005. *A Brief History of Neoliberalism.* Oxford: Oxford University Press.

Humphreys, Stephen. 2006. "Legalizing Lawlessness: On Giorgio Agamben's State of Exception." *The European Journal of International Law* 17, no. 3: 677–687.

Kolås, Åshild. 2014. "Degradation Discourse and Green Governmentality in the Xilinguole Grasslands of Inner Mongolia." *Development and Change* 45, no. 2: 308–328.

Kong Fanzhi. 1994. *Aoluguya de ewenke ren* [The Ewenki People of Aoluguya]. Tianjing: Tianjing guji chubanshe [Tianjing Ancient Books Publishing House].

Longworth, John W., and Gregory J. Williamson. 1993. *China's Pastoral Region: Sheep and Wool, Minority Nationalities, Rangeland Degradation and Sustainable Development.* Wallingford: Cab International.

Ong, Aihwa. 2006. *Neoliberalism as Exception: Mutations in Citizenship and Sovereignty.* Durham, NC: Duke University Press.

Ong, Aihwa, and Li Zhang. 2006. "Introduction: Privatizing China: Powers of the Self, Socialism from Afar." In *Privatizing China: Socialism from Afar,* ed. Li Zhang and Aihwa Ong. Ithaca, NY: Cornell University Press.

Pöyry. 2008. "Aoluguya Ethnic Reindeer Resort Master Plan," 21 March. Beijing: Pöyry (Beijing) Consulting Company Limited.

Taylor, James L. 2006. "Negotiating the Grassland: The Policy of Pasture Enclosures and Contested Resource Use in Inner Mongolia." *Human Organization* 65, no. 4: 374–386.

Wilkes, Andreas. 2006. "Innovation to Support Agropastoralist Livelihoods in Northwest Yunnan, China." *Mountain Research and Development* 26, no. 3: 209–213.

Williams, Dee M. 1996. "Grassland Enclosures: Catalyst of Land Degradation in Inner Mongolia." *Human Organization* 55, no. 3: 307–313.

Yeh, Emily T. 2009. "Greening Western China: A Critical View." *Geoforum* 40: 884–894.

Yeh, Emily T., and Gaerrang. 2010. "Tibetan Pastoralism in Neoliberalising China: Continuity and Change in Gouli." *Area* 43, no. 2: 165–172.

Zhang, Rongsu. 1988. "A Case Study on Mountain Environmental Management: Nyemo County (Tibet)." Occasional Paper no. 13. Kathmandu: International Centre for Integrated Mountain Development.

☺⟫ 4

THE MANY FACES OF NOMADISM AMONG THE REINDEER EWENKI

Uses of Land, Mobility, and Exchange Networks

Aurore Dumont

In the aftermath of the 2003 Reindeer Ewenki resettlement, the Chinese media reported extensively on "the last reindeer nomads of China." At first the media covered news about the move of the Ewenki and their reindeer from old Aoluguya to a new settlement near the city of Genhe. Later the media continued to follow the story as the reindeer fell ill due to lack of appropriate fodder and the herders returned to the forest. Was this a case of failed sedentarization? Did the Reindeer Ewenki succeed in maintaining their nomadic lifestyle? Responses to these questions must recognize that "nomadism" has many faces among the Reindeer Ewenki. Though they continue to move between the settlement and their camps in the taiga, the herders' present situation is ambivalent as they try to adapt reindeer husbandry to state development, moderniza-tion policies, and expectations of the benefits of sedentarization.

Spatial mobility is essential for nomads, as numerous studies on the importance of flexibility and adaptation in herd management strate-gies, social organization, land tenure, and interactions with outsiders have shown (Humphrey and Sneath 1999; Khazanov [1983] 1994, 1998; Stammler 2007). Based on fieldwork conducted between 2008 and 2011, this chapter will analyze how the Ewenki of Aoluguya maintain and adapt their reindeer herding practices to the current Chinese context. I argue that despite state interventions to change the course of their traditional herding,[1] the Ewenki have adopted flexible strategies to adapt to changing conditions. Giving special attention to variations over space and time, the first section takes a look back at the period before Communism and collectivism to better understand the Chinese state's political and ecological land use. The second section highlights the continuities, changes, and substitutions that shape Ewenki herders' simultaneously nomadic and settled way of life. Taking into account the reindeer herders' cultural and social practices and more specifically their "mobility" for different purposes, I explore how the herders themselves rearrange their social and spatial organization in the nomadic camp. The final part focuses on informal economic networks established between Ewenki herders and Han Chinese people from small towns.

State conceptions of land use and reindeer herding

While conducting fieldwork among Reindeer Ewenki clans of Manchuria in the early 1930s, the anthropologist Ethel J. Lindgren (1938: 609)[2] noted that the surface area of their nomadic pastures was about 7,000 km[2]. Reindeer Ewenki were then moving in a large territory covering the northern Daxing'anling Mountains along the Amur (Chinese: Heilongjiang) and Argun (E'erguna) rivers on the Sino-Russian border. Known by the places where they once traded with Russian partners (called *andak*),[3] they fell into three distinct groups: the Mohe, the Qiqian, and the Dubova (Neimenggu Zizhiqu Bianji Zu 1986: 209).[4] Incidentally, these barter exchanges were designated by the Russian verb *andačit*, "to barter" (Kaĭgorodov 1968: 124). The trade in game with the Russians allowed the Ewenki to maintain the mobile lifestyle dictated by their domestic economy, moving in small groups according to seasonal hunting and herding activities.

In winter, the high season for hunting, the nomads pitched their tents wherever game animals were abundant, whereas in summer their movements sought fresh pasture for the herd. Like other reindeer herders of northern Eurasia, the Ewenki usually kept small herds of domesticated reindeer and used them for milking, riding, and carrying loads. Ingold (1980: 24–25) has contrasted this "milch pastoralism" to the tundra's "carnivorous pastoralism," which keeps animals for meat production. Herding and hunting activities satisfied almost all the needs of the nomads, who used animal products for food, clothing, and housing. The taiga, as provider of reindeer forage and good hunting game, had symbolic as well as instrumental value (Fondahl 1998: 3).

In the twentieth century, state policies became a crucial consideration in identifying elements of change and continuity in nomadic peoples' traditional economy. Over the past decades, "modernization" has become an acute and still unsolved problem for pastoralists, whether they live in the Middle East, Central and Inner Asia, or the far North (Khazanov 1998: 8). How, then, should the concept of "modernization" be understood in the Chinese context? Dedicating his chapter to the modernization process among the Kirghiz pastoralists of Xinjiang, Kreutzmann stated that "from a viewpoint of modernization theory,

Figure 4.1. Reindeer at camp, January 2009, Galaya. Photograph by Aurore Dumont.

classifications apply that highlight the backwardness of peripheral societies, their outmoded economic strategies and their adherence to traditional behavioural patterns" (2012: 110). Regarding the Reindeer Ewenki, the state's approaches toward "modernization" have shifted over time. Whereas collectivization policy followed "the Soviet project of abandoning 'nomadism as a way of life' in favor of 'nomadism as a way of production'" (Habeck 2005: 141), recent environmental policies are based on the belief that China's grasslands are suffering pasture degradation due to livestock overgrazing.[5] Whether the multiple relocations of the Reindeer Ewenki settlements between 1957 and 2003 were guided by political, economic or ecological reasons, they are meaningful in explaining the state's conception of modernization.

A brief summary of the economic and political situation shows how, over time, the most influential events affected the Reindeer Ewenki, who have tried to conform to different kinds of environments. As understood by authorities, the task of "modernization" is implemented in phases, the first of which is sedentarization. In 1957 the first Ewenki "ethnic township" (*minzu xiang*) was created in Qiqian. However, around 1965 the prospect of a full-scale Sino-Russian conflict motivated the authorities to resettle the Ewenki away from the banks of the Argun

River to a newly built village named Aoluguya. Wooden houses were built, and their residents enjoyed modern amenities such as a school, medical and shopping services, and marketing assistance in selling hunting products. Some residents were employed in the local administration as teachers or administrators, but many went on with their life of hunting and herding.

In the 1960s, recognizing reindeer antlers' economic potential as raw material for Chinese medicine, the government initiated measures to turn the formerly small-scale reindeer herding into a more intensive reindeer-breeding business. Every year the antlers were sold to the government for work points. As in the former USSR, the "production nomadism" (or "nomadism as a way of production") introduced as a key model for reindeer herding reduced the care of the reindeer to a tool of production and isolated it from its social base (Vitebsky 1990: 348). From the 1960s on, the traditional hunting grounds and grazing land of the Reindeer Ewenki became a major attraction for the forestry, which led to the immigration of many workers, followed by the construction of small towns, roads, and railways in the middle of the forest.[6] This corroborates Aubin's (1974: 86) description of sedentary Han Chinese people who regard nomadic territory as fallow land that should be farmed or put to other uses. Despite these experiments, many reindeer herders embraced the possibility of continuing reindeer herding and hunting in the taiga under the Chinese authorities, as the sale of antlers was still a lucrative business. However, the growing appropriation of land by the forestry authorities has resulted in a pressure on the land and a reduction of reindeer pastures.

The reforms of the 1980s introduced the Household Contract Responsibility System in pasture areas. The system integrated people, livestock, and grasslands, and redefined herders' rights and responsibilities (Wu and Du 2008: 17). In Aoluguya, the reindeer were redistributed among herding families; however, the antler industry remains under state control to date. Beach (2012: 123) has called this a "system of partitioned rights and multiple holders" in which milk accrues to herders while antler crops are controlled by government authorities, although profits are shared in part with the herders.

In the mid 1980s, reform policies greatly promoted livestock businesses in the grasslands, ignoring the carrying capacity of the pastures. A decade later, restoration of damaged grasslands became a political priority, leading to the launch of large-scale projects aimed at "ecological restoration." In 1996, the state adopted the policy of Two Rights and One System, which Wu and Du (2008: 18) summarized as "demarcating pastures, forbidding free nomadism, adopting settled residences and controlling livestock stocking rates." Two years later it was succeeded by the Converting Pasture to Grasslands (*Tuimu huancao*) program, aimed at moving herding families away from the grasslands. Emily Yeh (2005: 9) has judiciously proposed the term "green governmentality" to describe ecological restoration programs meant to improve the conditions of nature and population by introducing new environmental logics.[7]

Finally, to realize modernization, the central state pursued the strategic goal of reducing regional economic disparities between the Han-populated eastern areas and the "underdeveloped" western region,[8] through a campaign to Open Up the West (*Xibu da kaifa*).[9] Prohibiting hunting was part of this process, and in 2003 the Aoluguya local government undertook to resettle the Ewenki and their reindeer via "ecological migration" (*shengtai yimin*) to a new Aoluguya township near Genhe city, 250 km to the south. The herders, the authorities, and the media saw this measure as a major event because it was intended to end reindeer herding in the forest. At the resettlement site, however, many reindeer died from lack of lichen, their principal food source, and the herders had to return to their remote camps.

The failure of this aspect of the resettlement put both the authorities and the herders in an uncomfortable situation. Herders who have chosen to continue living from animal husbandry cannot ignore the call of the taiga, which offers pastures that the settlement area lacks. They therefore must move between the new village where they are supposed to be settled, and the camps where they herd reindeer. Local authorities meanwhile have to deal with what they call "settling but not living" (*ding er bu ju*). In this context of "failed resettlement," the notion of adaptive mobility and adaptation has become a key challenge and perhaps also an example of the contradiction between economic development and environmental conservation.

The settled sphere and the status of herders

The 2003 resettlement also shed light on the confused situation prevailing in the herders' village. A brief look at the Aoluguya ethnic township provides an interesting overview of the complexity of the herding engagement in the community. Xie (2005, 2010) has pointed out the problem of "hunter status" (*liemin shenfen*)[10] and the distribution of housing following the resettlement. Ewenki "hunters" are priority recipients of houses in the new settlement, and hunters, whether they possess reindeer or not, do not have salaries or jobs.[11] The state's conceptualization of "hunter" is constructed on the basis of opposing categories and functions as part of a system of hierarchical dualism: Han/minority, city dwellers/village residents, hunters/workers. But this classificatory device does not reflect the viewpoint of those so labeled. For the Ewenki, the term *liemin* has a certain meaning and value and reveals one's mastery of herding and hunting skills. As Xie (2005: 104, 2010: 128) noted, it is quite illogical to assign hunter status to people who do not speak the Ewenki language and are unfamiliar with either hunting techniques or herding skills, while others who are counted among the best hunters but also have salaries and jobs are deprived of the status.

Following the same reasoning, some Chinese scholars have attempted to categorize the Ewenki into different groups according to social position and the extent of mobility in reindeer herding after resettlement. Qi (2006: 100) differentiated three types of people in the village: nomads (*yidong weizhu*), who have a traditional lifestyle and whose income comes from the sale of reindeer antlers; the seminomadic (*ban yidong ban dingju*), who have a modern lifestyle and whose income comes from salaries; and sedentary people (*dingju*) dependent on state funds. However, this classification fails to account for the complexity of the realities in the field. Although a large share of Ewenki do not possess reindeer, many are still directly involved in reindeer herding or engaged in a combination of reindeer herding and service sector activities, and even "sedentary people" who have salaries and apartments in Genhe may possess reindeer and engage in herding them. This illustrates the difficulty of settling on an analytical framework for studying changes in nomadic pastoralism and especially processes of sedentarization. Do the Reindeer Ewenki exhibit nomadic populations' general tendency to adopt a sedentary lifestyle and gradually give up "pastoral values"? Taking this point further, I analyze the strategies of Reindeer Ewenki engaged in reindeer herding.

The nomadic sphere: Rearranging social and spatial organization in the camps

The concept of nomadism remains controversial in the social sciences. While some definitions include all the communities whose primary resources extraction strategy—animal husbandry, foraging, trade, or services—is based on recurrent physical mobility, others prefer to restrict the term's usage to communities whose economy is based primarily on mobile herding (Rao and Casimir 2003: 5). Nomadism, commonly related to pastoralism as a cultural system with a characteristic ecology, involves highly mobile arrangements, and technologies and material culture adapted to mobility and movement of the group and its herds over socially recognized routes in annual cycles. Nomadism is a strategy that permits or enhances access to resources, implying a common set of ecological and economic practices. The notion of mobility is essential, since it answers the need for seasonal movements. Here the term mobility refers not only to seasonal migrations but also to the logic of adaptation and rearrangement followed by people involved in forest reindeer herding. The reindeer-herding economy depends on ecological knowledge of marked seasonality and mobility to maintain a regular supply of food for the herd.

Nomadism in its traditional form has been reduced in importance or transformed into sedentarized livestock breeding or stabling of animal stocks in Central Asia and Mongolia. Khazanov ([1983] 1994: 27) considered mobile pastoralism in its nomadic form dying, if not already completely dead. These changes have convinced many authors to rethink concepts of nomadism. Referring to the Nentsy reindeer herders of Russia, Stammler (2007: 23) used the term "lifestyle nomadism" both to define a mode of family migration and to describe something encompassing the conceptions of the Nentsy nomads, whose "real lifestyle" revolves around constant movements on particular routes. For Humphrey and Sneath (1999: 1–2), nomadism has disappeared virtually everywhere in Inner Asia, although mobility remains a central pastoral technique. Thus, both prefer the term mobile pastoralism to nomadism because it does not evoke the associations outsiders make about nomads as a category—free and egalitarian, a wandering type of movement, warlike tribes, and so on.

Among the diverse types of reindeer herding distinguishable along ecological, geographical, and cultural lines, taiga reindeer herding is considered to have the weakest economic future (Stammler 2007: 53). Ethnic groups who used reindeer mainly for transport and milking have seen herding for transport purposes dwindle (Stammler 2007: 69). In Russia, where snowmobiles have replaced animals, the number of domestic reindeer declined sharply after the collapse of the Soviet Union. Many authors thus consider domestic reindeer herding to be on the edge of extinction. In China, vehicles have replaced reindeer for transportation, with similar consequences. The mobile pastoral economy, dependent on a mobile way of life and the maintenance of herds year-round in the forest, has changed and diminished.

So when is the nomadic life over or "lost"? Does it even make sense to compare a certain way of life with an imagined ideal or "traditional" form of nomadism? As the reindeer becomes an ethnic tool and a tourist attraction, how should we understand the reindeer herding management of the Ewenki today? This mobile economy requires the organization of closely related families and individuals who, year-round or for part of the year, herd together and help and support each other. Thus, many Ewenki divide their time between residence in the settlement and regular stays in the nomadic camp (*liemin dian*).[12]

Rotation between the village and the camps

Seasonal herding determines the size of the community in a nomadic camp. From October to February the main activities consist of looking after reindeer and hunting, which has been banned since 2003. The herders regularly denounce the suppression of firearms, a restriction that deprives them of an essential part of their economy even as it tends also to restrain the symbolic value of hunting, which is a kind of regulation between men and spirits.[13] Despite the ban, hunting is still practiced without firearms: alone or with one or two others, men commonly track and trap small animals such as rabbits and Eurasian red squirrels (*Sciurus vulgaris*).

During the winter season, eight people at most share the encampment. In spring, reindeer cows give birth to calves. Throughout the summer, the reindeer come back to the encampment every day to benefit from the "smoky fire" (*maoyan*) that protects them from insects. The *maoyan* is made under a construction of vertical jointed poles called *sèrukan* (see Figure 1.1.). Summer is the time for milking and gathering different kinds of mushrooms, berries, and pinecones (*songshuta*). This is also when the reindeer antlers are cut.

Thus, from April to August all the nomadic tents are full of people sharing activities divided by gender. Men manage the herds, plan and execute migration strategies, hunt, cut wood, and sell hunting products; while women make food, look after the reindeer, and do the milking. Traditionally, several nuclear families gathered in the same encampment, but today these rules are less respected and members of a camp choose to be together according to affinity. Sometimes a herder leaves a camp to herd alone or with other families in another camp, mainly because of a disagreement.

According to the Aoluguya local authorities' records, fifteen herd owners are responsible for a total of eight hundred reindeer, which suggests that the reindeer herds owned by Ewenki households are actually very limited. A herd owner is often confronted with obstacles (e.g., children's needs, or an activity in the village) that create a need to involve relatives in herd management at the camp. Thus reindeer herding families must decide who will work with the reindeer and who will stay in the village. The settlement of Aoluguya is an indispensable space in Ewenki life. It is an administrative and reindeer herding headquarters, a marketing outlet, and a connecting point in visiting relatives. However, the village lacks essential economic and social infrastructure such as a food store, market, school, hospital and so on. The reindeer herders thus have to travel 4.5 km from the village to Genhe. Bus service is unavailable. Except for a few herders who possess a driver's license, they use bikes or motorcycles in summer and pay for taxi service during the rest of the year.

Herding used to be a family occupation, but young women and children are now largely absent. Women need to be with their children, who attend school in Genhe.[14] Thus women's traditional competences and responsibilities in the camp (cooking, repairing clothes, tending animals) have become men's tasks. A herder who needs to tend to other matters can usually get a family member to take care of the animals. Many unmarried men who do not possess reindeer also stay in camps working as herders. In return, they receive food and sometimes reindeer. A stay in the camp can be as short as a few hours or as long as two months. The herders' mobility depends on different factors. The great distance between Aoluguya and the different camps tends to encourage herders to form social networks of people whose services they can rely upon. Herders and their relatives or friends make the trip to camp to deliver fresh supplies and food, help with hunting and herding, participate in the move to a new campsite, or visit friends and relatives. Then they go back to Aoluguya, where they sell hunting products, buy fresh supplies for the camp, or visit friends and relatives. The organizational framework of the camp changes according to individual needs and seasonal activities, as described in the two following examples.

The first camp is composed of a couple—A (f.) and B (m.)—who own approximately thirty reindeer. A single man, C, the cousin of B, stays regularly in the camp to take part in hunting and herding. Thus, these three people periodically share the same tent. A and B have children, so when they leave the camp, D, the brother of A, comes to help C.

In the second camp are the couple E (f.) and F (m.), who have one child and own around thirty reindeer, and a widowed man, G, who inherited ten reindeer from his wife. As in the first camp, they all share one tent. During summer and winter vacations (July/August and January/February), the members of the nuclear family are together, while G, who has another activity in town, is absent. As soon as the vacation is over, E and her child return to the village, while G joins F in the camp.

In the examples above, we can see a rotation among individuals at the camp. In the first case, A and B regularly take turns with C and D, while in the second case, E and G join F successively. This kind of organization is typical of a "small camp," where a few people share the same tent. In bigger camps, which can have up to three tents, the mobility and presence of people in the camp is more complex. Herd owners who have jobs come a few times a year, especially in the summer. Their relatives work in the camp and take care of the herd. The members of a camp herd their livestock jointly, often in rotation and with other members. The local government applies the same logic of housing distribution in the village to the tents in encampments: one must have reindeer and be part of a nuclear family to obtain a tent. A single man who herds reindeer has to share a tent with relatives. Local authorities register all Ewenki households as residing in settled houses in Aoluguya and mostly ignore who goes to the camp and who comes back. Thus their records reflect administrative rather than residential reality.

Mapping the taiga: A reduced but flexible mobility

Various factors mediate the relationships Reindeer Ewenki maintain with their herding areas and how they deal with alternative uses of land and resources. It is essential to choose the optimal herding areas while simultaneously respecting the government's restrictions and divisions of the forest. Understanding different ways of mapping the land and notions of territoriality are thus crucial aspects of herd management and mobility. Whereas the Ewenki see the forest as pasture and hunting grounds with specific migration routes, the forest authorities understand the taiga in terms of strictly delimited territories used for industrial purposes. Even when the herders' movements follow established "routes" allotted to them, they pay special attention to the general environmental conditions and the quality of pastures.

The taiga abounds with valuable natural resources, attracting many seasonal Han workers who arrive on trucks in the morning and leave in the evening. These continual daily journeys are made possible by the parceling of the forest. The taiga is divided by big roads (*gonglu*) radiating from every township, along with "lanes"[15] that go deeper into the forest. A forestry map (*linye ditu*) (see Figure 4.2) depicts this careful mapping and division.

As Yeh (2005: 16) has also noticed, creating boundaries to demarcate administrative entities like national parks and state forests expands state power by establishing greater control over both the resources and

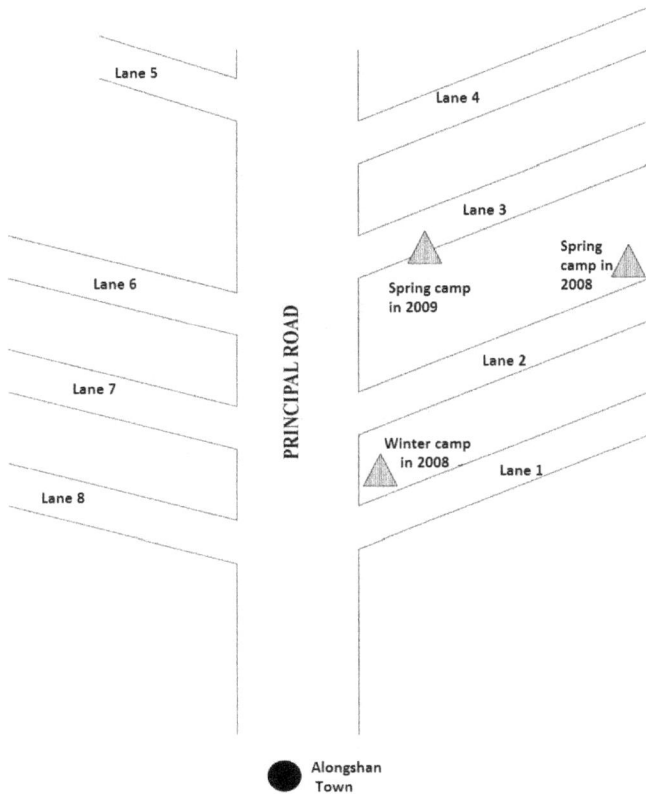

Figure 4.2. Division of the forest landscape in the Alongshan area. Created by Aurore Dumont.

the people who use them. Thus, mobility requires a specific work organization over space and time. Herders have to move with these demarcated areas in mind, respecting the frontiers and restrictions set by the forestry authorities. Their continuous movement across the taiga is no longer an act of free choice, as herders find themselves caught between state-imposed policies and nomadic life in the taiga.

Seven Reindeer Ewenki camps lie between Genhe city and Alongshan town, from south to north on the railway line that connects Genhe city to Mangui. The camp closest to Aoluguya is 30 km away, while the farthest is more than 250 km distant. A road links each camp to a township or forest station (*linchang*) at a distance of 15–80 km. Very often a herding camp is situated along a lane, or even deeper in the forest.

Before 2003, provincial frontiers and environmental legislation had drastically reduced the territory available for migration. Lavrillier (2011) noted Siberian Evenki reindeer herders' capacity for and knowledge about discovering new territories while traveling around 1,000 km per year. In winter they shifted camp "every 20 or 30 days, moving 40–80 km to the next site," whereas in summer they moved shorter distances more frequently, "for example 5–20 km every 3 to 10 days" (Lavrillier 2011: 217). Aoluguya Reindeer Ewenki movements are nowhere near such distances, annually moving only 15–20 km. The local government plays a central role in managing their herding activities. The policy of "modernizing" the camps was also implemented for the comfort of the herders. The first step was to replace the traditional cone-shaped tent of the Reindeer Ewenki (Ewenki: *palatka* or *djiu*)[16] with the modern ridge tent (Chinese: *zhangpeng*).[17]

   Where the traditional tent remains, it bears a touristic value. Certain other items have been introduced outside and inside the nomads' tent. A solar panel may allow TV reception, and shelves, tables, and wooden beds have become part of the interior of the tent (Figure 4.3). These heavy objects make it difficult to move everything on the backs of reindeer, and each of the two to four annual migrations requires a specific organization. The biggest devices, such as the solar panel and wooden

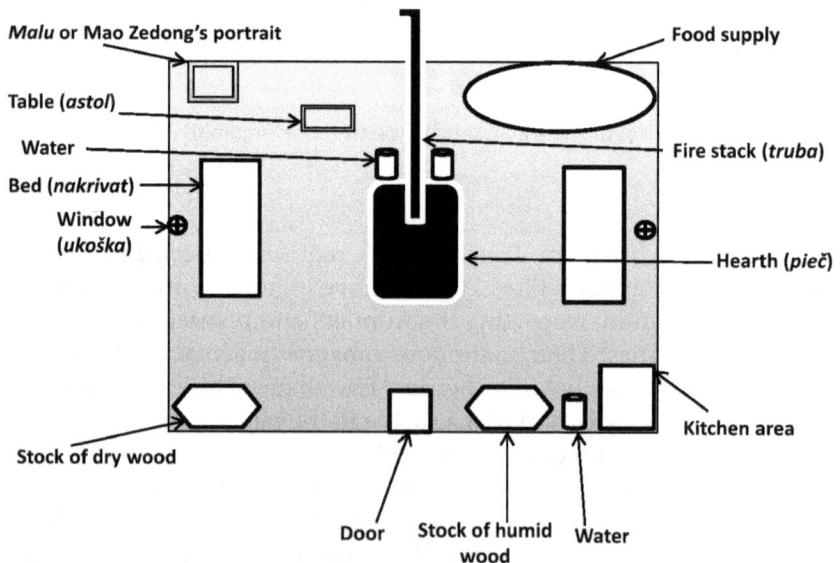

Figure 4.3. Interior of the tent. Created by Aurore Dumont.
Note: The interior arrangement may take several forms or change according to family. The sleeping area, the food supply, and the table can be moved around inside the tent. Russian words commonly used by Ewenki are bracketed.

beds, are moved by car while herders lead the reindeer on foot to the new camp. If the new camp is far away, the reindeer are transported by truck. However, the ever growing use of motor vehicles to carry materials, people, and at times reindeer has made the Ewenki and their herds less mobile than in the past. In Siberia too, Anderson (2006: 91) noticed the current lack of reindeer trained for saddle riding among Evenki herders, concluding that the conditions of post-socialist herding do not leave time for a high culture of domestication.

Despite the continuous interaction between sedentarization policies and herding practices, I prefer to perceive the Ewenki as mobile reindeer herders rather than "fully sedentarized" or "fully nomadic" people. Spatial links tying Reindeer Ewenki to urban areas are visible in the configuration of three major movements: between Aoluguya and Genhe city; between Aoluguya and the nomadic camps, and between the small towns and the nomadic camps. Although the nomadic territory of the Reindeer Ewenki has been reduced, their mobility is very strong, a fact easily explained by the absolute necessity of moving between all the places where they are connected. The geographical distance between the camps and urban spaces ranges from 15 km to more than 250 km. In this specific context, mobility requires knowledge of contacts and connections outside one's local area.

After the resettlement of 2003, many Han people who once worked in the old Aoluguya township were left unemployed. Some of them became taxi drivers and conduct regular transportation services, sometimes daily, between Genhe and the camps. In some cases, people can take the train from Genhe to the railway station nearest to their camp. Although the train ride covers part of the journey, the distance between the nearest small town and the camp is rarely less than 15 km. Here as well, taxi drivers are crucial. Han people from the town are paid to take herders into the lanes of the taiga up to their camp. When herders stay in the camp a long time, they also contact taxi drivers for food. The connection with the town provides the Reindeer Ewenki with the resources of an informal economy based on relationships between Ewenki in the camps and Ewenki in the settlement, and between Ewenki in the camps and Han Chinese people of the small towns.

Informal economies: Hunting game and reindeer as media of exchange

Until the 2003 resettlement, hunting was widely practiced by Ewenki. Game supplied food, wild animal parts used as materials, and high-value commodities for trade. The Chinese law for nature conservation and protection of endangered species made hunting illegal[18] and subjected hunters to penalties. Nonetheless, limited, clandestine hunting continues among Ewenki herders, providing an interesting framework for analysis of informal exchanges. Reindeer herding and hunting connects the Ewenki with their neighbors, geographically and economically. Khazanov (1998: 9) pointed to written sources demonstrating that nomads acquire a substantial part of their material culture from sedentary peoples, as well as other aspects of culture, and even ideologies. Regular contacts for barter trade between Reindeer Ewenki and their Russian *andak* partners were well documented by Lindgren (1938) and Yong (1991) in the 1930s and 1940s. Both stressed that these reciprocal exchanges were crucial for both sides, as Ewenki relied on Russian products (sugar, tea, flour, cotton, gunpowder, etc.) and the hunters' game was indispensable to the Russian fur market. At this time, the practice of hunting maintained a subsistence economy and afforded specific commodities.

Although the reindeer herders receive local government funding, their economic situation remains fragile due to the high rate of unemployment, the low price of reindeer antler, and the obligation to move constantly between the camp and the settlement, which requires money. Thus Reindeer Ewenki rely on their traditional domestic economy to improve their economic prospects.[19] Known as good hunters and the only reindeer herders of China, the Ewenki have opportunity to create "valuable networks."

In the context of recent governmental restrictions, hunting is practiced for two main purposes. The first concerns the herders' community consumption, while the second is within the scope of informal exchanges.[20] The latter comprise transactions and networks articulating many exchange logics, from monetary trade and sharing to services. I argue that this complex network of social relationships between the Ewenki and their Han partners is driven by external demand (the chance to obtain "forbidden goods"), favors, and monetary income. The reindeer herders hunt several types of game, primarily deer and small game. Each type of game corresponds to values and symbols ranging from qualities of taste to ritual functions and market value.

Both Ewenki and Han use rabbit, roe deer, and black grouse[21] primarily as food, but their ways of doing so differ. The animal parts preferred by the Ewenki are commonly unwanted by the Han community. For example, the hunters appreciate the ears, blood, eyes, and liver of the roe deer. Consumption of certain parts, in their view, provides better hunting skills. Eating the animal's ears sharpens hearing; consuming the eyes improves one's sight. The deer meat is part of prestige dishes while the grouse is recognized by the Chinese for its nutritional qualities and taste.

The sable (*Martes zibellina*),[22] Siberian weasel, and Eurasian red squirrel are hunted during the winter for their luxuriant furs. As hunted game, they fetch the highest market value and can also be a means of exchange and payment. After Ewenki community members take their share of game, the remainder has different "destinations." Most of the time, hunted game is sold to Han storekeepers and merchants of the small towns surrounding the camps. Then the "forbidden goods" end up in restaurant dishes such as "dragon bird soup" (*feilong tang*), whereas high-value animals like sable will probably be resold on any fur market. These goods are often assessed in terms of monetary value: a black grouse goes for ¥50;[23] a sable, ¥500–800. This "shadow trade" goes on mainly between Ewenki who are regularly present at the camps and Han people of the township—to which, as we have seen, every camp is linked. Apart from monetized transactions, another type of exchange, this one without financial compensation, occurs with forestry and township officials when valuable hunting game such as sable is "offered" in exchange for some "arrangement." This can be a better use of land, a blind eye toward discreet hunting, or loans of firearms—in brief, various bureaucratic or informal sanctions. This mutual exchange of reciprocal favors is clearly motivated by mutual service and assistance (see Figure 4.4).

Reindeer, whether dead or alive, are occasionally part of such exchanges. As a wild animal, the reindeer is protected by the state. Herded only in this part of China by a small population, it is also a high-value commodity. The local government takes part in herding decision-making and must be notified of any transaction or sale concerning reindeer. However, discreet transactions occur, mostly with people coming from the tourist industry. Reindeer may even be killed in some cases,[24] for example when they are affected by disease. In any case, the different parts of the animal are divided between the Ewenki portion and offerings to their partners. As for Ewenki personal consumption, some parts are shared between friends and relatives, and Ewenki women dry and soften the skins and use them to create traditional products such as bags. The finished handicrafts are offered or sold in the small shops of the village.

Both monetary and nonmonetary exchanges hinge on establishing a relationship (*guanxi*) and preserving companionship. The Chinese word *guanxi* literally means "relationship" between objects, forces, or persons (Yang 1994: 1).[25] Personal relationships are implicitly based on

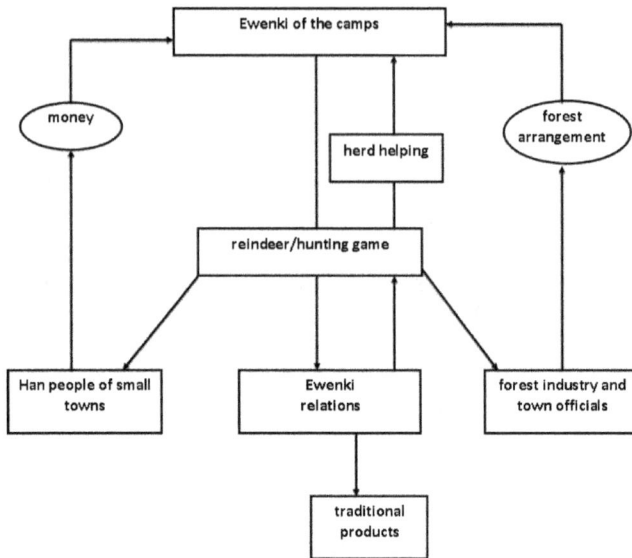

Figure 4.4. Reindeer and hunting game movements in networks. Created by Aurore Dumont.

mutual interest and benefit. Preparing to enter into *guanxi* involves establishing a basis of familiarity to shrink the barrier between insider and outsider. In the Ewenki case, once *guanxi* is established between the herder and a counterpart, either can ask a favor of the other, who is regarded as a friend (*pengyou*).

As Humphrey has shown in the case of Nepal, moral obligation means creating and preserving a sense of fairness and trust, with each side taking responsibility as a recipient of the satisfaction of each side (Humphrey 1992: 108). Maintaining trust is especially important in an informal economy context, where exchanges must be done discreetly. Such transactions take place in either the nomadic sphere (in the herders' camp) or the settled sphere (the township or city), according to the nature of the commodity. Herders are often more "mobile" in selling hunted game because they must frequently pass through a nearby town to buy food or make their way to Aoluguya. Meetings between the herders and their "friends" are occasions to share simple dinners or banquets that will strengthen confidence in the established relationship. Thus, each hunter has an "appointed friend" who is the preferred buyer of the hunted game. Friends are chosen with an eye to the benefits they offer as well as their capacity for mutual trust. Informal economic exchanges, arising not in a context of reciprocal dependence but rather in a situation of "mutual agreement," illuminate the ways Ewenki and their "friends" bypass laws and regulations.

Concluding remarks

Despite the political and environmental pressures on the social and spatial behavior of the Reindeer Ewenki, they have somehow managed to keep their domestic economy, in a rearranged form. The importance of movement and interactions in their multiple dimensions shows the herders' great flexibility in coping with new environments. Seen as a part of a complex interactive system, the lifestyle of the Ewenki reindeer herders in contemporary China is thus the product of a combination of many factors. However, the authorities regard their "nomadic way of life" more as an ethnic symbol than a traditional domestic economy. The government has come to recognize that reindeer herding is an economic sector that should be stimulated and developed to become a source of income as a tourist attraction. Thus, in the near future, the Ewenki will experience the effects of ethnic tourism, which can revive—or destroy—traditional values and practices. How do the Ewenki regard themselves in present-day China, and how do they interpret all these changes? They all agree that without reindeer, there would be no Ewenki people. The reindeer will long remain the ethnic symbol of the "last hunting tribe of China."

Notes

1. "Traditional herding" refers to the pastoral practices of the pre-socialist period.
2. Ethel John Lindgren's anthropological research focused mainly on the Reindeer Tungus of Manchuria (today's Reindeer Ewenki) and shamanism, but she also attempted to produce a comprehensive, detailed record of the "Khingan Tungus", today's Oroqen ethnic minority (Chinese: Elunchun), the Solon (Suolun), Russian émigrés, Han Chinese, and Mongols. Lindgren visited all these groups in the course of three expeditions to northeastern Inner Mongolia between 1929 and 1932 (See Lindgren 1935, 1938, 1939).
3. Common to several Altaic languages, the term *andak* means "friend."
4. Qiqian was previously named Ust-Urov in Russian. Dubova is today known as Shanghulin. The three groups were distinguished by their different hats: the Mohe group's hat was made of elk skin; the Dubova's was of red squirrel decorated with colorful material, and the Qiqian's was made of red squirrel skin alone (Neimenggu Zizhiqu Bianji Zu 1986: 209).

5. Most of the nomadic populations that are affected by these policies in China are scattered in the Tibet, Xinjiang, Qinghai, and Inner Mongolia regions.
6. In Inner Mongolia, the Han Chinese population increased from 1.2 million in 1912 to 24.70 million in 2010.
7. On land degradation and Chinese discourse from the Inner Mongolian grasslands perspectives, see Williams (2002) and Merkle (2013).
8. The definition of "the western region" remains unclear. When the campaign began, the region included nine provincial-level jurisdictions, but in 2000 three other areas were added, including Inner Mongolia (Goodman 2004: 6).
9. Opening the western regions to tourism is one strategy of the Open Up the West campaign for economic development. This is particularly true for Inner Mongolia, promoted as "the cradle of Mongolian culture." In Aoluguya, a large tourism project undertaken since 2008 has turned the village into a big "ethnic reindeer resort," following the tourism and marketing model of the Sami people of northern Europe. The local government has provided the inhabitants with new Finnish-style houses, a modern museum, and recreational areas (see other chapters in this book).
10. "Herder" (*mumin*) and "hunter" (*liemin*) are state-constructed professional categories. Pastoralist Ewenki are in the first category, but the Reindeer Ewenki are in the second, the state having recognized reindeer herding as a productive activity secondary to the primary activity of hunting. However, although hunting was officially banned and has not been a subsistence activity for a long time, the reindeer herders are still labeled "hunters' in the Chinese administrative nomenclature.
11. For a detailed analysis, see Xie in this volume.
12. *Liemin dian* literally means "hunters' point."
13. Hunting is a mediator between man and spirits among many hunter groups of the taiga. According to Hamayon (1990), sexual spirit partnerships, exchanges, and shamanic power were all born in the context of hunting rituals among the small nomadic groups of Siberia.
14. The old Aoluguya settlement had a school. Since the 2003 resettlement, all the children go to school in Genhe. The new village's proximity to the city was a strong argument for the resettlement.
15. Depending on the administrative division, the lanes are called *haoxian* in Heilongjiang province, while in Inner Mongolia they are usually *chaxian* or *zhixian*.
16. While *palatka* refers only to the tent, the Ewenki term *djiu* means tent as well as household.
17. This is the type of tent used by loggers—Han workers who may stay in the taiga several weeks. The workers' tent is commonly larger in size, housing ten to fifteen people.
18. The hunting ban included confiscation of hunting equipment.
19. This current situation has little in common with that of Siberia's Evenki herders, who turned to barter for consumer goods among other things. About barter in post-socialist Russia among Evenki, see Ssorin-Chaikov (2000).

20. Here I refer to all activities that are officially banned by the state, including hunting, selling and buying game, and providing illegal services.
21. The Chinese commonly call this bird the "dragon bird" (*feilong*).
22. The sable's nickname is "soft gold" (*ruan hangjin*) and its fur is one of the "three jewels of the Northeast" (*dongbei sanbao*), the other two being ginseng and deer antler.
23. ¥1 = US$0.16.
24. In the past reindeer could be sacrificed for ritual purposes.
25. Some other authors translate *guanxi* as "personal connections" or "social networks" (Yan 1996).

References

Anderson, David. G. 2006. "Is Siberian Reindeer Herding in Crisis? Living with Reindeer Fifteen Years after the End of State Socialism." *Nomadic Peoples* 10, no. 2: 87–104.
Aubin, Françoise. 1974. "Anthropologie du nomadisme." *Cahiers internationaux de sociologie* 56: 79–90.
Beach, Hugh. 2012. "Milk and Antlers: A System of Partitioned Rights and Multiple Holders of Reindeer in Northern China." In *Who Owns The Stock? Collective and Multiple Property Rights in Animals,* ed. Anatoly M. Khazanov and Günther Schlee. Oxford: Berghahn Books.
Fondahl, Gail A. 1998. *Gaining Ground? Ewenkis, Land, and Reform in Southeastern Siberia.* Boston: Allyn and Bacon.
Goodman, David S. G. 2004. "The Campaign to 'Open up the West': National, Provincial-level and Local Perspectives." In *The Campaign to "Open up the West": National, Provincial-Level and Local Perspectives,* ed. David S. G. Goodman. Cambridge: Cambridge University Press.
Habeck, Joachim Otto. 2005. *What It Means to Be a Herdsman: The Practice and Image of Reindeer Husbandry among the Komi of Northern Russia.* Münster: Lit Verlag.
Hamayon, Roberte. 1990. *La chasse à l'âme. Esquisse d'une théorie du chamanisme sibérien.* Nanterre: Société d'ethnologie.
Humphrey, Caroline. 1992. "Fair Dealing, Just Rewards: The Ethics of Barter in North-East Nepal." In *Barter, Exchange and Value: An Anthropological Approach,* ed. C. Humphrey and S. Hugh-Jones. Cambridge: Cambridge University Press.
Humphrey, Caroline, and David Sneath. 1999. *The End of Nomadism? Society, State and the Environment in Inner Asia.* Durham, NC: Duke University Press.
Ingold, Tim. 1980. *Hunters, Pastoralists and Ranchers: Reindeer Economies and their Transformations.* Cambridge: Cambridge University Press.
Kaĭgorodov, Anatoliĭ Makarovich. 1968. "Evenki v Trechrec'e (Po lichnym nabliudeniiam)" [The Ewenki of the Three Rivers Area (Personal Observations)] *Sovetskaîa Etnografîa,* no. 4: 123–131.

Khazanov, Anatoly M. 1998. "Pastoralists in the Contemporary World: The Problem of Survival." In *Changing Nomads in a Changing World,* ed. J. Ginat and Anatoly Khazanov. Brighton: Sussex Academic Press.

———. (1983) 1994. *Nomads and the Outside World,* translated by Julia Crokkenden. Cambridge: Cambridge University Press.

Kreutzmann, Hermann. 2012. "Kirghiz in Little Kara Köl: The Forces of Modernisation in Southern Xinjiang." In *Pastoral Practices in High Asia: Agency of "Development' Effected by Modernisation, Resettlement and Transformation,* ed. Hermann Kreutzmann. London: Springer.

Lavrillier, Alexandra. 2011. "The Creation and Persistence of Cultural Landscapes among the Siberian Evenkis: Two Conceptions of 'Sacred' Space." In *Landscape and Culture in Northern Eurasia,* ed. P. Jordan. Walnut Creek, CA: Left Coast Press.

Lindgren, Ethel J. 1939. "The Khingan Tungus (Numinchen)." *Man* 39: 19.

———. 1938. "An Example of Culture Contact without Conflict: Reindeer Tungus and Cossacks of North-Western Manchuria." *American Anthropologist,* n.s., 40, no. 4, Part 1: 605–621.

———. 1935. "The Reindeer Tungus of Manchuria." *Man* 35: 44–45.

Merkle, Rita. 2013. "Fifty Years of Transformation: The Decline of Nomadic Pastoralism in China; A Case Study from Inner Mongolia." *Études mongoles et sibériennes, centrasiatiques et tibétaines* 43–44. Accessed 1 July 2011 at http://emscat.revues.org/2166.

Neimenggu Zizhiqu Bianji Zu [Inner Mongolia Autonomous Region Editorial Unit]. 1986. *Ewenke zu shehui lishi diaocha* [Survey of the Social History of the Ewenki Nationality]. Hohhot: Neimenggu renmin chubanshe [Inner Mongolia People's Publishing House].

Qi Huijun. 2006. "Xunlu Ewenkeren shengtai yimin de minzuxue kaocha" [Ethnographic Survey of Ewenki Reindeer Herders' Ecological Migration]. *Manyu Yanjiu* 1: 98–105.

Rao, Aparna, and Michael J. Casimir, eds. 2003. *Nomadism in South Asia.* New Delhi: Oxford University Press.

Ssorin-Chaikov, Nikolai. 2000. "Bear Skins and Macaroni: The Social Life of Things at the Margins of a Siberian State Collective." In *The Vanishing Rouble: Barter Networks and Non-Monetary Transactions in Post-Soviet Societies,* ed. P. Seabright. Cambridge: Cambridge University Press.

Stammler, Florian. 2007. *Reindeer Nomads Meet the Market: Culture, Property and Globalisation at the "End of the Land."* Münster: Lit Verlag.

Vitebsky, Piers. 1990. "Centralized Decentralization: The Ethnography of Remote Reindeer Herders under Perestroika." *Cahiers du monde russe et soviétique* 31, nos. 2–3: 345–358.

Williams, Dee M. 2002. *Beyond Great Walls: Environment, Identity, and Development on the Chinese Grasslands of Inner Mongolia.* Stanford, CA: Stanford University Press.

Wu, Zhizhong, and Wen Du. 2008. "Pastoral Nomad Rights in Inner Mongolia." *Nomadic Peoples* 12, no. 2: 13–33.

Xie Yuanyuan. 2010. *Shengtai yimin zhengce yu difang zhengfu shijian: yi aoluguya ewenke shengtai yimin weili* [The Ecological Migration Policy and Its Application by Local Authorities: A Case Study of the Aoluguya Ewenki Ecological Migration]. Beijing: Beijing daxue chubanshe [Peking University Press].

———. 2005. *Aoluguya Ewenke shengtai yimin: yige guihua xiandaihua de ge an* [The Aoluguya Ewenki Ecological Migration: A Case of Planned Modernization]. Ph.D. Thesis, Beijing: Beijing University.

Yan, Yunxiang. 1996. *The Flow of Gifts: Reciprocity and Social Networks in a Chinese Village.* Stanford, CA: Stanford University Press.

Yang, Mayfair Mei-hui. 1994. *Gifts, Favors and Banquets: The Art of Social Relationships in China.* Ithaca, NY: Cornell University Press.

Yeh, Emily T. 2005. "Green Governmentality and Pastoralism in Western China: Converting Pastures to Grasslands." *Nomadic Peoples* 9, nos. 1–2: 9–29.

Yongtian Zhenxin [Haruka Nagata]. 1991. "Xunlu Elunchun" [Reindeer Oroqen], translated from Japanese by Ao Denggua. In *Ewenke zu yanjiu wenji* [Collected Studies of the Ewenki Nationality], ed. Neimenggu Zizhiqu Ewenke Yanjiuhui, vol. 2. Nantun: Neimenggu zizhiqu ewenke yanjiuhui [Inner Mongolia Ewenki Studies Association].

PART III

REPRESENTATIONS
Defining the Reindeer Ewenki Culture and Identity

◉⟩ 5

A PASSAGE FROM FOREST TO STATE

The Aoluguya Ewenki and their Museums

Zhang Rongde and Bai Ying

In August 2009, the Aoluguya Ewenki Reindeer Culture Museum was reopened after more than a year of reconstruction. This is the museum of the Ewenki people who live on the northwestern slope of China's Daxing'anling Mountains in Hulun Bei'er, Inner Mongolia. The museum is located in the Aoluguya Ewenki Ethnic Township, the third settlement built for the Ewenki community, which is just 4.5 km from the capital of Genhe on state highway S301. The municipal government describes it as "the only place for reindeer breeding in China, where the hunters have maintained an ancient, simple and unique lifestyle."[1]

The Aoluguya Ewenki Reindeer Culture Museum is the fourth museum constructed by the government in settlements it has built for the Reindeer Ewenki. The first such museum was established in 1985 in the settlement now known as "old Aoluguya," built in the 1960s at the confluence of the Jiliu and Aoluguya Rivers. This first museum was one room exhibiting the Ewenki hunting culture. Since then, museums have continued to feature prominently in the construction of Reindeer Ewenki settlements. In 1995 the government built a larger museum of Ewenki hunting culture to celebrate the thirtieth anniversary of the community's resettlement from Qiqian to Aoluguya. In 2003, when the Ewenki community moved into its third settlement, another brand-new museum was completed. Having played a significant part in the Ewenki people's "ecological migration," it also marked the termination of hunting. In 2008, this museum was scheduled for reconstruction in connection with a major effort to make Aoluguya into a tourist destination. A Finnish consultancy firm, Pöyry, was contracted to design the museum's exterior, and sections of the local elite were engaged in planning new exhibitions and the interior design. The new museum employed advanced audio-visual and electronic techniques.

After reopening, the museum in "new Aoluguya" became a key attraction for visitors who wanted a better understanding of traditional

Ewenki culture, and an important site for the local government to display its achievements in the study and preservation of Reindeer Ewenki culture. Moreover, as the museum showcased the government's ability to represent the Reindeer Ewenki as an ethnic minority and make them visible, the technical quality of the representation was important as such. Its success in this regard is captured by a comment left by a Chinese American visitor to the museum: "Great! The American Indian Museum can't be better than this!"

How can we comprehend the emergence and development of museums for the Aoluguya Ewenki in modern Chinese history? How are the contemporary status and identity of the Reindeer Ewenki connected to the museums through which they have been represented? Our preliminary observations suggest several avenues by which to approach these questions. These will be explored and analyzed in the following pages.

The emergence and development of museums

Since the founding of "New China," the Reindeer Ewenki have experienced more than half a century of governmental sedentarization efforts. The first Ewenki settlement was Qiqian, established in the early years of the People's Republic on the Sino-Russian border on the eastern bank of the E'erguna River. In the following decades, the Ewenki community was twice displaced in resettlement projects implemented by the local governments. A brief survey of the history of Ewenki resettlement and community reconstruction sheds light on the role of exhibitions and museums in the planning and development of each settlement.

The government built the settlement now called old Aoluguya (Chinese: *Lao Aoxiang*) in the 1960s.[2] Gu Deqing, author of "A Diary of the Exploration of the Life of Hunters in the Xing'an Mountains," visited this settlement for the first time in 1983. According to his records, Aoluguya had a total of 164 residents, including government cadres and workers, hunters, and their dependents. At that time more than thirty people living in three camps herded a total reindeer population of about a thousand animals. A township team was charged with managing production. Leaving its base in the settlement, the team went into the mountains to organize the work of the hunters, pay their wages, collect hunting produce, and cut the reindeer's antlers. The team was also responsible for vehicle transportation and communication between campsites (Gu 2001: 65). In 1985, while Gu Deqing was carrying out his study, the township government set up a cultural exhibition that portrayed Ewenki hunting culture by displaying the tools and equipment used for hunting, as well as photographs of Ewenki hunters.

Ten years later, the Genhe county government built a museum to commemorate the thirtieth anniversary of the Aoluguya settlement. The Museum of the Aoluguya Ewenki Nationality, a single-story building with several adjacent structures, covered an area of two hundred square meters. It featured more than twenty showcases displaying about a thousand items, including documents, objects, and photographs. Scenes from the forest were displayed using the technique of scene recurrence, and a special exhibition zone demonstrated reindeer culture with the help of a stuffed reindeer specimen. Artwork was also on show in the museum in the form of drawings on hide created by Liu Ba (Ljuba), a talented Reindeer Ewenki artist.[3]

In 2003, the government carried out its project of "ecological migration" (Chinese: *shengtai yimin*), moving the Reindeer Ewenki people from Aoluguya to a new settlement constructed in the suburbs of the city of Genhe. The new settlement, known as new Aoluguya, had a township government office building, residential houses furnished with central heating and modern plumbing, pens and sheds for the reindeer, a factory for reindeer products, and a museum. Construction of the museum building was part of the ecological migration project, but the funding to create the actual exhibits came from the State Cultural Relics Bureau. In the exhibition hall, presentations of the natural environment and folk culture displayed a total of 172 photographs, 126 material objects, and 17 specimens. Unlike the former museum, the new museum held exhibits of life-size figures—three groups in scenes of hunting and dancing around a campfire—created using advanced contemporary exhibition techniques such as scene recurrence. Meanwhile, a huge tablet displayed the museum's name: China's Aoluguya Ewenki Reindeer Culture Museum.

As of June 2008, the government earmarked funds for the reconstruction of the museum. The first stage of this project was to refit the exterior of the building with wooden materials, adding wooden lattice boards to the original walls and roof. The designers were consultants employed by Pöyry. While the architectural design drew mainly on Scandinavian influences, the use of wooden materials was reminiscent of the log cabins of the old Aoluguya settlement and served to highlight the forest lifestyle of the Reindeer Ewenki. The museum's interior was also rebuilt to house exhibition halls, a literary information center, a handicrafts showroom, a souvenir shop, a café and a projection room (see Figure 5.1). As for the contents on display, a limited number of original exhibits were re-used, but under a very different guiding

Figure 5.1. Exhibition at the new museum, November 2009, Aoluguya. Photograph by Bai Ying.

concept. This time Ewenki and other ethnic minority cadres were in charge of the exhibition design. The exhibition of Reindeer Ewenki culture covered hunting, shamanism, the material culture of animal hides, and the culture of birch bark. In addition, a section of the museum presented the Arctic reindeer culture, introducing different reindeer herders living in Finland, Norway, Sweden, Russia, and Canada, including the Sami, Yakut, Chukchi, Ulchi, Evenki, Even, Nanai, Nenet, Khantie, Inuit (also known as Eskimo), and North American Indians. As summarized by the township government's 'Aoluguya Scenic Introduction' (Aoluguya Minzu Xiang 2009), these five exhibition rooms represented different cultures including "Aoluguya Ewenki hunting culture, Shaman culture, birch bark culture, reindeer culture and Arctic culture," all of them "sparkling with their special cultural charm that uniquely belongs to the northern nationalities."

The development of museums: Themes and functions

Marxists view museums as part of the superstructure of society. While reflecting a given society's politics and economy, museums also serve as a political tool of that society. Thus museums in different societies differ in their attributes and functions (see Karp and Levine 1991; Macdonald and Fyfe 1996). In the People's Republic, museums were mandated to inculcate patriotism, help raise awareness of history, disseminate knowledge about nature, promote love for the country, improve political consciousness, and arouse the people's will to work productively (State Cultural Relics Bureau 1985: 2). In the New China, the mission of museums and exhibitions was to introduce the masses to the great achievements of the ongoing social reconstruction, understood as a revolutionary transition of the forces and relations of production. Marxist social evolutionary history was also the key framework underlying exhibits representing newly identified ethnic minorities or nationalities (*shaoshu minzu*). Exhibitions would thus identify the evolutionary stage of the group in question and showcase its achievements toward the highest stage of evolution—namely, the socialist society embodied by the New China.

As part of this endeavor, the hunting culture exhibition room established in Aoluguya in 1985 identified the evolutionary stage of Reindeer Ewenki society and presented its lifestyle and cultural features. Drawing on the Marxist theory that social evolution depends on the transformation of forces and relations of production, the exhibition emphasized the transition of the Reindeer Ewenki from the deprivation of the lower stages of evolution toward their liberation as masters of socialism, inspired by a newfound patriotic enthusiasm and productive passion. According to Gu Deqing's diary (Gu 2001), the exhibition was viewed mainly by visitors from other places, including Han-nationality officials and party cadres, television crews and their directors, journalists, photographers, and cultural workers such as musicians and dancers. When higher officials came to inspect the settlement, the exhibition was a way to gain exposure for the newly discovered or previously unknown nationality so that its difficulties could be addressed—a practice that continues today.

The Museum of the Aoluguya Ewenki Nationality, established in 1995, was an ethnographic museum presenting the unique characteristics of the Reindeer Ewenki culture and means of production, and displaying the material objects and articles of their social and family life. The museum's portrayal of their history and culture highlighted the livelihoods, religious beliefs, customs, and traditions that defined the Aoluguya Ewenki as a unique group. The new museum was built after the Reindeer Ewenki had exchanged their more portable cone-shaped tents for military-style ridge tents and begun using heavy cast-iron wood-burning stoves. The growing importance of reindeer horn production and their dependence on vehicles and logging roads for transportation were changing their lifestyle and material culture. The museum offered the Aoluguya Ewenki a way to show guests how they had once lived in the forest. Ewenki people would also drop by on their own to take a look at the cone-shaped tent that had housed their forebears, and the fire pokers, bows, arrows, and birch-bark boats that those ancestors depended on to survive in the forest. Another feature of this museum was its attention to cultural change, including the transition from a nomadic to a sedentary lifestyle. The significance of the nomadic lifestyle was illustrated by several pieces of artwork depicting migration scenes, created by Reindeer Ewenki artists.

The China Aoluguya Ewenki Reindeer Culture Museum opened its doors to visitors to the new Aoluguya settlement in 2003. Its exhibition techniques were more advanced than its predecessors', but it continued to highlight the characteristics that defined the Aoluguya Reindeer Ewenki as a unique group, focusing especially on the notion of "reindeer culture." This approach endured in the reconstructed Aoluguya Ewenki Reindeer Culture Museum opened in August 2009. However, a new theme set the Reindeer Ewenki against the backdrop of "reindeer peoples" of the Arctic, highlighting their cultural similarities. To advance this idea, a whole section of the museum was devoted to presenting the reindeer herders of the circumpolar region, locating the Reindeer Ewenki within this broader cultural setting. The new museum's mission and target group changed as well: unlike the earlier museums, which had catered mainly to visiting cadres, government officials, and the media, this museum was set up to serve the tourism market, targeting visiting tour groups as its key audience.

Over the four experiences of museum construction in the Reindeer Ewenki community, the museums were transformed to suit their changing functions, going from a mere tool for disseminating information to the public to a showroom for the marketing of ethnicity, or the production of visibility (Dicks 2007). The next section will describe the Aoluguya Ewenki Reindeer Culture Museum as a centerpiece of the government's project to construct the "Aoluguya scenic zone" for the development of ethnic tourism. In the cultural economy of tourism, the museum thus acquired a new and vital task in the production of visibility.

Museums and the production of visibility

When the new Aoluguya Ewenki Ethnic Township was constructed near Genhe city in 2003, the key goals were a better standard of housing and infrastructure for the former hunters and a convenient administrative seat from which local government could manage the community's internal affairs and the state could carry out its preferential policies to benefit the minorities. The goal of rebuilding the settlement was to make it a scenic zone for tourism, combining the attractions of the traditional "folk" culture with modern recreational facilities. Planners envisaged the entire community's involvement in the reconstruction.

The opening of the new Aoluguya Ewenki Reindeer Culture Museum in 2009 concluded the first stage of the Aoluguya scenic zone's construction. Unlike earlier museums, the new museum was not seen as an isolated construction project but as an integrated aspect of the settlement's reconstruction as a scenic zone for tourism. The 'Aoluguya Scenic Introduction' (Aoluguya Minzu Xiang 2009) maps out the government's vision of the scenic zone and the museum's significance in its construction. Its virtual tour of the Aoluguya scenic zone starts at the museum, where visitors enter "the gallery of the historical development of the Aoluguya Ewenki herders." In the lobby, marble sculptures depict scenes from the "life and production" of Aoluguya Ewenki herders, and the "wonderful scene of harmony between northern hunting nationalities and nature." With the help of tour guides, the introduction explains, "visitors can not only get to acquire the unsophisticated folk custom from cultural relics and photographs, but also witness the past and current situation of Aoluguya Ewenki herders as well as local pictures from in and around the Daxing'anling Mountains via hi-tech exhibition methods including audio devices, light-sensor devices and other electronic equipment" (Aoluguya Minzu Xiang 2009).

After portraying the visitors' experience of the museum itself, the scenic introduction continues its imaginary tour as the visitor exits the museum and arrives at an exhibition providing a "visual platform" for learning about the achievements of Genhe County during the last half century. The progression through Genhe's development segues into an exhibition of Aoluguya Ewenki herders' handicrafts. In this area people can not only watch craftspeople practice their arts but also participate in the crafting, experiencing the joy of making a handicraft product. An exotic cafe offers free tea to resting visitors. Outside the café there is a square with two cone-shaped concrete and brick "tents", giving tourists a sense of exoticism. Here visitors can take photos or purchase souvenir postcards. On the north side of the square are the sixty-two houses of Aoluguya Ewenki people, renovated and outfitted for tourism and shopping. In this area tourists can find out how Aoluguya Ewenki herders live today while also collecting high-quality special and local products at low prices. Having left the Ewenki houses, visitors arrive at the tribal zone, where they see the reindeer and sacred tree, and experience the unique form of life and production of the Ewenki herders. As the Aoluguya scenic trip ends, the visitor walks out of the forest (Aoluguya Minzu Xiang 2009, citing Pöyry 2008).

The Aoluguya Ethnic Reindeer Resort Master Plan (Pöyry 2008) described the settlement as divided into six functional zones, including the core tourist area (where the museum is located), the folk customs demonstration area, the residential area, the forest village (a theme park located across the highway), the reindeer park (including a proposed reindeer research center), and a camping and outdoor recreation area. The township government divided the implementation of this plan into several stages. The first stage (from 2008 to 2009) included the reconstruction of residential houses, the rebuilding and enlargement of the museum, the first phase of hotel construction, planting, construction of wooden houses for the demonstration area, the development of key tourism products, and personnel training. The second stage (from 2009 to 2010) covered the second phase of hotel construction and house reconstruction and the development of tourism products and tourist routes for the winter season. In the third stage (from 2010 to 2011), the hotel entered its third phase of construction, the forest village houses were built, and the reindeer park was established. The fourth and final stage (from 2011 to 2012) included construction of holiday villas, a reindeer research center and camping area, and the development of promotion materials for international marketing. The plan envisions the Aoluguya Ethnic Reindeer Resort hosting 1,200 tourists every day, reaching a total capacity of about 400,000 visitors per year. According to this plan, Aoluguya has the potential to become an ethnic tourism site unparalleled in China.

For its part, the township government has contributed a series of additional projects in support of the scenic zone construction. In 2005, it organized the first Cultural Festival of the Reindeer Ewenki to attract more visitors. In March 2009, the government applied to organize the fifth congress of the Association of World Reindeer Herders in Aoluguya in 2013. The congress provided a golden opportunity to create publicity for the scenic zone, though it was eventually hosted in the prefecture capital, Haila'er. In May 2009, the Aoluguya township government website went online, giving the community a presence on the Internet. The local government also applied to the Inner Mongolia Autonomous Region and central state organs for funding to become a site of Intangible Cultural Heritage and Protected Areas of Culture and Ecology. At last it obtained an official certificate for Aoluguya Folk Culture, and a total of five cultural items—Aoluguya Ewenki fairy tales, folk music, the shaman's dance, traditional medicines, and the cone-shaped Ewenki tent (Chinese: *cuoluozi*)—were added to China's Intangible Cultural Heritage list. In 2010, the first regional-level batch of Protected Areas of Culture and Ecology included the Aoluguya Ewenki Reindeer Cultural and Ecological Protection Area, to ensure prioritized compilation and protection of the Reindeer Ewenki language, techniques of traditional handicrafts, medicines, and folk customs.

The government has also organized cultural heritage projects to collect and arrange traditional music and dance, as well as folk songs and dances in new forms. In May 2010, the township government started a training course for family tourism, open to all sixty-two Ewenki households in the Aoluguya township. Its curriculum covered folk knowledge as well as manners, tourist reception, rules and regulations of family tourism, room service, and table settings, so as to equip residents of Aoluguya with the basic skills needed to enter the tourism business.

The development of ethnic tourism has focused the local government's economic development strategy on commodifying Ewenki heritage and customs, and the characteristics of "reindeer culture." Great efforts are thus made to reconstruct local cultural elements as marketable commodities for tourist consumption. The new museum, as a site where the Reindeer Ewenki culture is (re)constructed and made visible, is vital to this strategy.

A passage from forest to state

For the Reindeer Ewenki, unlike sedentary peoples, the emergence and development of museums corresponded to their gradual transition from forest life to settled life. From the state's perspective, this has been a process of attempting to integrate the forest-based nationality into the structures of the multinational state—that is, a passage from forest to state. Governmental projects aiming to sedentarize and integrate the transhumant Reindeer Ewenki have been ongoing since the New China came to be, and founding and reconstructing museums is part of these projects.

The Marxist theory of social development holds that human societies are constantly evolving from primitive society to slave society, followed by feudal, then capitalist, and finally socialist society. When the New China was founded, Reindeer Ewenki people were considered to be at a very early stage of social development, namely, the patriarchal society at the end of primitive society. Socialist China and its Communist Party saw it as their duty to develop primitive nationalities, including the Reindeer Ewenki, and bring them in "a single leap" into socialist society.

In September 1949, at the first plenary meeting of the Chinese People's Political Consultative Conference, representatives of the Communist Party and other political movements discussed the construction of the new state and administrative structures. Delegates of some minority nationalities were also invited to the conference. The Common Program of the Chinese People's Political Consultative Conference, approved at the conference, made it clear that ethnic minorities—together with the working class, peasants, revolutionary servicemen, intellectuals, the petty bourgeoisie, the national bourgeoisie, and other "patriotic" people—should all be represented at the Chinese People's Political Consultative Conference. Moreover, the Common Program identified the key goal of socialist China's "ethnic work" as assisting minority nationalities in their political, economic, cultural, and educational development; this was also written into the Chinese constitution.[4] These documents envisaged the minority nationalities as a united, active force in the construction of the new socialist China, and an object of transformation for the full realization of the socialist state. The passage of the Reindeer Ewenki from the stage of late primitive society to the socialist stage was therefore of key significance to agents of the state (see Rozman 1981).

Marxism stipulates that the socialist transformation toward full realization of the socialist society requires the extermination of exploitation. However, having found that the Reindeer Ewenki were still at the stage of patriarchal, late primitive society and had not yet developed into a class society, the ethnologists who first studied them saw no need to transform the structure of their means of production and ownership so as to eliminate exploitation. The fundamental socioeconomic unit of the Reindeer Ewenki, the *urilen* was understood as a patriarchal unit based on blood relations. Hunting guns and reindeer belonged to the household and furs to the individual hunter, but the community still played a key role in their life and production, and the household had not yet become an independent economic unit (Lin et al. 1997: 275). The scientists therefore proposed that the Reindeer Ewenki bypass the "democratic reforms" process and transit directly into socialist society via the promotion of cooperative production, while making every effort to develop their economy and culture with the support and assistance of the state. The central government later adopted this strategy, and the Reindeer Ewenki were finally recognized as a case of direct transition from primitive to socialist society.

The Reindeer Ewenki were previously known as the Yakut. In 1957, under the Chinese government's ethnic categorization project, they were lumped together with the Solon, who practiced animal husbandry and settled agriculture, and the pastoralist Tungus to form the Ewenki nationality, one of fifty-six nationalities in the New China. The settlements built for the Reindeer Ewenki were an important factor in raising their standard of living and also became the foundation of their political, economic, cultural, and educational development.

Since the 1950s, the Reindeer Ewenki community has experienced three planned (re)settlements. The first sedentarization efforts took place from 1949 to 1965 at Wuqiluofu village, under the auspices of the Qiqian Township People's Committee. The government's initial efforts centered on the trading station where Ewenki people used to gather, and the supply of goods to the station. A volume edited by the Editorial Office of the Ethnic Affairs Commission under the National People's Congress (Zhongguo Renmin Daibiao Dahui Minzu Weiyuanhui Bian 1958) describes the establishment of the trading center and relevant organizations to attract the hunters. During this period, the small-scale hunting economy and private ownership of hunting produce came to an end with the transition to a socialist collective economy. The Reindeer Ewenki were thus incorporated into the people's commune, which was geared toward collective ownership, concentrated production, and equal distribution.

The Qiqian Township People's Committee was the earliest administrative organization or local assembly. In this committee, Ewenki people were actively encouraged to take part in founding their own political organizations and voicing their aspirations. The new administrative seat was established at the trading center, and the first organization—a cooperative for supplies and the sale of hunting produce—was set up as early as 1949. The cooperative was commissioned to sell the game bagged by Ewenki hunters, and to supply the hunters with commodities. The building of the first school and health center at Qiqian village followed. By June 1953, construction was completed, and the new school opened, serving twenty-eight students aged eight to twenty-five. That August, the public health center was inaugurated and began providing the community with free medical care. A survey team from the Ethnic Affairs Commission that visited the settlement in 1957 reported that the "nationalities primary school" in Qiqian was equipped with an atlas and musical instruments (including an organ), and that the classrooms had wall calendars promoting hygiene, posters of human anatomy, and maps (Zhongguo Renmin Daibiao Dahui Minzu Weiyuanhui Bian 1958). As this and other reports affirm, in the first few years of the New China the trading station at Wuqiluofu had been turned into a bustling village with modern tastes, and an organic part of the new multinational state. However, as of July 1957 only a few Ewenki households had taken up residence in the village. Some hunters had settled there, but most residents were government cadres and forest guards.

After Khrushchev came to power in the Soviet Union, Sino-Soviet re-lations deteriorated. Tense relations with the Soviet Union made border security an issue, so the government decided to build a new settlement for the Ewenki hunters farther away from the Sino-Soviet border. The new settlement, named Aoluguya, was built at the confluence of the Jiliu and Aoluguya Rivers in E'erguna Banner. On 1 September 1965, all thirty-five Ewenki households originally based in Qiqian were moved to Aoluguya. The new town's population was nearly 500, of which 152 were hunters. After the displacement, the inhabitants of the new settle-ment continued moving around in the taiga but now drifted back and forth from taiga to settlement. Once hunting was reorganized as the primary task of the production brigade, the forest became a space of "socialist production" rather than a place of "residence."

Nearly forty years after the Ewenki community was settled in Aolu-guya, it was again displaced and resettled in "new Aoluguya," for sev-eral reasons. For one, gradual depletion of the wildlife they hunted for food had eliminated a dependable food supply. Also, reindeer numbers remained stable at around eight hundred head as inbreeding weakened the quality of the reindeer stock, raising concerns about the viability of antler production as the key source of income. Meanwhile, the infra-structure in Aoluguya was becoming dilapidated, and irregular flood-ing of the river caused further damage and inconvenience. Finally, the implementation of laws on gun control and the protection of wildlife, as well as the nationwide Forest Resources Conservation Project, meant hunting was no longer allowed. In accordance with the new policies and programs, the Reindeer Ewenki were moved out of the mountains and their hunting guns were confiscated.

Once they were resettled in "new Aoluguya," the Reindeer Ewenki were no longer able to hunt. However, it was soon apparent that the government's plan to raise reindeer in pens was unviable and had to be abandoned. Some former hunters chose to return to the mountains and keep herding their reindeer in forests 200–300 km away from the new settlement, creating new patterns of movement between the forest herding areas and the settlement in the township. Left without liveli-hoods in the new settlement, the Reindeer Ewenki who gave up rein-deer herding were even worse off after the displacement.

The reindeer as metaphor

As the government carried out its development programs, the Rein-deer Ewenki people were subjected to the passage from forest to state.

As an increasing number of people spent ever more time in Aoluguya, they were gradually taken farther from the forests and closer to the administrative center. The settlement provided an ever growing range of facilities, starting with the trading station and supply of market goods; then the school, health station, library, cultural center (screening free films), and hospital; and later the child care center, retirement home, veterinary station, cinema hall, bookstore, post office, and bank. Construction of the museum finally started in 1985, three decades after the settlement was established. The development of facilities in the settlement brought rapid change to the hunters' lifestyle. With that change came complex and intricate challenges to their adaption.

A significant trend in the development of Aoluguya Ewenki museums is the increasing emphasis on "reindeer culture" as the community's key characteristic, and the corresponding identity transformation from hunters to reindeer herders. The process and features of this transformation are well illustrated in the museums' evolution from the simple exhibition hall presenting the "hunting culture" in the old township to the state-of-the-art museum of "reindeer culture" constructed as the tourist resort's centerpiece.

With the 2003 resettlement, the reindeer became a key ethnic marker. This reflected the changing relationship between the Ewenki and their reindeer. Before the turn of the millennium, studies of the Reindeer Ewenki invariably described their economic livelihood as hunting and the reindeer as their mode of transportation. As the Ewenki themselves put it, "people move and hunt in the mountains with hunting guns and reindeer, and none of them can be omitted." Reindeer are smaller than horses, but they have bigger hooves and thus can walk through wetlands that no vehicle or horse can traverse. Back when Ewenki hunted hundreds of miles away from the trading center, all supplies had to be carried by reindeer. Game was butchered in the forest and then carried to the tent on the backs of reindeer. When the hunters moved between forest campsites, the reindeer carried supplies and equipment. Women, children, and the elderly rode the reindeer. Clothes, boots, and mattresses were made of reindeer hide, and the main drink was reindeer milk boiled with tea. A reindeer was a valuable gift. Upon marriage, the groom gave his bride a number of reindeer, and the bride was then required to supply the same number in return. Reindeer were never slaughtered for food unless there was an emergency, because reindeer were indispensable to hunting.

After the 2003 resettlement, hunting was prohibited, so most of the former relations between the Ewenki and their reindeer vanished. The government intended to put an end to the forest lifestyle not only by prohibiting hunting, but also by moving the reindeer out of the forest and into pens at the new settlement. Altogether, forty-eight reindeer pens were built with the purpose of industrializing reindeer husbandry. There were also plans to develop new marketable products, such as tinctures of alcohol containing reindeer horn. However, the reindeer failed to adjust to captivity, and the project had to be discontinued. Now the reindeer are herded in forests 200–300 km away from the settlement, and some Reindeer Ewenki still manage to continue their transhumant lifestyle, moving back and forth between the settlement and their herds.

As the identity of hunter became obsolete, the identity of reindeer herder started to be emphasized, and the reindeer came to epitomize the Reindeer Ewenki people. The reconstructed Aoluguya Ewenki Reindeer Culture Museum is the confirmation of this process. Built to represent the ethnic identity of the Reindeer Ewenki, the museum employs the reindeer as its primary symbol. With the reindeer as intermediary, the museum promotes the reindeer herder identity by highlighting the links and similarities between the Reindeer Ewenki and other reindeer herders of the Arctic region. Among the Arctic reindeer herders, the Sami people of northern Scandinavia are the primary example of the aspired-to reindeer herder identity.

The local planners of the new museum see the Sami as modern reindeer herders who lead a settled lifestyle while still maintaining close relations with their reindeer. Having visited Sami areas in Finland and Norway, they had seen firsthand how the Sami continue using reindeer hides to make clothes, boots, mattresses, and tents, while antlers and bones are used as raw materials for handicrafts as well as tools. They also observed that reindeer skins make popular souvenirs for tourists, who buy them to decorate their homes; and that reindeer hide can be made into leather suitable for clothing and luggage. The Sami people still enjoy eating the reindeer bone marrow and venison, and reindeer meat has become a profitable product. Moreover, the Sami case shows that reindeer can play an important role in the development of tourism—in Finland, for instance, reindeer are harnessed to pull Santa Claus's sleigh for winter tourists. The example of the Sami suggests that given the right circumstances, the Reindeer Ewenki might also be able to combine reindeer herding with a settled lifestyle.

Exchange visits to Russia, Finland, and Norway have enabled the Reindeer Ewenki to develop contacts with the Evenki people in Russia as well as the Sami in Scandinavia. In 2009, a delegation from Aoluguya participated in the fourth World Reindeer Herders Congress in Kautokeino, Norway, organized by the Association of World Reindeer

Herders. At this congress, the Reindeer Ewenki formally joined the association's representative assembly and agreed to host the fifth World Reindeer Herders Congress in Aoluguya in 2013. Their aim was to foster more communication with reindeer herders from countries like Norway, Finland, Sweden, and Russia, so as to learn how best to promote the development of reindeer husbandry and related tourism. In response to the new prospects, local stakeholders use the display of "reindeer culture" in the museum as a tool to reenvision and consolidate the Aoluguya Ewenki identity as reindeer herders.

Museums and modernity

Museums, while commonly known for preserving and arranging cultural relics, are less well understood as producers of cultural knowledge. Before the emergence of the nation-state, the chief task of the museum was to materialize history. But since the global spread of capitalism and nationalism, state museums have become highly uniform, structured institutions of cultural knowledge production. In China, museums were first used to teach members of the majority about the state's marginal populations, to inform the public about the multiethnic composition of the state, and to describe the local way of life. The museums established for the Reindeer Ewenki not only reflected the modernization agenda of the Chinese state but also served as avenues for the expansion of state power. As the Ewenki passed from forest to state, the significance of museums apparently increased, as did the distance between the Reindeer Ewenki and the forest, and the intensity with which development policies were implemented.

China's opening up to the global market had far-reaching socioeconomic consequences. As marketization expanded into areas inhabited by ethnic minorities, both cultural and natural resources became vital to the development of ethnic tourism. Modernization and globalization, especially in the twenty-first century, pushed museums to shift their focus to the pursuit of visibility as both ethnic minorities and their museums became resources for economic development. The original motivation had been to improve the minorities' living standard, but the result was also to assimilate them further into the multiethnic state. In Aoluguya, this process is evident in both the construction of the new museum and the development of the scenic zone for tourism.

The construction of museums in Aoluguya reflects the passage from forest to state in several ways. First, it can be seen as an expression of the expansion of state power. Second, it is a manifestation of the blueprint for creating a united, multinational Chinese state. Third, it highlights the core idea of ethnic equality as the foundation of political mobilization. Fourth, the development of the "ethnic" museum illustrates how ethnic groups had to be identified to enable the realization of ethnic equality. Finally, the museum's development for tourism illustrates the transformation of ethnicity into a resource in the production of visibility and tourism marketization. This highlights the linkages between the construction of ethnic minorities and that of Chinese modernity.

In the Chinese nation-building process, a powerful state authority was needed—initially to mold ethnic minorities as marginal as the Reindeer Ewenki into discrete, stable social categories; and later, in the era of Reform and Opening Up, to manipulate these categories to make marginalized groups produce culture in ways that were consequential in the social order (Schein 2000: 16). Now, with the development of ethnic tourism, the traditions by which ethnic minorities were once recognized are being put to work in the modernization effort. Government officials are prominent players in this effort, but other agents also engaging in the cultural transformation of minorities for tourism's sake include urban visitors from all over the world, minority intellectuals and elites, and local villagers (Schein 2000: 105). To attract tourists, minority areas compete fiercely with each other to accommodate the ethno-touristic fantasies of visitors seeking the authentic and "typical" (*dianxing*). Museums and theme parks thus employ ethnic minorities to reproduce the traditional or even the primitive, imitating the "backward" in a totally modern setting while simultaneously catering to the tourist's feeling of being modern. In the case of Aoluguya, since the settlement's reconstruction as a tourist site the Ewenki community has come to live in the midst of a scenic zone and pseudo-community for visitors, deluged by government officials, photographers, journalists, ethnographers, and tourists from all over the world.

The study of social change among the Reindeer Ewenki offers important insights into modern Chinese governance practices. Analyzing the emergence and development of museums in the context of sedentarization reveals how the multiethnic state works to transform, develop, and integrate an ethnic minority, and finally how the production of ethnic visibility becomes the main thrust of the development effort. The Chinese authorities have not forgotten that ethnic unity and the development of minorities are among the key goals of the modernizing China. Thus they have harnessed Chinese museums to promote ethnic tourism and the development of minorities. The passage of the Reindeer Ewenki from forest to state is a process of sedentarization and modernization, and therefore essentially an effort to realize the socialist goal of a modern, prosperous China.

Notes

1. See the Genhe government website, online at http://www.genhe.gov.cn.
2. For detailed information on the name Lao Aoxiang and the use of the term Aoxiang in the identification of the Reindeer Ewenki community, see the survey of Ewenki geographical names carried out by the Ewenki research committees of Inner Mongolia and Heilongjiang (Neimenggu Zizhiqu Ewenkezu Yanjiuhui, Heilongjiangsheng Ewenkezu Yanjiuhui Bian 2007: 397–398).
3. Liu Ba (1960–2002) became famous in China after appearing in an award-winning documentary that portrayed her life in the mountains after she returned from her art studies in Beijing. In the documentary she gave voice to the predicament of the Reindeer Ewenki people, expressing her feelings of loss and sharing her personal experiences with the filmmakers.
4. The Common Program of the Chinese People's Political Consultative Conference was approved at its first plenary meeting, 29 September 1949. The Constitution of the People's Republic of China was approved at the first session of the National People's Congress, 20 September 1954.

References

Aoluguya Ewenke Minzu Xiang [Aoluguya Ewenki Ethnic Township]. 2009. *Aoluguya jingqu jianjie* [Aoluguya Scenic Introduction]. Aoluguya.
Dicks, Bella. 2007. *Culture and Display: The Production of Contemporary Visibility.* Beijing: Peking University Press.
Gu Deqing. 2001. *Tanfang Xing'anling liemin shenghuo riji (1982–1985)* [A Diary of the Exploration of the Life of Hunters in the Xing'an Mountains (1982–1985)]. Jinan: Shandong huabao chubanshe [Shandong Pictorial Press].
Karp, Ivan, and Steven Lavine, eds. 1991. *Exhibiting Cultures: The Poetic and Politics of Museum Display.* Washington, D.C.: Smithsonian Institute Press.
Lin Yaohua, Jin Tianming, and Chen Kejin. 1997. *Minzuxue tonglun* [General Survey of Ethnology]. Beijing: Minzu chubanshe [Nationalities Publishing House].
Macdonald, Sharon, and Gordon Fyfe, eds. 1996. *Theorizing Museums: Presenting Identity and Diversity in a Changing World.* Oxford: Blackwell.
Neimenggu Zizhiqu Ewenkezu Yanjiuhui, Heilongjiangsheng Ewenkezu Yanjiuhui Bian [Ewenki Research Committee of Inner Mongolia Autonomous Region and Ewenki Research Committee of Heilongjiang Province]. 2007. *Ewenke dimingkao* [Survey of Ewenki Geographical Names]. Beijing: Minzu chubanshe [Nationalities Publishing House].

Pöyry. 2008. Aoluguya Ethnic Reindeer Resort Master Plan. Beijing: Pöyry (Beijing) Consulting.

Rozman, Gilbert, ed. 1981. *The Modernization of China.* New York: Free Press.

Schein, Louisa. 2000. *Minority Rules: The Miao and the Feminine in China's Cultural Politics.* Durham, NC: Duke University Press.

State Cultural Relics Bureau, Ministry of Culture. 1985. *Brief Introduction of Museum Science in China.* Beijing: Cultural Relics Publishing House.

Zhongguo Renmin Daibiao Dahui Minzu Weiyuanhui Bian [Editorial Office of the Ethnic Affairs Commission, China's National People's Congress]. 1958. *Neimenggu zizhiqu E'erguna qi shiyong xunlu de ewenkeren de shehui qingkuang* [The Social Situation of the Reindeer Ewenki People of E'erguna Banner, Inner Mongolia Autonomous Region]. Beijing: Minzu Weiyuanhui [Ethnic Affairs Commission].

๑)) 6

THE ECOLOGICAL MIGRATION AND EWENKI IDENTITY

Xie Yuanyuan

In August 2003, the mass media captured public attention throughout China with the story of a unique and striking case of resettlement taking place in Genhe County, Inner Mongolia: Aoluguya Ewenki hunters were leaving the forest settlements where they had lived for generations, to be resettled in new concrete houses in an urban area 260 km away. The stated purpose of the relocation was to protect the ecological environment of the forest, but it would also, of course, dramatically change the Ewenki hunters' way of life. According to the media, the hunters would now lay down their hunting guns, stay out of the forest, and lead a modern city life. The local government viewed this as a necessary step toward "sustainable development" that would not only protect the forest ecology but also improve the minority group's standard of living.

The story that was presented in the media was essentially what the local government had planned, and what was also expected to happen. Actually, however, Ewenki hunters soon started to set up new camps in the forest near the resettlement site, resuming their so-called primitive way of life. As these events became known, serious questions arose about what had actually happened in the resettlement process, and why a project that the local government had so elaborately designed had produced such unexpected and (from the government's perspective) unsatisfactory results.

During long-term fieldwork in Aoluguya lasting about one year from September 2003 to October 2004, I observed and experienced firsthand the immediate reactions to the move in the community, and the engaged discussions sparked by the resettlement. Unsurprisingly, local people, whether government employees or hunters, raised various complaints about the resettlement process. The complaints were not uniform, and I soon discovered interesting contradictions in the complaint narratives. The identity of the "hunters" also became a contentious issue. When applying for national relocation funds, the resettlement planners had based the number of households and people to be relocated on old statistics from the 1960s. Consequently, the housing built in the resettlement site was insufficient to accommodate all the inhabitants of Aoluguya. When the local government was set to distribute the sixty-two houses constructed at the new site, a crucial question arose: Who were the hunters? Since the houses were designated "hunters' houses" (Chinese: *liemin fang*), they should be distributed to the "real" hunters. Even if members of other ethnic groups were excluded, sixty-two houses would not be enough unless the hunter identity was strictly defined.

Then who were the hunters, and which criteria could the government use to identify these hunters? These questions generated heated debates and disagreements among local government officials and members of the Aoluguya community alike. In this chapter I will present some of the findings from my fieldwork, to help readers understand what happened in the aftermath of the resettlement, and what the move, known as "ecological migration" (*shengtai yimin*), meant to the community of Ewenki hunters.

The ecological migration

Nomadic hunters raising reindeer have lived in the forests of the Amur River bend for over three hundred years. After the New China was founded in 1949, these people were identified as members of the Ewenki nationality (*Ewenkezu*) and became eligible to receive preferential treatment from the government. To improve their standard of living and make hunting easier and more efficient, the hunters were provided with housing, rifles, and bullets. With the development of infrastructure such as roads and railways, and the intensified exploitation of the country's forest resources, a growing number of immigrants came to Aoluguya, slowly impacting the lives of the Ewenki hunters.

The Ewenki hunters have undergone three sedentarization (Chinese: *dingju*) programs since the founding of the People's Republic. The first such program, implemented in 1957, provided hunters with housing in Qiqian, a small trading post on the bank of the Argun River at the border between China and the Soviet Union. When tensions arose between the two countries a few years later, the Chinese government built a new settlement for the Ewenki hunters, farther from the border. The new settlement was named Aoluguya, and the township was called Aoluguya Xiang, or Aoxiang for short. Ever since the Ewenki community was resettled there in 1965, they have been known as the "people of Aoluguya" (*Aoxiangren*). In August 2003 the local government carried out its plans to resettle the hunters a third time, to a new settlement constructed at the site of an old timber mill named Sanchejian, located 4.5 km to the west of the county capital, Genhe. Since the name Aoluguya was already well known and closely associated with the community of Ewenki hunters, the new settlement was also named Aoluguya, and from then on the old settlement site was known as "old Aoluguya."

Despite the government's plans to settle the Ewenki nomads, their hunting life was not discontinued until the third sedentarization program, the ecological migration in 2003. Thus, the two former events are called "settling down but not dwelling" and "dwelling but not settling down" respectively. In the third relocation program, the local government aimed to settle both the reindeer and the people to bring the nomadic lifestyle to an end and fully realize the community's sedentarization. Thus the new settlement site was equipped with stables and pens for the reindeer, along with housing and other facilities for the hunters-turned-reindeer breeders.

The identity of the hunters

On the eve of the relocation, only about two hundred of the residents of Aoluguya were scheduled to move into the sixty-two newly built residential houses at the new settlement. Longtime inhabitants of old Aoluguya who were not members of the Ewenki ethnic group were not allowed to move to the new settlement site. Yet all of old Aoluguya's residents had to evacuate the site, because the local government had sold the entire site to a private enterprise. Those who were not relocated to the new settlement were left to their own devices and had to find their own way to make a living in other places. The government justified this by designating the new settlement as reserved for "Ewenki hunters."

Literally, hunters may be described as hunting for a living, subsistence, or recreation. In this case, however, the term hunter has special significance: it refers to one branch of the Ewenki nationality. In China, the Ewenki ethnic group is divided into three subgroups or branches. One engages in agriculture in the valley grasslands south of Daxing'anling. A second works in animal husbandry in the Hulun Bei'er prairie. Finally, the branch known as Reindeer Ewenki has hunted and herded reindeer in the hinterlands of the Daxing'anling Forest. These are the Aoluguya Ewenki hunters, also known as the "reindeer-using tribe" (*shilu bu*). The local government decided to make all members of the Ewenki nationality eligible for housing, whether they belonged to the Reindeer Ewenki or another branch. Thus, although the sixty-two houses are all hunters' houses, some residents are members of other branches of the Ewenki nationality.

Apart from Ewenki ethnic identity, a second criterion for receiving a house at the resettlement site was that the household head should not be a government employee. Thus it considered anyone not receiving a salary from the government a "hunter." Within the community this criterion led to confusion about the hunter identity. Taking Ewenki hunters at the time of the founding of the People's Republic as the first generation of hunters, the hunters presently in Aoluguya belong mainly to the second and third generations. Few in the third generation have had long-term experience hunting and reindeer herding in the forest, and the vast majority cannot speak the Ewenki language. Many have one parent who is a hunter while the other is not. Few know how to take care of reindeer or hunt, let alone make traditional hunting tools like birch bark canoes, snowshoes, traps, or hunting knives. Moreover, they often know less about traditional hunting practices than outsiders who have intermarried with the second generation of hunters and lived a life of hunting. Still, as the blood of hunter ancestors is thought to flow in their veins, the Aoluguya community recognizes them as hunters by descent. This popular perception does not, however, override the second criterion regarding government employment, so not all of these third generation hunters were allocated hunters' houses.

In the local government's view, providing every Ewenki hunter with housing as proposed in the resettlement plan was an urgent matter. Since there were not enough houses to accommodate every Ewenki resident of old Aoluguya, the government made those with government jobs ineligible for hunters' houses. The planners reasoned that clerks working in the local government, school, or hospital had financial means sufficient to rent a house in Genhe, whereas those without a government salary would be hard put to find a new place to live if they could not get a hunter's house. The exclusion of government employees was meant as a temporary solution to the housing problem, as in future the local government could apply for other funding to build new houses specifically for public servants.

When the local government decided government employees would not be allocated hunters' houses, the hunter identity became a contentious issue. In the past, "Ewenki hunters" had covered only the Reindeer Ewenki of Aoluguya; other branches of Ewenki were never regarded as hunters. But after the resettlement, any member of the Ewenki nationality, especially those experienced in hunting and animal husbandry, preferred to identify themselves as Ewenki hunters, since this identity could bring them a house. At the same time, hunters by birth could no longer claim the hunter identity if they had government jobs. Some other hunters by descent had previously worked as government employees for many years and then returned to the forest campsites to retire. Despite living in the forest and having lived there for many years, their hunter identity came into question because they still received pensions as government employees. Then there were those who were not Ewenki but were married to hunters and had lived a hunting life in the forest since marriage. In the past they had been regarded as hunters, but after the move their hunter identity was in effect canceled due to their nationality. In sum, only thirty or forty individuals could indisputably identify as Ewenki hunters. These were Reindeer Ewenki by birth whose nomadic forest life had never been interrupted.

The issue of identifying the hunters worked subtle changes in the perception of the hunter identity within the Aoluguya community. Some saw those who were given a hunter's house as incompetent losers unable to find a job and in need of special care from the government. This notion stigmatized "hunters" as recipients of government aid.

The hunters: Victims or destroyers?

The national ecological migration policy was introduced as a way to promote sustainable development (*ke chixu fazhan*) in line with the central government policy on comprehensive advancement of sustainable development. The policy objective is to reduce and prevent devastating environmental consequences of the process of modernization (e.g., serious deterioration of the natural environment) by balancing development and environmental protection.

The ecological migration policy was designed to rescue seriously damaged natural environments from continuous human exploitation by giving the local ecosystem time to regenerate. Following the principles outlined in the global Agenda 21, the relationship between indigenous peoples and the natural environment is not a relationship of irreconcilable "subject" and "object," but an intersubjective one in which indigenous peoples can play an important role as protectors of the natural environment. In other words, indigenous peoples are not regarded as destroyers but as potential defenders of their natural environment. Accordingly, in ecological relocation policy discourse, human-induced "vandalism" of the natural environment does not re-

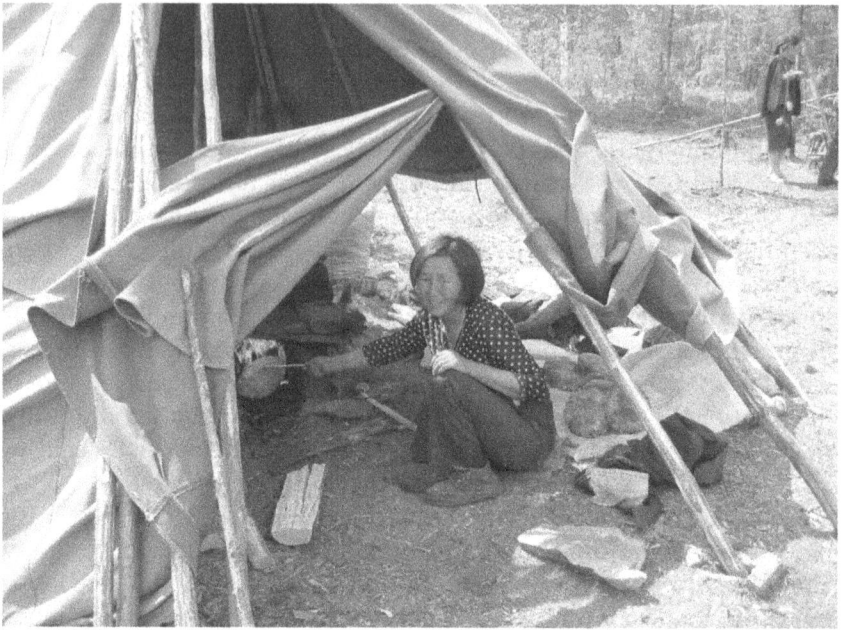

Figure 6.1. Marusja baking pan bread, July 2004, Arongbu camp. Photograph by Xie Yuanyuan.

fer to the behavior of indigenous peoples. In this logic the Aoluguya Ewenki hunters would, as local indigenous inhabitants of the vast forests for many generations, be seen as harmoniously integrated in the forest ecosystem.

Yet despite the national-level policy discourse, the local government viewed Ewenki hunters as destroyers of the natural environment and therefore targets for ecological migration. It described their hunting activities and traditional way of life as detrimental to the forest environment, arguing that hunting was reducing wild animal populations, and that hunters' habitation in forest camps and cutting of trees for encampments destroyed vegetation. In fact, history shows that the forest ecosystem was never damaged until the government initiated large-scale industrialization. At that time the hunters' population was larger and hunting activities were far more intensive, but the hunters never demanded excessively from nature.

Before industrialization, only a few hundred hunters lived in a forest covering over 20,000 km², where they had access to plentiful ecological resources. Drawing on Marshall Sahlins (1974), one could argue that the Ewenki lived in an "original affluent society." However, the consequences of the drive for modernization and economic growth impacted

Ewenki hunters in the form of environmental degradation, as wild animal populations shrank in a forest made sparse by extensive logging. In other words, the cause of environmental destruction was not the hunters' "primitive" way of life, but rather the government's policies for developing areas inhabited by minority groups, including large-scale deforestation and the commercialization of hunting. The hunters themselves were among the victims of environmental degradation, largely because of unsustainable or imbalanced modernization efforts.

Was it possible for hunters to destroy the forest environment for economic benefit? Apparently the government thought so. Therefore, under a "preemptive" policy attuned more to convenience than efficiency, the government requested all hunters to move out of the forest. From the hunters' perspective, they were being forced to move out of the forest as others went on destroying their previous homeland. Realizing that their situation might elicit strong outside support, they began to contest the local government.

Different complaints

Unlike the earlier relocations of the Ewenki community in 1957 and 1965, the 2003 resettlement fundamentally changed the hunters' way of life. This time they were forced to lay down their hunting guns and leave the forest. All Ewenki hunters suffered from the relocation, but the impact was not uniform within the community. During my fieldwork I found that in terms of their complaints, the Ewenki hunters fell into at least two different groups. For narrative and analytical convenience, I will call them modern and traditional hunters. Modern hunters were heavily influenced by discourses of modernization and had broken with the traditional values of the forest life. Traditional hunters still prized the forest life and took a dim view of the "modern life."

Throughout the resettlement process, the traditional hunters—mainly the senior ones—never consented to the relocation, preferring life in the forest. Despite their clear, unequivocal expression of their preference, the government treated their voice as merely a noise to be ignored. The modern hunters, on the other hand, had conscientiously internalized mainstream values. They regarded the hunting and gathering lifestyle as backward, primitive, and favored its elimination. They were willing to leave their seminomadic life behind for the promise of a modern city life and therefore supported the relocation as advocated by the local government. However, after the move they found the new settlement's conditions and the facilities unsatisfactory. Their complaints thus concerned the material conditions of the resettlement. Aware of the modern hunters' views, local government officials also knew it would be easy to placate them with offers of better services and conditions. Meanwhile, they merely ignored the "traditional hunters," largely because their views were more challenging and their complaints far more difficult to address.

When contesting the local government, the hunters cited national-level policy discourse to condemn the local government's practices. Interestingly, local government representatives used the same policy discourse to justify their actions. Drawing on the ecological migration policy discourse, these officials told the modern hunters: "Because your way of life is not in accordance with the protection of forest policy, you should alter it by laying down your guns and coming out of the forest to raise reindeer in stables. On the one hand, we can achieve forest protection, and on the other hand, you can say farewell to the past primitive and laggard lifestyle, and live a happier modern city life." The modern hunters found this argument acceptable: they had adopted mainstream values and rejected the value of their past life, so like the local government, they adhered to the theory of social evolution. But the local government's use of this discourse distorted the national ecological migration policy by labeling indigenous peoples as destroyers rather than protectors of the natural environment.

Soon after the relocation, after Ewenki hunters had returned to the forest around their new settlement to continue their old way of life, people started to question the premises of ecological migration. The local government's failure to take action against those who had returned to the forest raised further questions. For instance, if it was bad to destroy the forest environment near the old settlement site, was it somehow more acceptable to destroy the forest near the new site? To address these questions and justify its actions, the local government had to modify its interpretation of the policy of ecological migration. It now claimed that whereas environmental protection was just part of the rationale, the main purpose of the resettlement was to improve the hunters' living standard. However, by offering this explanation the local government again exposed itself to criticism, this time about the legitimacy of funding the relocation in the name of environmental protection. Relocation funds were explicitly meant for environmental protection, and it was unacceptable for the government to allow continued destruction of the environment near the new settlement. Caught in a dilemma, the local government had to admit either that the relocation had been a failure, or that the relocation funds had been used inappropriately. Adding to this embarrassment, they faced hunters' charges that their living standard had not improved, and that they were now even worse off than before.

For their part, the modern hunters also drew on ecological migration policy discourse to demand more benefits and better conditions, complaining that it was impossible to raise reindeer in stables as the government had assured them prior to the move. Many reindeer had died as a consequence of the failed attempt to keep them in pens and stables. Reindeer owners had no option but to return to the "primitive" life in the forest and therefore should receive compensation from the local government, they argued. This was especially so because reindeer herding was more difficult near the new settlement, as the surrounding forest was less suitable for herding. Former hunters also complained of economic losses due to the relocation, since they were no longer permitted to hunt and their hunting guns had been confiscated. After losing their livelihood they had to rely on government welfare and were prone to excessive drinking. Moreover, modern hunters claimed to have suffered psychological damage from discrimination in the new settlement.

After the relocation, the local government had to deal with a range of conflicts, for example by placating former hunters who wanted to make appeals to higher authorities. Tensions ran so high that one local government official was attacked and beaten up by hunters. Plagued by the controversies, local officials told the hunters: "Your living conditions have been improved immensely compared to the past, now that you have new houses instead of old tents, central heating instead of firewood, and flushing toilets that are far better than nothing. If you are still not satisfied, your complaints are unreasonable." The modern hunters refuted them, arguing: "You never carried out your promises. Our life is not as good as yours." Criticizing the local government for lack of proper implementation, they based their arguments on the national policy on ecological relocation itself. To sum up, modern hunters accepted the government's justifications for the move and were merely dissatisfied with the results of the relocation.

Traditional hunters, however, aimed their criticism at the basic premises of the relocation, questioning the justification itself and saying, "We dislike outsiders disturbing our normal life." Their "normal life" looked primitive and backward in the modern perspective, but traditional hunters genuinely loved and respected the old lifestyle, not only recognizing its value but enjoying it as well. These hunters used actions rather than words, resisting the relocation in silence. They absolutely did not accept the reasons the government had presented to persuade them to move out of the forest. They could not understand how the same state could make completely different policy decisions, encouraging hunting since the 1970s and then banning hunting in 2003. Nor did they understand the government's reasons for moving them out of the forest, namely, protecting the environment and improving their living conditions. How could the government know which life would be better for them, and what kind of help they wanted? Differences in cultural values were at the root of the conflict between traditional hunters and the local government. Since traditional hunters were mostly disadvantaged, the government saw no reason to listen to their views.

What can be learned from listening to minority voices?

Government actors most often prioritize the majority's viewpoint and disregard the voices of minorities. This seemingly commonsense democratic principle may lead to insensitivity to minority groups' concerns and interests, especially when the costs and benefits of policy decisions are ambiguous. Rather than proceeding cautiously and heeding the voices of all stakeholders, the government tends to be overconfident in its decision making. Such arrogance results in issues left unaddressed until serious conflicts and disastrous consequences arise (Scott 1998).

From the anthropological perspective, minority voices can appear as mirrors offering us a chance to reflect on our own notions and behavior. The relocation of the Aoluguya Ewenki may inspire us to rethink the problems of minority governance and the implementation of government policies targeting minorities. More importantly, this case offers an opportunity to rethink the question of environmental destruction and its causes. Who is responsible for the destruction of the forest, and how can the forest best be protected? These questions demand careful thought and investigation, and there are no easy answers. However, in addressing these questions, the government should provide a platform where different cultures and peoples can dialogue on equal footing. Carrying out such intercultural dialogues requires a break with the notion of a division between "backward" and "advanced." This simple dichotomy is a questionable standard by which to evaluate cultures and peoples.

It is a narrow, uncritical perspective on culture that prompts questions such as "Which parts of this culture are advanced and which are backward?" Thinking outside of the dominant discourse and paradigm, we should rather ask whether the culture in question is adaptable to the environment, or how it can be adapted to the environment. This line of thinking enables us to objectively evaluate others and to assess our own culture as well. Should the present wave of modernization and globalization roll on irreversibly, this way of thinking might give us a chance, no matter how slight, to adapt ourselves by drawing local knowledge from others (Geertz 2000). The people of Aoluguya still possess a wealth of knowledge about adapting to the forest environment. Unfortunately, the government, whether out of arrogance or insensitivity, continues to ignore the hunters' experiences.

References

Geertz, Clifford. 2000. *Local Knowledge: Further Essays in Interpretive Anthropology.* New York: Basic Books.

Sahlins, Marshall. 1974. *Stone Age Economics.* London: Tavistock.

Scott, James C. 1998. *Seeing Like a State: How Certain Schemes to Improve the Human Condition Have Failed.* New Haven, CT: Yale University Press.

◌𝄞 7

TENTS, TAIGA, AND TOURIST PARKS
Vernacular Ewenki Architecture and the State
Richard Fraser

This chapter provides an account of vernacular architecture among the Reindeer Ewenki of Inner Mongolia. Describing the vernacular characteristics of Ewenki dwellings and their transformation over time, the chapter offers insights into the changing nature of minority-state relations and the potential future of the community. The opening section describes the vernacular features of Ewenki architecture, specifically the birch bark and animal hide tepee tents (Ewenki: *djiu*) that were the community's sole dwelling until the mid 1980s but remain in limited use today. Here I show how the tents, made of materials from the immediate taiga environment, served to maintain the community's mobile hunting existence, physically structured people's everyday social relations, and reflected the broader cosmological aspects of the Ewenki lifeworld. I then offer an account of how the community's dwellings have changed over time, specifically by replacement of the birch bark and animal hide *djiu* with canvas-covered ridge tents.

Situating this in a context of increasing relations between the Ewenki and the Chinese state, I show how the state has influenced the characterization of Ewenki architecture by presenting the *djiu* (also known as *cuoluozi* or *xierenzhu*) as the archetypal dwelling of the community and the newer ridge tents as a nontraditional transformation. This evokes the state discourse of "cultural decline," which has been perpetuated in the contemporary era with the newly constructed Aoluguya Ethnic Reindeer Resort's display of reproductions of "original" tents at the expense of their canvas-covered counterparts. Contrary to this characterization, I argue that the adoption of ridge tents should be seen as a locally mediated, vernacular transformation that suited the demands and context of collectivization. This is correlated with the contemporary situation, where the present-day reindeer herders continue to experience the ridge tents as vernacular dwellings, responding to further transformations by featuring new architectural innovations.

Drawing inspiration from Evans and Humphrey's (2002) account of architectural afterlives, I argue that the reproductions featured in the Aoluguya Ethnic Reindeer Resort themselves signify a non-vernacular transformation, with the socialist state having appropriated the style and symbolism of Ewenki architecture in its politicized representation of "traditional culture." After exploring the changing nature of Ewenki architecture and the political implications associated with it, the chapter ends by offering insights into the potential future of the community, an issue of particular significance since the 2003 relocation. Here I argue for the continuation of taiga-based residence in ridge tents, something requiring recognition and support from the government. This is not to devalue the newly constructed dwellings in the Aoluguya Ethnic Reindeer Resort—on the contrary, by basing my argument on a phenomenological approach to architecture I emphasize the mutual interdependency of the two dwellings with regard to the viability of reindeer herding in the Chinese taiga.

Vernacular architecture among the Reindeer Ewenki

The Ewenki (Russian: Evenki) are a Tungusic people of Northern Asia. According to Russian sources, their origins can be found in the vicinity of Lake Baikal. From there, several groups are said to have migrated between the third and fourth centuries A.D., some making their way east to the Okhotsk coast, others north to the Lena River basin, and some northwest to the upper tributaries of the Yenisey River (Ermolova 2003). Prior to the formalization of the Sino-Russian border, numerous bands of Tungusic-speaking hunters traversed both sides of the Amur, or Heilongjiang River, moving across the remote region seeking suitable hunting grounds (Heyne 1989, 2007; Lindgren 1930, 1935, 1936; Nentwig 1991, 2003).

Often referred to in Chinese sources as Yakut, the ancestors of the Reindeer Ewenki entered Chinese territory from Yakutia in Russia's Sakha Republic in the late 1820s (Heyne 2007; Kaïgorodov 1968; Lindgren 1930, 1935, 1936; Nentwig 2003). Partially settled by the mid 1960s after relocation away from the Sino-Russian border, the community was again relocated in 2003 to a purpose-built settlement on the outskirts of the county capital. Since then, most Reindeer Ewenki have stayed permanently in the settlement, residing in concrete and wooden dwellings provided by the state and receiving free electricity and a monthly welfare payment. Concurrently, between thirty and forty individuals live and work from six campsites in the Daxing'anling taiga, practicing mobile reindeer pastoralism, by which they procure and sell antler and other reindeer products (Fraser 2010).

When they first entered Chinese territory, the Ewenki[1] resided in tepee-like tents called *djiu*. These dwellings, used sparingly in northeast Inner Mongolia today, consist of twelve to sixteen larch poles erected lengthways and tied to form a conical hut secured with strips of bark. The *djiu*'s surface was covered with animal hides in winter and birch bark in summer. Measuring five to six meters in diameter and having an open fire in the center, a single dwelling housed four to six people and is an apt example of vernacular architecture. As Forsyth remarks, "[the Ewenki] lived in easily transportable conical tents consisting of a few larch poles and a covering of reindeer-skins or sheets of birch-bark. Here, within a diameter of some fifteen feet, they disposed their fire, their sleeping places, and their meagre accoutrements" (1994: 49).

Although "architecture" is typically associated with the built environment, connoting urban structures such as houses and buildings, a more accurate vision uses broader terms: it is the material manifestation of human *dwelling*, including that in so-called rural or non-urban environments (Ingold 2000). As Lawrence and Low (1990) have pointed out, architecture is the product of humans' building *activity*, comprising not only houses, plazas, buildings, and streets, but all built forms such as shelters, enclosures, and semipermanent coverings. In regards to hunter-gatherers' dwelling types, for example, Ingold remarks: "The fact remains that hunter-gatherers do build shelters of various kinds. So who are we to say that they have no architecture?" (2000: 180). This suggests a need for a more grounded conceptualization of architecture, not as material "construction" but as the dwelt effect of fulfilling practical and existential requirements. In a comment directly related to Heidegger's own rearticulation of this human capacity for dwelling, Ingold states: "The concern is to regain that original perspective, so that we can once again understand how the activities of building—of cultivation and construction—belong to our dwelling in the world, to the way we are" (2000: 185–186).

Here it is useful to distinguish between two kinds of architecture; namely, vernacular and non-vernacular. The latter, otherwise known as "polite" architecture, is characterized by stylistic elements of design intentionally incorporated for aesthetic purposes, specifically going beyond the functional requirements of the dwelling. By contrast, vernacular architecture refers to the product of built activity geared solely to local physical needs and using materials drawn from the immediate "natural" environment. Apt examples include the igloos of the Inuit, the Mongolian yurt, and the Native American tepee, but as Brunskill

(2000) has pointed out, it may also refer to more static dwellings such as the South African banda and the Swiss log cabin. In Rudofsky's (1987) famous words, vernacular architecture is "architecture without architects." Typically the individual or group behind its construction is guided by local considerations and needs rather than style or fashion, "a series of conventions built up in (their) locality. … The function would be the dominant factor, aesthetic considerations, though present to some small degree, being quite minimal. Local materials would be used as a matter of course" (Brunskill 2000: 27–28).

This characterization is readily applicable to the *djiu,* which comprises construction materials available in the immediate taiga environment. Indeed, the environment where the Ewenki reside abounds in the larch and birch trees that provide wooden tent-poles, strips for the lashings, and the outer covering of the dwelling. Also, the *djiu* is designed to satisfy the traditional needs and subsistence of the mobile Ewenki: it is easily transported and erected, specifically ensuring mobility between hunting grounds. As Brunskill has noted, "all forms of vernacular architecture are built to meet specific needs, accommodating the values, economies and ways of life of the cultures that produce them" (2000: 28).

In this sense, vernacular architecture is intrinsically influenced by the occupant's way of life, as the activities and experiences going on around the dwelling influence the specifics of dwelling construction. For example, how big the family unit is and how space is shared within the dwelling both affect the layout and size of vernacular architecture, as seen in the case of the *djiu,* whose material features were clearly related to the social structure of the Ewenki themselves. Each tent was traditionally divided according to age, with sitting places distributed according to unit members' seniority and status. The place directly opposite the entrance of the tent (Ewenki: *malu*), for example, was reserved for honored men only, the upper right-hand side for the chief of the unit and his wife, the upper left-hand side for elders and children over a certain age, and the lower left-hand side for guests and outsiders (Shirokogoroff 1929). This spatial division served to visualize everyday social relations in the physical composition of the dwelling itself, embodying specific forms of interaction between unit members, such as the respect shown toward elders.

Here there are interesting parallels with Bourdieu's description of the Berber house and its underlying symbolic significance and domestic spatial arrangement. Indeed, consisting of a simple rectangular form, the Berber house is divided into two parts, a division that becomes the basis for an elaborate system of binary oppositions between male and

female (Bourdieu 2003). Similarly, in the case of the *djiu* a gender division kept women not associated with the unit from passing along the
right-hand side of the dwelling at all, externalizing normative assump-
tions of "male" and "female" specifically through the architecture of the
djiu. This further extended to the positioning of multiple tents within a
single encampment alongside one another in a specific order of status.
In Anderson's description,

> The circular space within the lodge was conceived as a sort of corridor,
> which wrapped around its hearth. During the day, the lodge mistress and
> other women would take up their places to the right (as one entered the
> lodge) while the master would sit at the very back at the place called the
> *malu*. Guests and children would occupy the left. At the night, a different
> arrangement would result with the lodge owners sleeping together to
> the left, the children and other relatives to the right. Belongings would
> be stored in various specific places in the lodge according to one's sta-
> tus. There was a prohibition against "circling" (or walking through the
> corridor). If a man entered the lodge, and having turned to the right, sat
> down, he would have to exit the lodge in the same direction (Anderson
> 2006: 3).

The vernacular characteristics of the *djiu* are evident in their use of local
materials and the relationship between the tent and the kinship networks that they contain. In this regard, the dwelling's internal structure
and external placement can both be seen as lived reflections of Ewenki
society as a whole, serving to structure people's everyday social relationships and inculcating normative modes of behavior. Staying in a
djiu in 2008, I myself remarked upon the tent's resemblance to an animal's ribs, with the vertical poles evoking imagery of a carcass. Similarly, Vitebsky remarked that the image reflects an old Eveny[2] legend:
"A reindeer rescues two little children from an evil spirit by turning its
body into a living tent, with its ribs serving as the framework and its
hide as a cover" (2005: 90). In both a literal and symbolic sense, therefore, the *djiu* can be said to "contain" or embody Ewenki social life.

Like other peoples of Northern Asia, many Ewenki do not construct
a conceptual division between the sociality of human beings and that
of spirits, animals, and nonhuman entities (Heyne 1999; Fraser 2010),
embodying what is generally termed an animist ontology (Pedersen
2001; Willerslev 2007; also see Bird-David 1999). This too is reflected
in the vernacular characteristics of the *djiu*, such as in the rule that the
entrance of the tent must always face the south, considered locally to
be the source of good fortune.[3] In a lived relationship with the agency
attributed to aspects of "the environment," the experience of good and
bad fortune is manifested in the Ewenki tent's positioning. At the same

time, a specific order traditionally governed the setting up of a *djiu* with the purpose of showing respect to the nonhuman agencies thought to reside in the chosen locale.

The tent's vernacular features are visible in its physical positioning within both human *and* nonhuman environs, a quality similarly demonstrated in the placement of fire at the center of the dwelling. Fire is sacred to many North Asian indigenous peoples, and the community holds it in great awe. Whenever a fire is lit, a person will first offer a portion of liquor into it as a gift, an act referred to locally as *feeding the fire* (Fraser 2010). Here fire is attributed a degree of personhood typically reserved for the human species, as one of my informants explained: "Fire is very important in our lives. The fire-spirit is like an old woman called Gulum-ta. We make an offering to her by pouring alcohol into the fire, before a meal." Several rules and taboos concern the treatment of fire, such as that one should never thrust a sharp object into it, an action believed to harm the fire spirit. Moreover, fire is said to exhibit a degree of personhood by "speaking to people" through its cracking, hissing, and burning: "Fire can … be perceived as a being that is able to communicate with humans. … If a person has troubles in hunting, sparks can be understood as the fire's wish to comfort the hunter's feelings" (Brandisauskas 2007: 103). The personhood attributed to fire is spatially marked in its positioning in the middle of the *djiu* directly beneath the opening (and sky) and its role as a centerpiece around which people interact, eat, drink, and communicate with the nonhuman domain. In this regard, Ewenki vernacular architecture becomes the material manifestation of not only human social relations but also interaction between human and nonhuman.

Vernacular architecture and indigenous "cultural decline"

At the time of their arrival in what would become Chinese territory, the livelihood of the Ewenki was hunting, using reindeer as pack animals and for subsistence milking. Upon the founding of the People's Republic in 1949, the new Communist administration actively integrated the community into the emerging nation-state, transforming the hunting economy into a "hunting production brigade" (*lieye shengchandui*) by procuring a portion of the hunted pelts, furs, and meat in exchange for production points, credits, and eventually monetary payment.

By the mid 1960s, the state had also conducted an analysis of the community's reindeer antlers and, recognizing their viability for use in traditional Chinese medicine, reorganized the hunting economy into a collective enterprise modeled on the Soviet *sovkhoz*. Approximately a thousand head of reindeer were collectivized, and the state paid Ewenki a salary to supply harvested antler on an annual basis.[4] Despite this transformation, the *djiu* continued to serve as an apt dwelling that facilitated the community's ongoing hunting practices as well as the recently collectivized reindeer economy.

Accompanying collectivization was the construction of Aoluguya, a settlement specifically designed for the community that boasted wooden houses and an antler-processing factory. As increasing numbers of people began distancing themselves from the hunting and herding economies, some found employment in the forestry industry and government. This created a division between those who prioritized the taiga-based lifeworld and those who, having found employment outside it, happily accepted the modern facilities of the new settlement.

By the early 1980s, a new dwelling type had emerged. The ten-foot-square ridge tent gradually came to replace the birch bark and animal hide *djiu,* and remains the most commonly used tent today. It houses five to six people and, like the *djiu,* has a frame of larch trunks; however, the ridge tent's frame is rectangular and hung with sewn canvas. Replacing the open fire at the center is a wood-burning stove connected to an iron chimney that disperses the smoke from the top of the dwelling. Whereas people in the *djiu* slept on the floor around the fire, the new tent held benches for sitting during the day and sleeping at night, adding an element of increased comfort and practicality.

Interestingly, in a similar transformation at this time some Siberian Evenki and Eveny also replaced their tepees with canvas-covered ridge tents (Anderson 2006; Vitebsky 2005).[5] Anderson mentions that "they were 'acquired' in some unspecified complex transaction from departing soldiers at the nearby, abandoned Soviet Army weapons testing range" (2006: 10). The Reindeer Ewenki in China effected a comparable transaction between herder-hunters and the forestry authorities, the latter having utilized ridge tents for work in the taiga. The state made them available with the intention of increasing productivity.

Thus the adoption of ridge tents appears to be part of a broader shift across Northern Asia, which harks back to earlier debates about the vernacular architecture of the region. Indeed, the peoples of Northern Asia provide much food for thought in the analysis of vernacular architecture, most of which has been framed in evolutionist terms. According to Anderson, "roughly one hundred years of published work on Ewenki vernacular architecture dictated certain ideals of how designs and behaviours should be exhibited in a pure form" (2006: 3–4). Indeed, drawing upon the writings of Shirokogoroff (1929, 1935), Suslov

(1936) and Turov (1975) have argued that changes in architecture reflect transformations in social structure, and increased complexity in
built structures is considered representative of cultural development.
This positioning of dwelling types along a taken-for-granted scale of
social evolution continues to influence research of the region to this
day: "Rather than writing in the ethnographic present, researchers
have tended to prefer the past perfective where documented behaviour
in the past is seen to hold up a standard for the living today" (Anderson
2006: 4; also see Ventsel 2006).[6]

The corollary of this preference is that as vernacular architecture un-
dergoes change, new dwelling types such as log cabins or altered tent
structures are inevitably interpreted as cases of "cultural decline," as
opposed to an idealized "traditional" architectural model from which
all subsequent dwellings are thought to have originated. Anderson observes that "when presented with hybrid structural forms, for example
conical lodges made of plastic sheeting, there is a great temptation to
evaluate them as denigration of a cultural ideal rather than a clever
adaptation of the same architectural intuition to new materials" (2006:
4). This, I argue, is precisely what occurred in the case of the Aoluguya
Ewenki: the state constructed a discourse about "traditional" Ewenki
architecture by characterizing the new ridge tents as a nontraditional
transformation. Indeed, the ridge tents had been provided to the Ewenki
as a form of modernization, so they could not, from the modern socialist state's perspective, be equated with "traditional culture." Thus the
djiu came to be seen as the "true" Ewenki dwelling, while the ridge tent
exemplified their apparent "cultural decline." As we shall see, this division continues to pervade contemporary attitudes and policy.

The origins of the division can be traced to the construction of Aoluguya, where the state erected a museum alongside the settlement to
"scientifically" position the community on a scale of social and economic development. It featured a diorama-like display with a repro-
duction of a *djiu* that, via its placement in an official "scientific" setting,
came to define the tent as the archetypal dwelling of the Ewenki lifeworld. As an anonymous government official explained to me: "The
aim of the old Aoluguya and its museum was to settle the community
and present the Ewenki people's real culture. It was important that the
museum did not show the changes they were experiencing. The *djiu* is
traditional and so it was featured." In fact, the entire character of the
settlement, including the museum and other quasi-museum trappings,
required that Ewenki architecture be used specifically to actualize the
state's representation of "traditional culture." Therefore the *djiu* came
to be defined as the "archetypal" dwelling of the Reindeer Ewenki, a

manipulation that can be seen as an early precursor to the "ethnic village" (Chinese: *minzu cun*; perhaps better described as ethnic theme parks) characteristic of contemporary China, which compartmentalize minority culture through the medium of, among other things, "traditional architecture" (Gladney 2004).

Contrary to this characterization, I argue that the adoption of the ridge tents in the early 1980s was a locally mediated, vernacular transformation that suited people's needs in an emerging context of opportunity, changing relations with the state, and the availability of new, more practical materials. This is so because, as I show below, the vernacular architecture of hunters, or any other people, responds to their ability to access certain materials. It is imperative to avoid looking at architectural change from the perspective of an idealized form or state-sanctioned discourse on cultural denigration. Instead, in keeping with the phenomenological perspective outlined above, architecture should be perceived as emerging from the context of people's everyday lives and practices, including their flexible adaptation to new materials and changing constituents of their environments.

From animal hides to canvas: A vernacular transformation

With collectivization the Ewenki were, for the first time in their history, integrated into a system that prioritized output at the expense of subsistence. I argue that this integration, coupled with early attempts at sedentarization, came to be manifested within Ewenki society itself, transforming the community "from hunters to herders" and inculcating a modernist production ethos. Although a foundation for this had already been laid with the formation of the hunting production brigade (*lieye shengchangdui*), I will show that the introduction of the antler industry has been the most notable attempt to bureaucratize the reindeer lifeworld, and its designation of quotas, targets, and deadlines has induced what Forsyth, writing in the context of Siberia, calls "a comprehensive social revolution" (1994: 296).

As noted above, before collectivization the Ewenki were hunters who used their reindeer as pack animals and their milk as a supplement to subsistence. Membership in the collective, however, redefined them as "reindeer herders" (*yangluren*)—employees of the state contracted to supply the antler crop to the state company. Although they continued to engage in subsistence and collectivized hunting until 2003, government statistics show that the economic importance of hunting began to decline at the time of collectivization, and that eventually the antler industry took precedence. Of course such a transition can never be pinpointed exactly; rather, as I show below, it emerged gradually over an extended period.

First, the Ewenki came to be integrated within a system combining "points" for credit with ration cards, which incentivized maintenance of a stabler, more predictable level of output amongst the herder-hunters. This was more easily achieved through reindeer herding, which was annually oriented rather than seasonal and not dependent on the availability of game. Another factor was the introduction of hitherto unknown time-scales within the reindeer economy. To crop and deliver antler during the early summer, the herders had to adjust their movements, which in turn affected the positioning of taiga encampments and altered the practice of hunting. In the process, the hunters became herders within the new structure of collectivized "employment," as reflected in the community's decision to increase their herds to meet the demands of the new antler industry (Nentwig 2003). The Siberian Evenki were similarly transformed "from hunters to herders" in the mid twentieth century: "In 1927, 92.7 percent of all far eastern (Evenki) economic units were oriented toward hunting and trapping. After collectivization … the average proportion of hunting and trapping income dropped to 24.2 percent, while the proportion of income derived from reindeer breeding rose to 39 percent" (Anderson 1991: 15).

In China, a corollary factor behind this change was the construction of Aoluguya. Although some in the community avoided the settlement and spent most of their time in the taiga, its mere presence was of consequence to the entire Ewenki population. Once it was built, increasing numbers of people began to identify with a "settled way of life," particularly those who had sought employment outside the reindeer economy and were drawn to modern housing and electricity. Inculcation of production-oriented "work" via their integration into the salaried antler economy inevitably affected the herder-hunters' self-perception. More and more herder-hunters began to divide their time between the forest and the settlement, whereby the latter became known as a feature of the Ewenki lifeworld. Meanwhile, Aoluguya indirectly connected the herders to the broader national economy by making consumer goods and foodstuffs available. As mentioned earlier, before arriving in Chinese territory the Ewenki had engaged in trade and barter with the Cossacks living along the Argun River and, following the establishment of the People's Republic, in the town of Qiqian (Nentwig 2003). Aoluguya was the next logical site for acquiring needed goods, including ammunition, salt, food, and alcohol. Inevitably, linkages were forged between the taiga and village lifeworlds, a state-mediated physical *and* conceptual relationship that integrated the community into the production-oriented structure of the collective economy.

Of course, I am not suggesting that "traditional life" was uniformly replaced by collectivized modernity. On the contrary, traditional practices and attitudes continued throughout the various "modernization" efforts, much as they do in the contemporary era. But at the same time, these practices increasingly intertwined with the policies of the socialist state, something also observed in the Siberian context. As Ssorin-Chaikov remarks, for example, the state came to be embodied not as an agent of overarching authority, but in everyday behavior and practice: "What appears as a visible centre of power, hides, in fact, an opposite move: that the power operates not between this visible centre and the overseen subjects but as a relation inside the subjects ... statehood operates by vanishing as an entity in the 'microphysics' of power" (2003: 116). Likewise, in the Chinese context some in the community continued to hunt and herd reindeer as they had done in the past, reproducing the practical skills and knowledge demanded from a taiga-based lifeworld. Yet transformations were inevitable at the level of practice and self-identification, and the herders came to identify themselves not just as reindeer herders but in terms of modernist ideology of "production" itself. In the language of practice theory, the Ewenki can be said to have come to identify with the *illusio* (Bourdieu 1996) of modernity and production rather than solely subsistence.

I argue that the adoption of the ridge tents must be elucidated within this complex series of entanglements. Indeed, in keeping with Ingold's phenomenological approach to architecture and Anderson's comments on architectural change, I maintain that the adoption of ridge tents was a vernacular modification—something that "made sense" in the context of collectivized reindeer husbandry, the shift from hunting to herding, the rise of a production ethos, and the availability of new, more practical materials. In this regard three specific points merit consideration. First, adoption of the ridge tents was *possible,* because by this time the taiga held increasing numbers of logging roads built for the burgeoning forestry industry, alongside which the herders could set up their dwellings. Close proximity to these roads ensured access to government-supplied vehicles, which not only brought provisions and support but also assisted the herders with their movements in the taiga. Having already begun to transition from hunting to herding, the herders could thus afford to use the ridge tents as they themselves had reduced their mobility enough to rely on state-supplied transportation. As we have seen, the ridge tents allowed for benches to be used for sitting and sleeping, something that would have been impossible in the *djiu,* which had to be lightweight and erectable at short notice. The benches served the growing number of herders who had become accustomed to higher levels of comfort while visiting the settlement.[7] The combination of the newly available tents, increasing presence of logging roads, corollary supply of transportation, and higher levels of comfort afforded by the dwellings made ridge tents a suitable option from the herders' perspective—a vernacular response to a series of interrelated transformations.

Second, adopting the ridge tents made sense because they needed no animal hides as a covering, and the hides now had value as a commodity. New materials, such as tent canvas and multipurpose plastic sheeting, served as suitable replacements for both tree bark and hides, being lightweight, low-cost, waterproof, and reparable. As Anderson remarks, "Plastic sheeting is highly valued since it is extremely light and can also be used to cover saddlebags at night. ... The lesson ... seems to be that architectural strategies are applied to materials that are on hand and that match local needs" (Anderson 2006: 17). This continues to be the case for the contemporary reindeer herders, who emphasize the importance of plastic sheeting and regularly acquire on visits to the settlement, as it remains the ideal material for covering tents and supplies.

The third and perhaps most important factor was that the ridge tents were heated by wood-burning stoves instead of open fires. Indeed, this was the most common reason the contemporary herders gave for the switch to ridge tents, as the stoves kept the new dwellings considerably warmer in the long winter months. Here the vernacular characteristics of the ridge tents correlated with people's own (shifting) physical and existential needs in a change that suited local needs and made practical sense within the herders' current social and economic circumstances. Thus, although the *djiu* had been an apt dwelling for subsistence hunting prior to collectivization, ridge tents were the more suitable choice for collectivized reindeer herding—a vernacular response to a new context of livelihood and production. According to Anderson (2006: 2), "transformations in the social and economic situation have allowed Evenki and other Siberian peoples the luxury of creating multiple living and working spaces of a transitory nature which, although 'non-traditional,' nevertheless bear a signature of taiga life." In a similar vein, I argue that collectivization gave the Reindeer Ewenki in China the opportunity to develop new kinds of flexibility and luxury, and that ridge tents suited local needs, being compatible with the antler industry of the contemporary era and easy to use thanks to new, more practical materials.

As in any case of social change, however, the adoption of the ridge tents produced contradictions. For example, the wood-burning stoves, being extremely heavy and requiring motorized transportation between encampments, reduced the mobility of the herders. This in turn limited their movements' scale and frequency to the detriment of the grazing of reindeer and especially hunting, making people more dependent on the state. Thus, the adoption of the ridge tents as a vernacular transformation did not preclude far-reaching consequences for herders' livelihoods, which had important implications for the 2003 relocation.

Vernacular architecture and forced relocation

In 2003 the state began its relocation of the Ewenki. It offered the community housing in a purpose-built settlement on the outskirts of Genhe City as compensation for relocating and accepting the newly implemented hunting ban.[8]

Significantly, some in the community had agreed to relocate, specifically those who had been separated from the reindeer economy earlier on. These people have, overall, adapted well in the new settlement. Opponents of the decision included former hunters, who are now unemployed and dependent on government payments, as well as current herders' family members who reside away from the forest campsites, typically because they have children in regional schools. These latter individuals have been most affected by the relocation: they try to maintain ties with the taiga-based lifeworld but find themselves disengaged from the herding economy and from subsistence hunting, now dissolved.

The new settlement holds housing for "hunters" (see Xie, this volume), an antler-processing factory, a cultural museum, a hotel, and several Ewenki-inspired constructions devoted to manufacture and sale of traditional handicrafts. Each house is divided into two halves, one per family. Each half has two bedrooms as well as a kitchen, bathroom, and living room; electricity and water are free. Assisted by a Finnish consultancy firm, local officials have planned to transform the settlement into the Aoluguya Ethnic Reindeer Resort, a residential-cum-tourism center intended to provide opportunities for tourism-related employment.

Architecture has played a fundamental role in the planning and construction of the settlement, with both the state and consultancy firm using designs inspired by "reindeer culture" to assist in the "preservation of Ewenki culture." Thus the settlement features reproductions of *djiu* and *djiu*-inspired buildings, and Finnish designs for the houses themselves. Tourists are encouraged to stay in the settlement's hotel—outfitted with comparable stylistic elements—to experience the cultural uniqueness of what is marketed as the "reindeer tribe." In this respect the settlement is akin to the ethnic village, where "traditional culture" is equated with tourism presentation (Gladney 2004). Across the street from the main settlement is the so-called forest park, an outdoor display depicting the reindeer herding lifestyle, featuring a birch-bark *djiu* (Figure 7.1), several other reconstructed dwellings (all cone-shaped) and a few reindeer kept in a fenced patch of forest. As part of the show, tour guides dressed in reproductions of traditional clothing demonstrate "how the Ewenki used to live," presenting activities such as crafting storage containers from birch bark, telling stories, and baking traditional bread (Fraser 2010).

The way the state (and consultancy firm) has maintained the discourse about "traditional" Ewenki architecture, with the new settlement featuring *djiu* reproductions at the total expense of the ridge tents, deserves emphasis. The discourse is reproduced at the new state-of-the-art museum, where a *djiu* stands as part of an exhibit, once again characterized as the "true" Ewenki dwelling. As in the old Aoluguya, the state is purposefully using Ewenki architecture for its own ideological and conceptual purposes by forbearing to associate a (new) feature—the ridge tent that has been the herders' primary dwelling for

Figure 7.1. Ewenki *djiu* at the forest park, July 2008, Aoluguya. Photograph by Tashi Nyima.

the past twenty-five years—with the Ewenki lifeworld. Herein lies a contradiction, however, because whereas the ridge tent was a vernacular response to the social and economic context of collectivization, the state has imposed a *non*-vernacular transformation in the form of *djiu* reproductions and the broader design of the settlement, appropriating the style and symbolism of Ewenki architecture in its politicized representation of "traditional culture."

This is comparable to Evans and Humphrey's (2002) discussion of architectural afterlives in the Inner Mongolia Autonomous Region. They argue that whereas in Mongolia itself the yurt has a vernacular afterlife in providing non-pastoral residence for urban dwellers on the outskirts of Ulaanbaatar, in Inner Mongolia, where yurt use is diminishing, a non-vernacular transformation has occurred, with the structure and style of the yurt inspiring the architecture of museums, restaurants, and tourist camps. Evans and Humphrey propose that this does not reflect a vernacular transformation because it is an imposed design—the yurt is being appropriated and replicated in the politicized Mongolization of the Chinese architectural landscape:

> The Chinese-built yurt is very different from the contemporary urban yurts of Ulaanbaatar. These are lived-in dwellings, and often consist simply of the standard pastoral yurt placed in a city compound. The Mongol urban yurt … may thus evolve through an unbroken practical vernacular architecture into a number of hybrids between the mobile dwelling and the house. This is in contrast to the Inner Mongolian case, where the Chinese "yurts" are a reintroduction as it were, of a building form that is ideologically held to belong to the past (even though there are regions of Inner Mongolia where yurts are still used). Our article suggests that the processes of substitution, quotation, and estrangement of "yurts" that are taking place in the Chinese environment are quite different from the vernacular evolution of yurts in the towns of Mongolia itself. (Evans and Humphrey 2002: 204)

Similarly, I contend that the reproductions featured in the Aoluguya Ethnic Reindeer Resort are themselves non-vernacular appropriations; indeed, as static dwellings permanently fixed to the ground, the featured *djiu* are ill suited to a hunting and herding lifeworld. At the same time, they feature stylistic modifications such as furniture, seating-places, and electricity, all added not to enhance the practice of reindeer herding but to allow tourists to feel comfortable while they experience "traditional" Ewenki culture. Seen in this perspective, the *djiu* reproductions are reintroduced versions of an idealized "original" tent, erected for ideological purposes and without regard for vernacular considerations.

As Ingold observes, unlike life in the substantial buildings of the village settlement, "most of life, for hunter-gatherers, goes on around dwellings rather than within them" (2000: 180). This comment aptly characterizes the specificity of hunter-gatherer ontology by drawing attention to the divergence between building and dwelling as modes of being-in-the-world. *Building* captures a Cartesian ontology, epitomized by the notion that "worlds are made before they are lived in" (179); whereas *dwelling* refers to direct perceptual engagement, so that "acts of dwelling preced[e] acts of worldmaking" (179). In this sense, the hunter-gatherer mode of apprehending the world is one of engagement and practical immersion, "not of building but of dwelling, not of making a view of the world but of taking a view in it" (Ingold 1991: 121). This distinction is readily applicable to the Ewenki and the Chinese state, as well as to the divergence between vernacular and non-vernacular architecture. As we have seen, the ridge tent, though radically different from the "original" *djiu*, remains a *lived-in* dwelling evolving along an unbroken line of practical vernacular architecture. By contrast, the reproductions displayed at the Aoluguya Ethnic Reindeer Resort were erected according to a *building* ontology, intended to imitate the vernacular dwelling for a purpose beyond use and functional design. Epitomizing this latter perspective, Rapoport writes, "the organization of space cognitively precedes its material expression; settings and built environments are thought before they are built" (1994: 488). Likewise, the Chinese state seems to have cognized the organization and use of (Ewenki) architecture *before* its material expression, in direct contrast to the vernacular ridge tents' emergence from the ongoing dwelling of the herders themselves.

As I shall show next, the state's failure to recognize the ridge tent as vernacular architecture is problematic because although the appropriated dwellings of the new settlement may entertain tourists, ridge tents are the vernacular architecture of contemporary reindeer herders. This has important implications for the community's future, especially in maintaining a flexible reindeer economy and symbolizing contemporary Ewenki identity.

Vernacular architecture and the contemporary reindeer lifeworld

Thirty to forty Ewenki herders live and work in the Daxing'anling taiga, herding reindeer and harvesting antler on an annual basis. Their numbers fluctuate according to the seasons and personal preference.

Many spend all their time in the forest and rarely visit the settlement, while others visit periodically, primarily to purchase supplies, deliver harvested antler, and visit family and friends (Fraser 2010). Together the herders own seven to eight hundred head of reindeer and reside in ridge tents and a few *djiu*. A single encampment holds between two and six dwellings, and the *djiu* is found in only two encampments (see also Kolås 2011).

As noted above, a hunting ban accompanied the relocation and construction of the new settlement, leaving the antler industry as the last remaining feature of the reindeer lifeworld. Thus the ridge tents continue to serve as vernacular dwellings—all the herders I spoke with emphasized their ongoing satisfaction with the tents as a low-cost, reparable, practical option. At the same time, they do not see the ridge tent as an unchangeable dwelling but as one that responds to new circumstances and contexts by allowing incorporation of architectural innovations, a feature that showcases the tents' ongoing vernacular characteristics. For example, the herders have developed a new practice of leaving the tent poles or frames standing after an encampment has been moved. Thus, when traveling through the taiga one may come across the empty "shell" of an encampment from which the herders have removed the canvas cover and transported it to the next site. The herders have several favorite locations to which they return at different times during the year, taking advantage of their dependence on the state's motorized vehicles, and of their exceptional status as the only people legally entitled to reside in the taiga. As a result, they are able to leave the frames standing when moving between camps, a vernacular response to the increasingly sedentarized herding of the contemporary era.

Another example is the emergence of a new dwelling type, specifically a larger canvas tent with more sleeping positions and no stove in the center. Elucidated within the context of the contemporary reindeer economy, this "nontraditional" transformation once again makes practical sense and demonstrates the ongoing flexibility of vernacular architecture. The need for seasonal workers has increased, as the Ewenki have to rely on antler cropping as their primary source of income and the number of permanent herders has generally declined. The new tent is found only in campsites where large numbers of reindeer are tended, creating demand for additional workers—typically Ewenki men living permanently in Aoluguya or Han Chinese from nearby villages. There is no stove because the tent is used only during the mild antler cropping season, when there is less need for additional warmth. The combination of these factors induced a vernacular response on the part of the herders, who then acquired what I call the "workers tent."[9] As Anderson puts it in a remark directly applicable to this example, the key finding is that "the presence of ad-hoc or hybrid structures does not imply the collapse of architectural intuition. Instead it shows a clever marshalling of skill to make the best use of the resources churned up in post-Soviet conditions" (2006: 24).

Another transformation is the practice of using the *djiu* for cooking rather than sleeping. I found that when erected at the larger campsites, these tents were primarily used for baking a traditional bread in a brick stove built in the center of the dwelling.[10] In this case the *djiu* would typically be erected right beside a ridge tent. The individual performing the baking would use the former for cooking and sleep in the latter. Remarkably, however, in winter, when reindeer graze deeper in the mountains and are accompanied by only a few men, the *djiu* is still used in its mobile form as an easily transportable sleeping tent. This exemplifies not only the persistence of vernacular architectural intuition amongst the contemporary herders, but also their relationship to dwelling within a (changing) environment. The herders use different dwellings depending on context, such as in the adoption of the ridge tent; but they can also use a single dwelling for different purposes depending on the season, as in the case of the *djiu*. This brings the relevance of a phenomenological approach to architecture to the fore, deconstructing the division between traditional and nontraditional to focus instead on the practical articulation of people's dwelling-in-the-world via, among other things, vernacular architecture.

Another example concerns the cosmological features of the Ewenki lifeworld, which, as noted previously, once manifested itself in the community's architecture and still does today, though more variably. For example, each ridge tent is always erected with its entrance facing south, reproducing the assumption that good fortune comes from that direction. Offerings and libations to the fire-spirit continue to be made within the tent, as the herders still regularly communicate with their dwelling's fire-spirit. Now that the open fire has been replaced with an iron stove, however, the liquor is now offered by throwing the alcohol directly onto the stove itself, rather than "into" the fire. This, I was told, is just as effective as the original way of making the offering, since the fire-spirit is perceived to "take" the offering through the surface of the iron stove.

A final example concerns the relationship between the ridge tents and the social composition of the herders. Above I described the spatialization of age and gender divisions within the *djiu*, something that is less visible today as men and women, young and old, share multiple living and working spaces. Nevertheless, certain divisions continue to remain visible. For example, in all the new dwellings I stayed in, herders of the older generation were given sitting and sleeping positions at the far end of the tent, directly opposite the entrance. This "division" was not governed by strict codes of conduct described in the classical literature—young people occasionally sat in the seats of their elders and vice versa. At the same time, though, it continued to manifest itself as a normative mode of behavior: a young herder instinctively moves out of a senior's place, should the latter reenter the dwelling or clearly indicate a wish to occupy the space.

Thus, although the ridge tents differ in shape from the *djiu*, the *malu* is (partially) rearticulated as the most respected part of the dwelling, its position remapped onto the structure of the new tent. My own presence in the campsites also rendered this visible. For example, when I first arrived, I was seated at the far end of the tent directly beside the host, which marked my status as a guest. When it came time to sleep, however, my allotted position was not at the far end but the lower left-hand side of the dwelling, which, as we have seen, used to be reserved for guests in the *djiu*.

The relaxation of age and gender divisions is something that Anderson has also noted in the context of the Siberian Evenki, where post-socialism appears to have loosened the formalized divisions within people's vernacular architecture. However, as Anderson shows, this does not mean that age and gender no longer influence vernacular architecture or the practice of reindeer herding:

> After repeated residence one quality of the residential architecture began to stand out. If, in the relatively deep Soviet past, members of one family, or even brigade, were confined to one tent, today the people in a hunting and herding unit were dispersed across many tents…
>
> Correspondingly, gendered and status activity that would have been structured under the roof of one tent … has now been broken up into different spaces—but it is nevertheless structured. (Anderson 2006: 12)

In this regard, while post-socialism can be said to have relaxed divisions within individual tents, new divisions have emerged across *multiple* tents. Similarly, new divisions are now emerging *between* different Reindeer Ewenki encampments, again manifested in vernacular architecture. For example, of the campsites currently operating, three are in the same area as prior to relocation, while the remainder are located closer to the new Aoluguya. As described by local government officials, the closer one travels to Genhe and new Aoluguya the more "modern" the campsite is said to become. One encampment even features solar panels as part of its vernacular architecture, while those farthest away rely on more "traditional" architecture such as the *djiu*. This division has become one way the local government rates the "modernity" of the reindeer herders. Speaking with members of the local administration, for example, I was told that camps farthest from Aoluguya are the most "traditional," specifically because, as one official put it, "they continue to use traditional tents."

Vernacular architecture and the future of the Reindeer Ewenki

The appearance of new divisions between different encampments through vernacular architecture pertains specifically to the viability of the dwelling perspective outlined above. In contrast to normative definitions, a phenomenological approach to architecture includes the totality of sites people engage with, whether they are local, foreign, permanent, or temporary. In this regard, Ewenki vernacular architecture cannot be equated solely with "fixed locations" of tents or campsites, but must include the storage sites, plastic sheeting, solar panels, rivers, roads, and even urban settlements associated with the practice of reindeer herding, with everyday life "going well beyond the walls of a conical tent and the hearth at its centre" (Anderson 2006: 2). This perspective extends the "built-environment" of the Ewenki outward into the landscape itself.

This has important implications for assessment of the future of the Reindeer Ewenki, now that reindeer herding is ever more integrated with life in the settlement, particularly since the latest relocation. Indeed, I argue that the settlement and newly constructed houses too should be seen as part and parcel of Ewenki vernacular architecture. Here it is imperative to coalesce the ridge tents and new houses as multiple sites of opportunity for the practice of reindeer herding, regardless of divisions between the traditional and modern, or the authentic and inauthentic. This shifts the focus from the walls and hearth of the tent to the ways in which the Ewenki themselves order the world around them, "maximizing flexibility in relation to various kinds of architecture" (Anderson 2006: 2).

The relevance of this perspective is evident among herders' family members who are integrated into the taiga-based lifeworld but reside permanently in the settlement, and among the numerous herders who divide their time between travel in the taiga and Aoluguya. Here a phenomenological approach reveals emerging new uses of vernacular architecture, as in the case of individuals who set up shops to sell reindeer antler from their houses (Fraser 2010), or who have capitalized on the increased access to technology in the settlement by launching websites from their houses to facilitate delivery of antler products. These people can be seen as flexibly "making use" of the settlement's architectural appurtenances, incorporating their houses into the herding enterprise much as their predecessors did with a birch tree, ridge tent, or logging road. Viewed in this way, the new houses in Aoluguya are experienced not in opposition but rather in addition to the ridge tents as another site of opportunity, and not as inauthentic dwellings but as part of contemporary vernacular architecture. Indeed, as is clear from the case of the Aoluguya Ewenki, vernacular architecture can include tents *and* houses, and divisions between the settlement and taiga can be mediated by strategies that cut across the divide.

Despite the increasing number of herders dividing their time between the settlement and the taiga, this does not suggest a uniform pattern of sedentarization—on the contrary, new architecture facilitates the reindeer lifeworld *alongside* sedentarization, enabling herders to move from one location to another depending on the season, the number of people currently in the campsites, and personal preference. This was made clear during one of my campsite visits, when an Ewenki youth arrived to spend the summer in the taiga after completing his school exams. Now, he explained, was his time to "live in the forest" and "be a reindeer herder"—at least, until the end of summer, when he would return to the settlement.

To be sure, despite such cases of flexibility, it would be misleading to present the situation in overly simplistic terms. While some herders develop strategies that cut across the divide, for others the taiga-settlement division remains problematic. As noted, some Ewenki almost never visit the settlement, remaining at the campsites for over three hundred days a year. These individuals' dislike of the new Aoluguya and what they perceive as its radical divergence from life in the forest (Fraser 2010) was thrown into relief when I traveled with two herders from a campsite back to the settlement. Embodying their unease at the prospect of travelling to Aoluguya, the two individuals drank heavily throughout the duration of the trip, arriving at "their" houses disoriented and physically uncomfortable. After collecting supplies they rushed back to the vehicle, and we returned immediately to the campsites. Later that evening they explained their unease, telling me that they simply did not feel comfortable in the settlement: "Life is hard in the forest but it is better than the settlement. There is nothing to do there. There are no animals, no reindeer. I can never visit for too long. I cannot live in a place like that."

Thus, although some in the community are able to "use" the settlement to their advantage, creating new kinds of vernacular architecture, this is not the case for all individuals. Indeed, for some herders what matters most is not the newly constructed dwellings or layout of the settlement but the existential security provided by living in the taiga. As I have noted elsewhere (Fraser 2010), the lifeworld of the Ewenki necessitates a specific ontology of human and nonhuman personhood that is grounded in the ongoing relationship between the community and its lived environment. Here ecological relations are intertwined with those of human sociality, and the environment is experienced not "out there" but "ready-to-hand" (Heidegger 1962). For many, this contrasts directly with the new Aoluguya, where the lack of person-based networks results in the de-*person*alization of the settlement, capturing the divergence between life in the taiga and the settlement. "Getting used to" life in Aoluguya is an ongoing process of embodiment and skill, an ability to incorporate new architectural features into one's everyday lived experience. So whereas vernacular architecture has, for some, come to include multiple types of dwelling such as tents *and* houses, for others it refers *only* to taiga-based residence, a variation that has important implications for both the state's intention to "preserve traditional culture" amongst the community, and the viability of contemporary reindeer herding.

Conclusion

This chapter has provided an account of vernacular architecture among the Reindeer Ewenki. I have argued that, contrary to the division promulgated by the state, vernacular features of Ewenki architecture continue to be evident in ridge tents, both at the time of collectivization and in the contemporary era. The herders do not construct a division between "traditional" and "nontraditional" architecture. Instead, they experience transformations from within the exigencies of the reindeer herding lifeworld, making changes to their architecture as they see fit and acquiring useful new materials whenever they become available. In this regard, the ridge tents and new houses should not be seen as non-vernacular transformations, but rather as dimensions of contemporary Ewenki architecture.

The history of the Reindeer Ewenki in China demonstrates that reindeer herding requires a fixed center through which the reindeer lifeworld can be facilitated. Meanwhile, however, the relocation and construction of the settlement has created a series of new constraints. It is therefore imperative that the Aoluguya Ethnic Reindeer Resort be seen as only one dimension of the contemporary Ewenki lifeworld—

something that exists alongside, not instead of, taiga-based residence. Here an understanding of vernacular architecture might serve to demonstrate how herders can live in both the settlement and the taiga simultaneously. This way of life would be easier with more regular transportation between the taiga and settlement, government support for the maintenance of ridge tents, more flexible schooling and health care provision, and recognition of the specific needs of individuals who are less accustomed to life outside the taiga.

Notes

1. Hereafter, "Ewenki" refers to the reindeer-herding Ewenki unless otherwise specified.
2. The Eveny or Even are a people in Siberia and the Russian Far East. A 2002 census described them as a population of 19,071 people living primarily in Magadan Oblast, Kamchatka, and northern parts of Sakha. The Eveny are closely related to the Ewenki, sharing similar origins in the Transbaikal region and traditional occupations as hunters and reindeer herders.
3. The practice of setting up a south-facing tent also has practical implications, specifically that it allows more sunlight into the dwelling and blocks the cold northern wind. Mongolians also always set up their yurts with entrances facing south.
4. Reindeer antlers grow throughout the year and are cut before any bone substance has formed. They contain high levels of rantarine, a highly prized substance in Asia, said to increase the immune system and build masculine virility. Antlers that are not cut will be shed naturally but are less potent and hence less valuable.
5. In an interesting parallel, the reindeer-herding peoples of both the Russian North and China have embodied a quasi-militarization of the reindeer-herding lifeworld through the use of canvas tents and army boots and clothing, which have all become "hallmarks" of contemporary reindeer herding.
6. Pikunova's (1999) Evenki dictionary aptly portrays the structured distribution of space within a standing Evenki dwelling as a solemn cultural ideal (Anderson 2006).
7. The transformation from sleeping on the floor to raised "beds" has important implications in terms of changes in bodily experience that cannot be dealt with here. However, this correlates with a series of other transforming "techniques of the body" such as the experience of electricity.
8. At the national level, the relocation was characterized as a *necessary* step in the environmental protection of Inner Mongolia, defined as "ecological migration" (*shengtai yimin*). For example, Wun Nanlan, former mayor of Genhe, noted about Ewenki subsistence practices that "their living methods resulted in a sharp decline of wild animals and environment degra-

dation. Mushrooms and bryophyte on which reindeer feed have almost disappeared in the area due to overgrazing. It will take at least 25 years to grow back to its original state" ("Reindeer Ewenki" 2003).

9. Other examples of such use include the yurts that Mongolian pastoralists in Inner Mongolia set up alongside their brick homes. In winter and autumn, they are often used for storage, as it is more practical to reside in the (warmer) brick house. In spring and summer, however, the yurts are taken out to the pasture to serve as lived-in dwellings.

10. The Ewenki bake a yeast-free pan bread on an iron plate. This practice continues in the campsites even as it is simultaneously appropriated at the Aoluguya Ethnic Reindeer Resort. It exemplifies the kinds of skills still maintained by the herders that are gradually being presented in a tourism setting.

References

Anderson, David. 2006. "Dwellings, Storage and Summer Site Structure among Siberian Orochen Evenkis: Hunter-Gatherer Vernacular Architecture under Post-Socialist Conditions." *Norwegian Archaeological Review* 39, no. 1: 1–26.

———. 1991. "Turning Hunters into Herders: A Critical Examination of Soviet Development Policy among the Evenki of Southeastern Siberia." *Arctic* 44, no. 1: 12–22.

Bird-David, Nurit. 1999. "'Animism' Revisited: Personhood, Environment, and Relational Epistemology." *Current Anthropology* 40: S67–S91.

Bourdieu, Pierre. 2003. "The Berber House." In *The Anthropology of Space and Place: Locating Culture*, ed. Setha M. Low and Denise Lawrence-Zúñiga. London: Blackwell.

———. 1996. *The Rules of Art: Genesis and Structure of the Literary Field.* Stanford, CA: Stanford University Press.

Brandisauskas, Donatas. 2007. "Symbolism and Ecological Uses of Fire among Orochen-Evenki." *Sibirica* 6, no. 1: 95–119.

Brunskill, Ronald. 2000. *Illustrated Handbook of Vernacular Architecture.* 4th ed. London: Faber and Faber.

Ermolova, Nadezhda. 2003. "Evenki Reindeer-Herding: A History." *Cultural Survival Quarterly* 2, no. 1 ("The Troubled Taiga"): 23–24.

Evans, Christopher, and Humphrey, Caroline. 2002. "The Afterlives of the Mongolian Yurt: The 'Archaeology' of a Chinese Tourist Camp." *Material Culture* 2, no. 2: 189–210.

Forsyth, James. 1994. *A History of the Peoples of Siberia: Russia's North Asian Colony 1581–1990.* Cambridge: Cambridge University Press.

Fraser, Richard. 2010. "Forced Relocation amongst the Reindeer-Evenki of Inner Mongolia." *Inner Asia* 12, no. 2: 317–346.

Gladney, Dru. 2004. *Dislocating China: Muslims, Minorities, and Other Subaltern Subjects.* London: Hurst.

Heidegger, Martin. 1962. *Being and Time.* New York: Harper & Row.

Heyne, F. Georg. 2007. "Notes on Blood Revenge among the Reindeer Evenki of Manchuria (Northeast China)." *Asian Folklore Studies* 66, nos. 1–2: 165–178.

———. 1999. "The Social Significance of the Shaman amongst the Chinese Reindeer Evenki." *Asian Folklore Studies* 58, no. 2: 377–395.

———. 1989. "Die Jagd in den Wäldern des Großen Hinggan. Ein Beitrag zur Wirtschaftsethnologie der chinesischen Rentier-Ewenken." *Jahrbuch des Museums für Völkerkunde zu Leipzig* 38: 32–100.

Ingold, Tim. 2000. *The Perception of the Environment: Essays on Livelihood, Dwelling, and Skill*. London and New York: Routledge.

———. 1991. "Becoming Persons: Consciousness and Sociality in Human Evolution." *Cultural Dynamics* 4: 355–378.

Kaĭgorodov, Anatoliĭ Makarovich. 1968. "Evenki v Trechrec'e (Po lichnym nabliudeniiam)" [The Ewenki of the Three Rivers Area (Personal Observations)]. *Sovetskaja Etnografija* 4: 123–131.

Kolås, Åshild. 2011. "Reclaiming the Forest: Ewenki Reindeer Herding as Exception." *Human Organization* 70, no. 4: 397–404.

Lawrence, Denise, and Setha M. Low. 1990. "The Built Environment and Spatial Form." *Annual Review of Anthropology* 19: 453–506.

Lindgren, Ethel J. 1936. "Notes on the Reindeer Tungus of Manchuria: Their Names, Groups, Administration and Shamans." PhD diss., Cambridge.

———. 1935. "The Reindeer Tungus of Manchuria." *Journal of the Royal Central Asian Society* 22, no. 2: 221–231.

———. 1930. "North-Western Manchuria and the Reindeer-Tungus." *Geographical Journal* 75: 518–536.

Nentwig, Ingo. 2003. "Reminiscences about the Reindeer Herders of China." *Cultural Survival Quarterly* 27, no. 1: 36–38.

———. 1991. "Jagd und Wanderviehwirtschaft in der Taiga Chinas: Zur Situation der Rentier-Ewenken im Großen Hinggan-Gebirge." In *Nomaden, Mobile Tierhaltung. Zur gegenwärtigen Lage von Nomaden und zu den Problemen und Chancen mobiler Tierhaltung*, ed. F. Scholz. Berlin: Verlag das Arabische Buch.

Pedersen, Morten Axel. 2001. "Totemism, Animism and North Asian Indigenous Ontologies." *Journal of the Royal Anthropological Institute*, n.s., 7: 411–427.

Pikunova, Zinaida Nikolaevna. 1999. Kartinnyi Slovar Evenkiis-koga iazyka [Evenki Picture Dictionary]. Saint Petersburg: Prosveschenie.

Rapoport, Amos. 1994. "Spatial Organization and the Built Environment." In *Companion Encyclopaedia of Anthropology: Humanity, Culture, and Social Life*, ed. Tim Ingold. London: Routledge.

"Reindeer Ewenki on the Move." 2003. *China Daily*, 1 May.

Rudofsky, Bernard. 1987. *Architecture without Architects: A Short Introduction to Non-pedigreed Architecture*. Albuquerque: University of New Mexico Press.

Shirokogoroff, Sergei Mikhailovich. 1935. *Psychomental Complex of the Tungus*. London: Kegan Paul, Trench, Trubner.

———. 1929. *Social Organization of the Northern Tungus*. Oosterhout: Anthropological Publications.

Ssorin-Chaikov, Nikolai. 2003. *The Social Life of the State in Subarctic Siberia*. Stanford, CA: Stanford University Press.

Suslov, Innokenty. 1936. *Shamanstvo I bor'ba s nim.* [Shamanism and the Struggle against It]. *Sovetskii Sever* [Soviet North] 3–5: 89–152.

Turov, Michail. 1975. "K probleme proiskhozhdeniia i evoliutsii evenkiiskogo labaza-'noku" [On the Problem of the Emergence and Evolution of Evenki labaza-'noku]. In *Drevniaia istoriia narodov iuga Vostochnoi Sibiri (Irkutsk)* [Ancient History of the Peoples of Southeast Siberia (Irkutsk)] 3: 193–209.

Ventsel, Aimar. 2006. "Hunter-Herder Continuum in Anabarski District, NW Sakha, Siberia, Russian Federation." *Nomadic Peoples* 10, no. 2: 68–86.

Vitebsky, Piers. 2005. *Reindeer People: Living with Animals and Spirits in Siberia.* London: HarperCollins.

Willerslev, Rane. 2007. *Soul Hunters: Hunting, Animism, and Personhood among the Siberian Yukaghirs.* Berkeley: University of California Press.

PART IV

Local Voices

◯》 8

CAMPFIRE
Weijia

Campfire—it's burning
Lighting the Ewenki
Our long history floating through time
Remaining strong
Has the history been recorded?
Nobody has recorded it
It's been burning throughout history
For the Ewenki people's culture it's burning brightly
This is the meaning of the campfire
The Ewenki people see the campfire as a god
Because she gives warmth and light to her beloved people

໑ 9

My Homeland
Gong Yu

I was born in the early 1980s, at a time when China was going through unprecedented social changes. I was born in Aoluguya, although the name now needs to be preceded by the word "old." This is because today's Aoluguya is not the same as the Aoluguya of my birthplace. In the Ewenki language, the name Aoluguya means the place where the poplar grows densely. The Aoluguya where I was born lies seventeen kilometers from the town of Mangui. I've heard that Ewenki hunters found this beautiful place while they were out hunting. As a village, old Aoluguya had a very small population. It was usually called Aoxiang, or "Ao Township." It was inhabited from 1965 until 2003.

My father *amin* and mother *eni*

In the Ewenki language, father is called *amin,* and mother is *eni.* I am an Ewenki but my lineage is mixed, since my father belongs to the Han nationality. Despite this circumstance, my parents wrote "Ewenki" in the "nationality" box when they filled in the residency registration form. In the box for "given name," they put my Chinese nickname, Yu, meaning lotus flower. Although my mother initially thought they should put an Ewenki name in the form, they eventually followed the Han custom of giving a Chinese name, along with the father's surname. When I started school, Gong Yu was also my formal school name. At that time the people of Aoluguya were gradually accepting the use of Chinese names for their children.

Within Aoluguya, everybody called me "lotus," and outside the village I was called Gong Yu. But in my heart I had yet another name: Niurika. This was a result of my mother's influence. She thought that an Ewenki person ought to have an Ewenki name. Hence my mother asked Maria Sologon, whom she held in high regard, to give me an Ewenki name. Maria named me after our last shaman Njura, who died in 1997. I have understood that the old woman named me in this way because she hoped I could do many good deeds for the Ewenki people, just like this shaman had done in the past. The four Ewenki clans are named Buljotin, Sologon, Kudrin, and Kaltakun. Since my mother's clan is Buljotin, I use the Ewenki name Niurika Buljotin.

My father's name is Gong Xuewen. His hometown lies in a remote area in Sichuan province. He came to Inner Mongolia in the 1970s, when railroads were being built. After that he stayed on in Aoluguya. He still remembers clearly the exact time when he came to Aoluguya. It was in July of 1979 that he and a few others from his hometown arrived in Aoluguya together. Besides my father, three of his fellow townsmen also married Ewenki women. My father started working as a tractor driver. Later he became the leader of the hunting brigade, the director of the wood processing factory, the head of the grain supply center, the head of the local United Front Work Department of the Communist Party, and finally the Party Secretary until his retirement. My parents both experienced the introduction of the Household Contract Responsibility System in 1984, when thirty reindeer were distributed to every Ewenki hunter. In 1994, the reindeer contracting system was modified. The reward for reindeer breeding was canceled, and the hunters' pay was based solely on their production of reindeer horn. The income was shared between the individual hunter and the hunter's cooperative at a ratio of 70 percent to the individual and 30 percent to the public.

My father knew well how laborious the life of reindeer herding could be. At that time he would go to each campsite in the forest at least twice a month, driving a small truck on the rugged forest roads. As he explained, he had to go there to supply them with food, medicines, and news. The hunters usually stayed in the mountain forest for at least half a year, and even one year at a time. Now the situation is better than before. At the campsite they have solar power lighting, and most people have a motorcycle. Also the roads are better. But the overall condition is still very poor, according to my father. At the same time my father misses all those herders he got to know then, and the way of life at that time. It was a sweet life, though also really bitter, happy while hard.

My parents were married in 1980. When I was to be married in June of 2011, my father said that their wedding had been simple, costing only five hundred yuan. My father told me: "We have nothing to give you for your marriage. We brought you up and let you have a good education, although we ourselves never had any higher education. We have given you whatever we were able to offer you." My father and mother had to retire before the resettlement in 2003. My father knew well the feeling of leaving one's native place, since he had left his own hometown earlier. Nor was this the first time the Ewenki people were resettled. But my father never wanted to leave Aoluguya, and he wasn't given a residence in the new Aoluguya after the relocation. My parents bought a residence four kilometers away from new Aoluguya in order to be close to their old Aoluguya friends.

I've never been to my father's hometown, but I believe that his native place is also beautiful. Last year my father went to his home place to celebrate my grandmother's eightieth birthday. Before he set out, he told us he would return after the lunar New Year, the Spring Festival. In fact, he came back a month earlier than planned. I think Sichuan is the home of my father's dreams, while Aoluguya is the home that he could never leave for long.

My mother's name is Alaike. Her hometown is the village of Qiqian, a place that can hardly be found on a map. Whenever my mother mentions Qiqian, a happy look appears on her face. It seems that the place is a heaven. In fact, she only lived there for six years. My mother belongs to the Buljotin clan, which is the largest of the four Ewenki clans. My mother's parents lived as hunters in the Greater Hinggan Mountains, as the Reindeer Ewenki have done for generations. My grandfather and grandmother had five children. Their last child died very young. The winter of 1988 was extremely cold, and my grandfather and grandmother, uncle and aunt were all taken away by the cold weather, leaving my mother suffering in great pain. After this, she had only one younger brother left, named Dawa. My mother helped Dawa to marry a good young girl. The young couple continued herding the reindeer he had inherited from my grandparents. Now Uncle Dawa's family has almost a hundred reindeer. They have two children, a girl and a boy. Both of them lived in my home while they went to primary and middle school, until they left for high school in Haila'er. The younger brother Daweier has joined the school choir. His elder sister Daliya is studying tourism and works as a tour guide in Aoluguya on her holidays. She often guides tourists on visits to Ewenki campsites, to let more people know about Ewenki culture and the contemporary situation in the forest.

My mother's birthplace Qiqian is located on the border between China and Russia. Since they moved away from there in 1964, my mother never returned. Nor did most other Ewenki people, except her grandfather and a few others who went back to hunt. Old people say that in 1964 they became victims of unforeseeable events. There was a serious deterioration in relations between China and Russia, and consequently the Ewenki were forced to leave Qiqian. They were first given temporary lodging in Qiqian, and after one year, under the leadership of Nicolaj, 113 people from thirty-five families settled down in Aolu-guya. When my mother started school in Aoluguya, she lived in the school's dormitory together with her schoolmates. My mother told me that they didn't know any Chinese when they started school, but the teachers taught them Mandarin. Gradually they would also practice by speaking with Han people. Whenever holidays were approaching they would wait eagerly to go into the mountain forest, to keep the reindeer company and play among the larch and silver birch trees. In my moth-er's words, the vast woodland was their paradise. However, in the early 1970s tuberculosis began to spread in Aoluguya. At that time the dis-ease was difficult to cure. Although the government helped the Ewenki by providing free hospital treatment, many of the infected still lost their lives. Luckily my mother and a few others managed to recover. She is still not willing to recall those terrible times, when many relatives and friends passed away.

As a girl, my mother showed that she had inherited the Ewenki marks-manship. She would often go hunting with the adults in the densely forested mountains, taking the birch-bark boat to hunt for big game. Mother could shoot with great accuracy, and because of this she was chosen to attend Hulun Bei'er Sports School. When she left home, she thought she would never return. She missed her hometown very much. However, as she was preparing for a big competition she was affected by some kind of eye disease. The drugs and treatments she was given were ineffective, so she had to give up and return home. But when she saw the reindeer and forests, her eyes recovered quickly, as if by magic.

After middle school, my mother was employed by Aoluguya Town-ship. She worked for the service team for hunters, the cultural station, and the township government until her retirement. My mother worked hard and did her job well. In 1982 she became a delegate to the sixth ses-sion of the People's Congress of Inner Mongolia. This was her proudest achievement. Later she joined the Evenki Association of Inner Mongo-lia Autonomous Region, taking active part in all kinds of social activi-ties and nongovernmental organizations. Drawing on memories from her childhood, she recorded old Ewenki legends, stories, and customs.

After retiring, my mother began to make all kinds of traditional handicrafts. She says that although these handicrafts have gone out of use today, she and her elders often used them the past. These things have been important for the survival of the Ewenki until the present. My mother thinks they are treasures that our ancestors left us, and that they should be kept alive. She says that actually, we have already lost too much. That's why she plans to recreate all the traditional Ewenki handicraft products for future generations. Now many young people ask my mother to teach them the Ewenki language and culture. She instructs them patiently, but when reporters come for interviews, she usually offers the young people the place in front of the camera. In anything that concerns the Ewenki, my mother always accepts people's requests and tries her best to help others. Starting in 2005, my mother taught the Ewenki language every other week in the Aoluguya township government building. In 2011, she began to teach Ewenki in the Aoluguya nationality school. She goes to work even when she's not well. She says that the children all like learning the Ewenki language, so she needs to teach them well. My mother works hard for this, especially now that the education bureau is paying more attention to the teaching of ethnic minority languages.

My *heka* and *ewo* relatives

In the Ewenki language, relatives who are elder to one's father are called *heka* if they are male and *ewo* if they are female. These terms are used for the relatives of both parents. My maternal grandfather's grandfather was the elder Pjotr Buljotin, and his son's name was also Pjotr Buljotin. My great-grandfather's wife was named Matrjona Sologon, and their son, my grandfather, was called Silij Buljotin. Dagera Sologon was his wife and my grandmother. They lived their entire life in the forest, never leaving their reindeer. When I was a little girl I met my mother's parents.

My great-great-grandfather, the elder Pjotr, was the most spiritually powerful shaman of his time. People say that till this day, no shaman has been more powerful than him. He was called Apollo, and he had a bear as his protector. When the bear spirit entered his body, he could have a conversation with the spirit, and wielded the power of driving out evil. His shaman's song was acclaimed as the most beautiful and most allegorical. Among the Ewenki, only the shaman could sing the shaman's song, so after the last shaman passed away, few people could remember the song. People believed that the shaman always knew the number of reindeer, and could predict hunting results just from looking into the palm of one's hand. As the story goes, Apollo once told his son: "You will hunt five moose in five days." His son was young at the time, and he didn't trust his father's predictions. But as it turned out, he really hunted five moose in five days. After this, his son started to believe in his father's powers.

My great-great-grandfather was the *ataman* or leader of the Ewenki hunters during his time. He had one iron seal inscribed in Russian with the words "Tungus Buljotin tribe mayor's seal." He also had one reindeer-skin book that recorded the history of our Ewenki people. He regarded these two things as treasures and took good care of them, rarely showing them to others. Few people saw them, and the memories of those who did have now become faint. He eventually left them to his son, but after the Cultural Revolution, no one saw them again. People say they were put in a *kolbo*, which is a storage place in a tree, and that they were burned. Our family members have kept looking for the seal and the reindeer-skin book, but their resting place is as opaque as the passage of the dark era. They are still like exhortations from *heka* and *ewo*, bonding us together across time.

The elders all describe my great-great-grandfather as a tall and handsome man. During his time, his family was the most populous, and so were their reindeer. People think that God rewarded him like this because he was a shaman and did many good deeds. Now he often appears in the dreams of his granddaughter Maria Buljotin, dancing to bless the Ewenki people. Across time and space, conversation and dance link us together.

My great-great-grandfather had three sons. He gave his own name to his second son, my great-grandfather. When the father and son share the same name, this is regarded as the most precious blessing. My great-grandfather was married twice. His first wife passed away from disease soon after their marriage. He married his second wife Matrjona Sologon when she was only fifteen years old. She gave birth to twelve children, eight boys and four girls. Their eldest daughter Maria was born in 1916. She married Alexij Kudrin. In 1952, her husband passed away, so she and her four sons and three daughters joined the family of her husband's father. Pasha, their second daughter, was born in 1919. She never married. She passed away in 2009. Their eldest son Daweigede died in the Cultural Revolution. Their second son Wuluji only reached the age of twenty-six. Their third son was Siliji (1927–1989). He is my maternal grandfather. Their fourth son was Nea (1932–1945). Their fifth son was Andrei (1933–1977). His wife's name was Lisike, and she was a shaman. Their sixth son, Gelisike, was born in 1934. When he was young he went to school with the Japanese officers' children and learned to speak Japanese. After Liberation he became a forest policeman, responsible for protecting the forest and preventing forest fires. He never married. Now he lives in the retirement home. Their seventh son was Magela (1936–1975). Their eighth son was Kuka (1939–1948). Their third daughter was Getilina (1943–1953). Their youngest daughter Anta was born in 1945 and was married to a Han.

My grandfather and his siblings were all baptized in the church. The Russians built an Orthodox church in the area where the Ewenki lived.

They forced them to go to church and pay church tax. Russian names are common among the elder Ewenki generations. A male pastor and a female pastor carried out baptizing ceremonies. As described by Maria Buljotin, there was a big basin of water in the middle of the church. Around the basin, some candles were lit. The pastor would cut off a lock of the child's hair and throw it into the basin. If the hair kept afloat, the child could live a long life, otherwise not. The pastor would write the child's name on his or her forehead and cheeks with a red pen, repeatedly praising God. Then the pastor would hold the baby while circling the basin three times, singing a song of blessing.

Ewenki men are all excellent hunters. My great-grandfather hunted a big moose when he was over seventy years old, all by himself. People admired his energy and strength. Before the Liberation, he once earned a whole bag of money from hunting. He put the money into the family *kolbo*. The Ewenki did not give much importance to money. All their needs could be met by nature. Every family had a Russian merchant as trading partner, known as *andak*. As described by Gelisike: "My family had some *andak*. When I was young, nine sable furs could be exchanged for one bag of flour. But the flour was very bad. We didn't know the value of our furs. In fact, sable, otter and lynx furs are valuable. We used these furs to barter whatever we didn't have, such as cloth, tea, beef tallow, flour and cream."

At first the Ewenki used flintlock rifles that could shoot twice successively. Later they used Russian-made rifles that could shoot only once but with more power. Then came sleeve guns and other kinds of weapons from the Nationalist government (1912–1949) and the Japanese. In the 1980s they began to use shotguns and semi-automatic rifles. This ended in 2003, when hunting was prohibited and guns were confiscated.

The Japanese arrived in the Ewenki homelands around 1935. My great-grandfather and his three eldest sons were forced to leave the mountains for training in camps set up by the Japanese. They experienced much cruelty and suffering in the camps, and all the food had to be supplied by the Ewenki. While the men were away, the women were burdened with all the work on the mountain. They were all starving. There was an Ewenki man named Tarapei who refused to join the training and resisted the oppression by the Japanese soldiers. In the end he was whipped badly by the Japanese. He jumped into the river to end his own life. This incident aroused the Ewenki people's anger. The Japanese had to hold a traditional funeral for Dalafei according to Ewenki custom. It has been calculated that more than two hundred people in fifty-three households died of causes related to the Japanese reign, wiping out some Ewenki clans. In August of 1945, my great-grandfather and many other Ewenki men launched several deadly assaults on the Japanese.

The Ewenki who live in the forest all have a mental map of the Greater Hinggan Mountains. My great-grandfather Pjotr was acclaimed as a "living map" of the mountains, by virtue of his knowledge and accuracy. With the coming of the "New China," explorations were made into the Greater Hinggan Mountains, and my great-grandfather became a guide. He first led a joint exploration team from China and Russia. As they entered the unknown territory, he helped them collect plenty of firsthand material on the geography, geology, mineral reserves, and resources of the mountains, which was crucial for the region's later development. By the end of the 1960s, the Chinese government had begun to develop the forest resources of the Greater Hinggan Mountains. Regardless of their family situation, almost all Ewenki men were required to lead expeditions into the virgin forests, using reindeer for transportation. One after another, Ewenki men served as guides for expeditions engaged in forestry planning, railway design, and road surveying, leading teams that might include more than fifty people. While the reindeer carried the equipment, the guide was the expedition's flag-bearer.

This is my story, and the story of my family, my clan, Aoluguya, and the Reindeer Ewenki. We lived in the forests, nearest to heaven. We led a happy life, though always accompanied by puzzles and pains. My Uncle Dawa is still in the forest herding the reindeer inherited from my grandfather. But the forest is steadily dwindling and becoming sparser, and there is not enough fodder for the reindeer. The herds are shrinking, and the hunting rifles are gone.

Reindeer, hunting rifles, forest, big nature: this made up the entire world of the *heka* and *ewo*, and was also the world of my mother during the first stage of her life. This is my mother's treasure, which she would protect with her very life. This is also what fills my childhood memories, and gives me a sense of responsibility that I cannot deny. This world is inhabited by the sacred reindeer, and by the shaman that the Ewenki cannot find, nor give up or forget. It fills us with grief that no one can answer our questions: Who will we be, if we lose our reindeer? Who are we, since we lost our hunting rifles? We lived here, generation after generation, so why are we no longer allowed to stay here? Every nationality springs out of a unique source that runs through the long history of its cultural development. Though it cannot persist without its own stubborn vitality, outside support is also vital to its survival.

🌀 10

HUNTING ALONG THE BEI'ERCI RIVER

Gu Xinjun

My memories take me back to the spring of 1990…

The Greater Hinggan Mountains were just welcoming the first breath of a budding May, with scattered azaleas as ornaments. Su're, Kuyile, Maqiala, and Baoaodao were rowing a wooden boat on the limpid Bei'erci River, to go hunting downstream. This was a wonderful season for hunting, and the best for catching deer. The party was ready to cover some distance, unless they were lucky enough to get a deer on the way, which would stop their advance to the lower reaches. At this time of year, the Bei'erci River was very shallow. Walking in it would have been no problem, except for some deeper waters where dark vortexes made it more unpredictable. The sun shone warmly, but the water was still freezing.

Baoaodao was rowing. He was a great fisherman, always hanging around on the river. He would be the company of Su're, Kuyile, and Maqiala along the way to the estuary of the Aonian River. This was where he kept his base, although he tended to leave it frequently to fish and trap.

On this trip, Su're and Kuyile were carrying model 56 guns on their backs. These were military semi-automatic rifles authorized by the old township leader He Lin, and belonged to the second set of such rifles provided for the Aoluguya Ewenki hunters. The first of such weapons, fitted with rounded bayonets, were distributed in 1980. The second set, distributed in 1985, was better than the first, and had flat bayonets. These rifles were provided free of cost, although the hunters had to pay for their bullets. As opposed to the other two hunters, Maqiala carried a small-bore shotgun, so only small game could prove his hunting skills.

Su're, Kuyile, and Maqiala were planning to return after reaching the estuary of the Aonian River, but might also continue to drift downstream, depending on what they caught. The day was drawing to a close.

"Okay, stop here! Let's camp here for the night." Kuyile, hugging his semi-automatic, sat at the head of the boat, pointing with his right hand at the riverbank to the left of them.

"I think we should go ashore and spend the night here. Traveling in the dark could be dangerous," Su're agreed.

"Get the boat ashore!" Kuyile commanded the paddling Baoaodao.

Soon after, the boat was driven up onto the bank. Everyone was busy unloading their bags and rifles. Kuyile jumped out of the boat first, stepped through the shallow water, and found a flat place on the bank to put down his bags and gun. Then he took out a big knife from his bag and found his way into the woods. Su're and Maqiala put their bags on the ground and got busy. Baoaodao took out a piece of fishing net from his luggage, put on his waders, and moved upstream. Su're went to fetch water from the river, carrying a black and pitted water bottle and an aluminum pot that was just as rough. Maqiala collected wood from fallen trees nearby. After a little while, Kuyile returned from the woods carrying a smooth larch rod over his right shoulder, and two shorter sticks under his left arm. Those were for the construction of a tripod for cooking, as the Ewenki people usually do.

Maqiala set down the firewood he had collected, found a piece of birch bark and brought out some matches, and lit the bark with a sudden swish. Then he foisted the burning bark under a pile of tinder. After the fire was lit, he made it flare with some fist-sized pieces of dry wood. Su're hung the black bottle and pot, both filled with water, onto the crossbar over the high fire.

"Baoaodao will return with his catch soon, and we're going to boil the fish. After eating them up, we can cook fine dried noodles in the broth!" The fish was not even caught yet, but Kuyile was already imagining the feast.

Su're and Maqiala opened their bags, brought out furry hides and padded cotton mattresses, and put them on their selected seating places. The campfire burned ardently now, bursting forth sparks. As the fire grew, the day retreated, leaving the crackling flames and chattering river streaming past the camp. Baoaodao returned, carrying the fishing net and some fish strung on wickers. There seemed to be more than a score of them, in various sizes. Baoaodao hung the net on a willow branch and threw a wicker of fish in front of the seats of Maqiala and Kuyile.

"This is all for today. I've caught as much as we can eat. In this river we can fish any time we want," Baoaodao said while taking off his waders.

"That's a lot already! How many are there?" Kuyile asked as he picked up the skewered fish.

"There's plenty of fish swimming against the river. This is the catch from two nets," Baoaodao replied.

"Come on! Let's pick out some good ones and cook them quickly. We're going to have fish in clear soup!" Kuyile urged the others to get busy, as if they were doing nothing.

The catch was all trout, the most delicious of all coldwater fishes. As the water began to boil, Baoaodao grasped a handful of grainy salt from the salt bag and scattered it into the pot.

"Don't put in too much, or we'll suffer from too salty soup!" Kuyile yelled, as soon as he saw what Baoaodao was doing. From a teabox made of birch bark, Su're picked up a handful of tea, opened the black bottle, dropped the tea into it, and put back the lid.

"Maqiala, bring out the drink, please! How can we have fish without alcohol?" Kuyile advised.

"Get me a spoon! I would love to start tasting the soup!" Baoaodao sat down next to Kuyile, ready with his bowl and chopsticks. All their chopsticks were handmade of willow twigs cut into similar lengths and smoothed with a knife, making the best of local materials.

Kuyile got the spoon from Su're, its grip broken in half. He dipped it into the pot and blew hard before tasting the soup, afraid that it would scald his lips.

"Wow! What a fresh flavor! It's too good to be true!" He was so happy that he couldn't help smacking his lips. "Let's lift it down from the fire."

"It's not too cold today, and we can save some firewood as well," Su're said, lying wrapped in his blanket.

"Why don't you guys eat more? What delicious fish sou... soup!" Kuyile's mouth was obviously full of soup, with noodles plumping his cheeks.

"No more! You go ahead and finish the soup and noodles alone!" Su're and Maqiala chortled at the same time.

They didn't feel too cold sleeping outdoors that night. The feast at dusk seemed to have added several degrees to the nightly temperature. The break of dawn saw the four of them packing busily as smoke rose from the extinguished campfire. They set off early, without taking time for breakfast. Once again Baoaodao was rowing. Drifting with the current required little of his strength, but all the more of his skill at steering a boat. The water bubbled downstream, leaving behind endless vortexes near the banks. On the river ahead of them, wild ducks sometimes flew up with a flapping sound, like helicopters hovering above water; sometimes fish bounced through the surface.

"Don't talk! We're likely to find roe deer drinking or foraging by the riverside! Keep your eyes on the banks!" Kuyile said to Maqiala, who was seated in the middle of the boat, and Su're, sitting in the bow holding his rifle. The tranquil woods muffled his voice. The sun shone warmly on the pine tree forest crowning the peak of a hill, where nightingales sang silvery songs echoing among the trees.

"Hey! The water ahead seems shallow! Watch out for rocks in the water!" Kuyile yelled as he scouted the river in front of them.

"Isn't that a big rock making waves ahead?" Maqiala asked as he moved over to get a better view, clutching the side of the boat. They drifted closer and closer to the breaking waves.

"But there's a tail! Dear mother! Those are three huge fish!" Maqiala shouted.

The river flowed rapidly but the water surface was unbroken, and the boat moved closer. Su're and Kuyile had already picked up their rifles and were staring at the surface. Soon, the three fish could be seen swimming painstakingly upstream in line with the side of the boat. The two rifles were drawn and everyone in the boat got busy. Baoaodao tried with all his might to stop the boat for a while in the turbulent stream. The fish were all around 1.5 meters long, weighing at least twenty kilos each. Kuyile and Su're shot two of the fish, spraying the surface. They sighted the white belly of one of them, gutted by a big bullet hole. Kuyile put his rifle aside and jumped into the knee-deep river as soon as he had fired, to grasp the fish they had shot. He first caught hold of the tail of one of them, holding it with its head down. The fish buckled and whipped its powerful tail, and Kuyile had to shield his face from being smashed. Just when he was about to put the fish into the boat, it broke loose from his grip and left him reeling backwards. The fish leapt into the water and made a desperate escape upstream, where it quickly vanished from sight. Kuyile then lifted up the other fish, which was floating stably in the water with its white belly up. This one was much weaker, probably due to more serious wounds. With the assistance of Su're, he loaded the fish safely into the boat.

Maqiala, carrying his small-bore shotgun, waded through the stream trying in vain to find the escaping fish, and so did Su're. Baoaodao docked the boat at the riverside. Kuyile, Su're and Maqiala had not even taken off their shoes or wrapped up their trouser legs, but jumped directly into the river with extreme excitement and enthusiasm at the sight of so many big fish at once.

"What regret!" Kuyile patted the bow of the boat and sighed, "We should have unfolded the bayonets on our rifles to stab the fish! We would have caught all three of the big things!"

"Sure! Those fish couldn't have escaped if we had taken our hunting knives out and stabbed them in the back!" Su're added.

Kuyile couldn't stop his self-accusations: "Alright! What a stupid mistake!"

"Let it go! It's been fine! We may run into more fish downstream!" Baoaodao said while he continued to row.

Su're finally raised a key issue: "I think we're kind of lucky! I suggest we go to Yikemasha and exchange the fish for some food and supplies that we need for hunting. It's the red deer we're looking for, rather than the fish!"

"Su're is right! Where have we just been, and how much distance have we covered? Of course there will be something bigger waiting for us ahead!" As he spoke, Maqiala waved his fingers towards the fish lying in the cabin.

The wooden boat continued its journey and finally docked at a small beach. There they had the day's first meal, prepared in a very simple way. It was afternoon when they finished eating. They boarded to continue drifting downstream. The sun was almost setting when they stopped the boat at a place about five kilometers from Yikemasha. From this anchorage they could see the Yikemasha Bridge in the distance.

"Great! Baoaodao and I can finally take a rest!" Maqiala lay on the bundles in the cabin, murmuring lazily. "Su're, why don't you carry the fish out of the boat and take it to the forestry station up the road, together with Kuyile? I'll be here waiting. Come back soon!"

Su're and Kuyile understood that Maqiala was afraid of being caught by the fire inspectors. This was the fire prevention season, and their hunting trip would be stopped if it was discovered by the inspectors. That was why the boat had to be docked at a distance, in a sheltered place. Baoaodao left the boat and went off into the woods by the riverside for some willow twigs to be twisted into a rope, as well as a two-meter long larch pole. He jumped back onto the boat, slipped the willow twig rope into the mouth of the fish, threaded it through the gills, and bent the willow twig into a loop, tying both ends together.

"Come on! Slip the pole into the loop!" Baoaodao stretched the willow twig loop, and Kuyile put the pole into the circle. Kuyile asked: "Will the loop break?"

"Nope! I promise it will last all the way to the forestry station." Baoaodao answered.

With their semi-automatic rifles over their shoulders, Su're and Kuyile carried the shoulder-height fish up the road, its tail dragging along the ground. Both men were 1.77 meters tall, which only proved the size of the fish. After a day's exposure to the sun, the skin of the fish was a little dry and tough. Gradually they got closer to the Yikemasha Bridge. They didn't need to cross the bridge, since the forestry station was on the northern bank of the river. As they approached the station, a Jiefang truck carrying red bricks drew up to them. Its driver had spotted the big fish on their shoulders.

"How did you fish this?"

"With guns." Kuyile answered.

"Where did you fish it? How much are you charging?"

"Near the hill area. You want it?" Kuyile said, "How about 150 yuan?"

"Nice! I have exactly 100 yuan for you here. You can keep that for now. The other 50 yuan will be paid after we arrive at the forestry station." While he talked, the driver took out a hundred-yuan bill and handed it over to Kuyile.

"Okay! Get onto the truck! Let's figure out the rest at the station!" The driver helped lift the fish onto the truck. Su're and Kuyile climbed onto the bricks in the back and got seated at the same time. Not long after, the truck arrived at the site where the station was constructed. The driver asked Su're and Kuyile to unload the big fish and gestured to them to follow him with it. Su're and Kuyile were still not sure whether the driver was the buyer of the fish. They lifted the fish and followed the driver closely. He looked perky as they walked up to the brick house. Su're had been here last summer, when the forestry station was being built. There had only been a wooden building, which had been used to house the forest police. Only one squadron was based here then.

Su're and Kuyile carried the fish, following the driver almost to the front of the brick house. A man came out from the house and posed at the gate, looking at them with an air of superior knowledge. The driver waved his hand to the man in a high and mighty way.

"Hey, Chairman Zhou! Are you busy? Aren't you returning to Mangui?"

"Not so much. How can I leave when it's not the weekend yet?" the man answered.

"Chairman Zhou, come and take a look! What do you think about this fish?" the driver asked again.

The man named Chairman Zhou walked up to Su're and Kuyile. After a short examination, he asked: "You two fished this? Where did you fish it?"

Kuyile answered: "Yes, we did. It was caught somewhere in the hill area."

"What a huge thing! A big whale like this is a rare catch!" Chairman Zhou continued to ask: "Did you use guns?"

"Yes!" answered Su're.

"Fishing with guns! Huh! Interesting! Hey, Li, go find a big pot! And you two, hand it over here!" Chairman Zhou looked like a director. "Get me the scales, also!"

The driver left. Su're and Kuyile handed the fish on their shoulders over to two other men and were then invited to the office of Chairman Zhou. Chairman Zhou soon poured tea for Su're and Kuyile, who had already taken their rifles off their shoulders and seated themselves on the sofa with the guns in their arms. Chairman Zhou offered the teacups to Su're and Kuyile, and said: "Zhou is my family name, and I'm in charge of the forestry station. You can come visit me in the station or in Mangui if there is any need. By the way, where are you going to hunt?"

"We planned to hunt downstream for red deer. Since we caught the fish, we'd like to exchange it for some food and daily necessities to supply our hunting trip." Kuyile said straightforwardly.

By this time a young man had entered the office and exclaimed: "Chairman Zhou! We just had the fish weighed. You'll never believe how many kilos it weighs!"

"How many?"

"It weighs 22.5 kilos!" the young man shouted.

"What a heavy and big fish! What do you two want in exchange? There is no food left here. What about some alcohol?"

"Alcohol is okay." Kuyile agreed reluctantly.

"Hey, Li! Please go to the cafeteria to pick up all of the alcohol that you can find, and some canned foods if there are any! They are about to take off!" Chairman Zhou said.

After a while, Li and another young man stumbled into the office with a box in their arms and brought all the bottles of alcohol out of the box and onto the desk. The brands were obvious; among them were the cubic bottles of Wujiabai, and the skirt-like bottles of Hongliang liquor. While Su're looked at these bottles he thought: How wonderful it would be if there were piles of bread and instant noodles on the desk right now!

"I'm really sorry, but there's actually nothing left to eat here!" Chairman Zhou said in a very apologetic and polite way. "The alcohol is for you to enjoy on the way to your hunting!"

Kuyile stood up and shook hands with Chairman Zhou. He said modestly: "Chairman Zhou, you are way too courteous! We'll return and give you venison if we get some deer."

By this time, Li, who was standing next to them, told Chairman Zhou: "Chairman Zhou, we have slit the fish and three lenoks were found inside!"

Chairman Zhou was engaged in the conversation with Kuyile, and said repeatedly: "Good! Good!"

Kuyile packed the bottles of alcohol on the desk one after another into his military knapsack. Su're was still seated on the sofa. From outside the door they could hear sporadic chattering, and it was obvious that this was from people talking about the fish.

"Okay, it's getting late and I've got to go! Thanks, see you around!" Kuyile finished packing, tied up the knapsack and put it on his back, and took the hand of Chairman Zhou.

Su're stood up, put the rifle over his shoulder, and reached out his right hand to give Chairman Zhou a handshake.

"Thank you, Chairman Zhou! See you next time! Welcome to our Aoluguya in the future!"

"Not at all. Let's keep in touch!" Chairman Zhou answered with a smile.

Kuyile grabbed his semi-automatic rifle and walked out of the office, with Su're following closely. Chairman Zhou showed them out of the room. As Kuyile and Su're left the station they could no longer see the driver, but Zhou and his subordinates stood watching them leave.

They returned from where they came, rushing with the setting sun. Walking very fast, they arrived quickly at the docking place.

"What have you two got? What took you so long?" Maqiala sat up from where he was lying. "What could we get? Just some alcohol! We asked for food, but they said they didn't have any. So, here's some alcohol to drink on the way!" Su're answered while he took his rifle off his shoulder. Kuyile took his off as well, handing it over to Baoaodao. Then he lifted the bag off his shoulder and carried it onto the boat, to the sound of clinking bottles.

"Come on, let's go! Let's set off now. We'd better pass Yikemasha before dark and go further downstream," Kuyile ordered from the cabin.

Baoaodao was busy rowing, but Maqiala was silent and seemed unhappy. Su're sat watching both banks; Kuyile was in the bow. It was getting dark as the boat passed Yikemasha Bridge and the forestry station on the northern bank. The setting sun made the Tebugejia Rocky Mountains seem much steeper and loftier. The boat drifted like a floating, swinging cradle. They went ashore on a beach near the mountains. As usual, they got busy with the camping and dinner preparations.

They spent more than two days covering the river route from Tebugejia to the Aonian River, during which they had nothing to eat except tedious rice and fine dried noodles with troublesome slippery mushrooms. As they were about to reach the estuary of the Aonian River, Baoaodao found a red deer lying in the Bei'erci River. It appeared to be two years old and had the usual biramous antlers on its head. There was a rump part near the tail missing. They docked the boat and dragged the deer ashore together. When they slit its stomach they found that there was no smell of decay in the intestines or abdomen, and neither was the flesh decayed. Kuyile adjusted the head of the deer and found a sharp axe to cut off the antlers together with the head. Maqiala took it from him and put it on the beach. Kuyile was in charge of pulling the hide off the flesh.

"It must have been bitten by a wolf no longer than two days ago!" Baoaodao explained as he pulled on the forelegs of the red deer while Kuyile pulled out its internal organs.

"Since it just died, its kidneys will be the pals of my drink!" Kuyile said, with his head lowered in a posture like that of a surgeon operating on a patient. Maqiala and Su're went back and forth, fetching the parts of the deer and immersing them in shallow water. Kuyile pulled out the heart of the deer, handed it over to Maqiala, and said: "Please pour the heart blood out first, and dry the heart in the air." Maqiala grasped the heart and put it upside down on a plastic cloth spread on the beach, so that he could squeeze the blood out of the heart.

Kuyile separated the four legs of the deer and said, "Let's immerse them in the water until we can find some spare time to separate them further and pull out the tendons." Baoaodao dragged the legs aside and immersed them.

"Old Maqiala, go and boil the water. We're making deer rib stew!" Kuyile shouted while cutting off the last parts of the deer.

Su're, seeing that the deer was almost fully butchered, went searching for dry wood for the campfire on the riverbank. Maqiala carried the black aluminum pot to fetch water from the river, while Baoaodao laid out the deerskin. Kuyile was holding the ribs with his left hand and cutting them up with a bloody hunting knife in his right hand. Su're set the tripod up for cooking while Maqiala lit the campfire. Flies were humming around them, attracted by the smells of flesh and blood. Close to noon, the cooking pot with the deer ribs was starting to steam.

Kuyile, seated by the campfire, took out a bottle of Hongliang liquor from his bag and put it on the ground. "We've finally got some real meat to eat! Having fish all the time has disgusted me a little! We should have changed that situation earlier!"

From some unknown place, Maqiala brought out onions, peeled some of them, and threw them into the pot to add flavor to the red deer ribs. "I'll save some for sauce."

Su're took his seat on the fur mattress next to Kuyile and poked the campfire repeatedly with a stick to make it burn brighter. Kuyile rolled the bottle of alcohol over in his hands, read the label and said: "This will be boring! The alcohol percentage is too low! Why do those people in the forestry station like this stuff so much?"

"Have you calculated how much these bottles of alcohol are worth?" Su're asked Kuyile.

"Roughly, these bottles are worth a little more than 50 yuan! Bottles of Hongliang are sold for about three yuan each in the township store, as far as I can recall, so they're not that expensive!" Kuyile answered with the bottle still in his hand.

Su're continued: "So, that huge fish was worth only 150 yuan in total? That's too cheap!" Actually, Maqiala and Baoaodao knew nothing about the 100 yuan in cash, because Kuyile had repeatedly told Su're on the way back from the forestry station not to tell the others about the cash. When Kuyile and Su're returned to the boat, Maqiala and Baoaodao saw that they had brought back nothing of value. Maqiala felt unhappy and unsatisfied with the behavior of Kuyile and Su're. However, he acted as if nothing had happened, and didn't say a word.

In order to dry the meat, hide and heart of the red deer, they had to stay there for another day, although they were not more than a day's travel from the estuary of the Aonian River. Their midday meal was a true feast. Having deer ribs to eat and antlers as bounty was heavenly! Before supper they put up a simple conical tent, not for fear of rain but to enjoy a good night's sleep. Next morning, Su're and Kuyile got up before the break of dawn, bringing their rifles with them as they climbed a bare hill to a watch post overlooking the river. They sat there until noon, but there was still no sign of red deer. On their way back they startled a hen that flew off into the distance. Kuyile walked to the place where it took off, only to find a nest with seven eggs in it. "Ah, that flying thing was brooding! Let's take these and fry them up!" Kuyile said as he bent and reached out his hand to pick them up, "Wow! They're still warm!"

"Put them down! Let the hen brood these! We'll get many chickens in the autumn!" Su're tried to dissuade him. Kuyile failed to listen to Su're's advice and stuck to his plan to take the eggs back to camp, fry them, and eat them up with alcohol. "It's less like having eggs than eating seven chickens in one meal!" Su're teased with obvious sarcasm.

They finally left on the third day, to follow the river current in the warm, clear sunshine. The boat kept on drifting with the slow flow of the Bei'erci River. Kuyile, carrying his semi-automatic on his back, left the boat and strolled along the river on his own. Every now and then he crossed into and out of the willow thickets by the riverside.

"Hey! Come on! There's a boat here! Hurry up!" The people on board heard Kuyile's shouts and soon had the boat docked. Su're and Maqiala jumped out of the boat and ran straight to where Kuyile was.

"What kind of boat?" Su're questioned.

"A wooden boat! Let's take this boat! Now what we should do is to lift it onto the river to check out whether it's usable!" Kuyile suggested while he examined the boat.

"Gorgeous! It's finely manufactured and painted a nice blue!" Su're said. "But it seems somebody is hiding this boat here. Are you sure we can take it?"

"It's no big deal! Anyway, who cares! Cut the crap!" Kuyile insisted. Maqiala was just listening. After realizing Kuyile's determination, Su're said nothing and followed him to lift it onto the river. Small as the boat was, it could easily carry three people.

"From now on, let's divide our team into two boats! Me and Su're can go in this boat, and you guys can go in the other one!" Kuyile ordered from the smaller boat.

"Whatever," Maqiala replied from their original boat.

The Bei'erci River in May was confident about her happy, rapid water flows, and the graceful, sublime scenery on her banks. Her waters streamed deeply and shallowly, rapidly and softly, pushing the boats constantly forward. Kuyile and his friends traveled in the two boats until they finally reached the estuary of the Aonian River at dusk. Kuyile, standing in the water, made great efforts to pull the boat ashore. It was no longer early, and they got busy with the campfire and food as usual, eventually preparing for sleep.

Baoaodao suddenly emerged from a willow thicket, without anyone knowing where he had been. He said: "There's a cellar in that higher place. Let's sleep there!"

"No! No! It's been wonderful outside, and I don't want to waste such good weather! Sleeping outdoors is better, not to mention the dampness and shade of a cellar! You want to live in that? Sure you can, after our departure and your return!" Kuyile said, seated by the campfire.

"That cellar is old! There's enough fish and meat here. And what's the cellar doing here anyway? Whose can it be, and when was it dug?" Maqiala wondered.

For supper, they used deer rib broth to cook fine dried noodles and made some tea in the sooty black bottle. Kuyile arranged his own drink, pouring spirits from a bottle of Wujiabai into his tea mug. Su're, Maqiala and Baoaodao enjoyed the steamy noodles with venison.

Kuyile poured a little alcohol from his mug onto the burning campfire. "Just paying my respects to Vulcan!" he said, taking a mouthful himself afterwards. "Come on! Come on! Just take a little sip! Especially you, my friend Baoaodao! You must be tired of boating and fishing these days. You should drink some more! Don't leave us tomorrow, please!"

"Huh! It's great to be with you guys! I realized that you Ewenki are good people just as soon as I had met you. Thanks!" With these words, Baoaodao took the alcohol and drank a big mouthful of it.

"Take it easy, there are still some bottles left. They'll be enough for us!" Kuyile then took out a bottle of Hongliang. From Yikemasha to here, he hadn't stopped drinking, so the 50 yuan worth of alcohol was running low.

"Baoaodao, man! Let me take those antlers of yours with two branches. We've got our own secret recipe for processing antlers in Aoluguya. You can pick them up from us when you come. Those will definitely bring in big money!" Kuyile opened up now, sharing his thoughts.

"Good! I'll follow your advice! Everybody knows that you Aoluguya people are experts in deer antlers! I believe in you, man. I can really benefit from this, unless of course the antlers have gone bad." Baoaodao spit out a piece of chewed noodle that got stuck while he talked.

"Okay! You can sell directly and settle the deal after you return home," Maqiala added.

Su're didn't give his opinion but took the alcohol and sipped a mouthful. Actually, Baoaodao had his own views about the antlers. He thought keeping them would be illegal and selling them was unjustifiable. Only Kuyile and Su're had the right to keep and sell the antlers, and what Kuyile had proposed was just an idea of his.

That night they all drank considerable amounts of alcohol, leaving the campfire burning low and indistinctly. The night sky was clear and the temperature mild. They quickly fell asleep to the echoes of melodies sung by the river. After breakfast, in the faint morning light, Su're, Kuyile, and Maqiala carried their belongings aboard. Then they shook hands with Baoaodao and said their final goodbyes.

"See you in Mangui after our trip!"

"See you around!"

"Take care!"

With his rifle beside him, Kuyile was seated in the quarter, holding the oars tightly. Su're held his rifle in the bow, and Maqiala was in the cabin. They left the estuary of the Aonian River in the boat they had picked up on the way. Taking a long look behind them, they saw Baoaodao reluctantly watching them leave.

This boat was lighter and easier on the rower than the original one, and allowed for faster travel. There was an area ahead where the river was deep, but strewn with rocks, one next to another, leaving gaps no larger than ten centimeters at the narrowest. Each rock was as big as a small room, and the river ran fast. These were some very big rapids.

"Uh-oh, it's not good. The flow is getting faster and the drop is too steep, so why not get ashore and give way to the waters?" Su're, seated in the bow, advised the paddling Kuyile.

"Stop, let's get ashore! The drop is getting closer amazingly fast!" Maqiala was also worried about the situation.

Kuyile rowed the boat to the eastern bank. After pulling it ashore, he said: "You two take care of your own belongings and my rifle! I want to row through here and have some fun on this expedition!"

Maqiala and Su're unloaded all the cargo. Su're told Kuyile: "Be careful!"

"Take it easy. I will," Kuyile answered before rowing the boat to the middle of the river.

The boat was soon pulled into the current. Kuyile kept rowing carefully to keep the boat balanced and avoid being thrown into the river. Maqiala and Su're, carrying heavy loads on the bank, walked in tandem while they stared at Kuyile boating in the stream. The boat was swept quickly from the top of the rapids to the bottom, and was then docked.

Maqiala and Su're walked up to the boat, only to discover that the wooden deck had come loose. "How are you? Frightened?" Maqiala asked.

"I'm more scared than hurt! That nearly ended in a shipwreck!" Kuyile responded.

"I told you to go ashore but you didn't listen to me. That was dangerous!" Su're said.

"Okay, no more talking! Just get back in the boat. I'll never return to this place." Kuyile said with a pale face.

"I've heard from older people that there are several miles of rapids downstream that are very hard to take on. Hunters have named these the Jaws of Death and some also call them the Waters Colliding with Mountains. From downstream, looking up, the river water is like a cataract hurling itself down," Su're said, back on the boat. The term "Waters Colliding with Mountains" means that the waters of the Bei'erci River fall from the top of the rapids to the bottom, where they run into the foot of a mountain and are forced to turn sharply to the west.

After the "jaws," the current relaxed, and the boat drifted stably downstream. Soon they reached the next camping place, the Snake Mountains, where tents were scattered here and there. Obviously there used to be quite a lot of people camping here. Rumor had it that this place was being prepared for the construction of a hydropower station, but after the first drafts were finished, nobody knew what was going on.

"Guys, look north! How tall and great! Those are the Snake Mountains. People say that red deer antlers can be found at the foot of those mountains. The antlers are from deer that were chased onto the summit and forced to jump off the cliffs to their death!" Maqiala said.

"I heard that too," Su're added.

The three had docked the boat, but none of them went ashore. The sun was about to set, but they had no intention of spending the night here.

"It's getting late. Are we staying here, or not?" Su're asked.

"No, we're not staying in such a place. It makes me weirdly uncomfortable. Let's leave this place and go downstream a little bit. I'm looking for a good beach!" As he finished talking, Kuyile pushed the bank with the end of an oar, and the boat moved.

"This place isn't far from E'erguna Left Banner. But we still haven't sighted a living red deer since we started our journey. We haven't even spotted a roe deer!" Kuyile gazed at the mountainside with a disappointed look on his face.

They stopped the boat for the night at a shallow beach. Maqiala and Su're took charge of the cooking. While Maqiala fetched water, Kuyile lay lazily on the beach, devoid of energy. He woke up only when the food was ready. The setting sun lit up the sky. They had no more words to exchange. It could be the long-term dullness of boating made them exhausted, or the daily chatting was getting tedious; it could also be the lack of gains during the trip that discouraged them. But there was clearly dreariness in this group, and in their hearts. The campfire went out gradually. They were so tired that they fell asleep early. Except for their snoring and the ripple of the Bei'erci River, the entire mountain forest was engulfed in silence. If there had been any alcohol left, they might have been drinking. But they had emptied all the bottles during the past few days. Kuyile never thought about sustainability when he drank, and because of the low percentage of alcohol in those bottles, he could easily drink two to three of them with each meal.

It was the tenth day of their hunting trip. The results were clearly less than promising. They had to disembark when they reached their destination, and that wouldn't take long. They spent another night near the Snake Mountains, had a simple breakfast, and took off early. The farther downstream they went, the wider the Bei'erci River became, and the slower it flowed. Their boat drifted only slowly, and the rower was soon exhausted, so they had to take turns rowing.

After a sharp turn, they followed a straight stream. Kuyile, who was rowing, saw a red deer on a barren hillside above the north bank in front of them. He lifted the oars and said softly: "Maqiala! Come and take over the oars please! There's something on the hillside ahead. You come and steer, and get close to it slowly!"

"I see! I see them! There are four deer, with antlers!" Su're stared at the barren hillside and spoke softly. The boat moved steadily closer to the target.

"Come on! We've got to get ashore as soon as possible for a better view! Be quick!" Kuyile said. He was the first to get out of the boat, moving quietly with his semi-automatic rifle in hand. Su're followed him closely, also holding his rifle while keeping the target on the hillside in sight. Their actions were silent as they found the best positions for shooting. Both rifles were aimed at the deer as Maqiala pulled up the boat.

"Bang bang! Bang bang!" Kuyile opened fire first, and Su're shot after him. The four deer were standing in two groups on the hillside. Three of them escaped quickly, while the one that was hit staggered and dropped to the ground.

"Stop firing! Stop firing!" Kuyile screamed. Because Kuyile was still shooting at the three escaping deer, he had no idea that Su're hadn't stopped firing on the deer lying under a pine. The wounded deer was keeping its antlered head upright. Su're kept shooting for a while, until he saw the deer struggle to stand up, only to fall down again.

"Gosh! No! The antlers are totally broken!" Kuyile, standing on the beach, held his rifle in his right hand and smacked his head repeatedly with his left hand. "I told you to stop shooting! Why didn't you listen to me? You see, now we'll get almost nothing for those wonderful high-quality antlers!" Kuyile complained.

"How could I stop? I was afraid it would escape like the other three! There would have been nothing for us then!" Su're argued. "Now ask Maqiala to row us over. We'll get the small axe before we go up the mountain."

Kuyile waved to Maqiala to get him to take them over to the other bank. Meanwhile, Su're returned the bullets from the bore of his rifle to the magazine, pulled the security wrench, and swung the rifle onto his back. Kuyile did the same.

Maqiala brought the boat, picked up Kuyile and Su're, and crossed to the northern bank. Kuyile took a small sharp axe from his bag, saying: "Maqiala, man! You stay here and get all the things ready. We two will go uphill to fetch down that wounded deer. Just prepare for stripping off the deerskin!"

Su're followed Kuyile up the steep hill, which was difficult to climb. About halfway up, they separated to look for the deer. Kuyile found the wounded deer caught in a bush only three or four meters away, its antlers bloody and broken. He shot it in the neck to make sure it wouldn't jump up again. "Stay still now!" he told it. After firing, Kuyile called to Su're to come over: "You hold the deer's head still, and I'll cut it off!" Kuyile started to cut carefully. "If they hadn't been broken, I guess these would have been amazing antlers, with four branches!" Soon, the antlers and head were cut off. Su're took them in his hands and examined them appreciatively. "What a pity! Should we look for the two broken-off branches?" He put the antlers softly down on the ground, and went to find the missing pieces of antler in the deer's path.

"Okay, I got them!" Su're held up the lost antler parts and showed them to Kuyile.

"You carry the antlers downhill, and I'll drag the body down. You take good care of the antlers, be careful on the way back!" Kuyile said. Then he began to pull at the deer's body. Since the hill was steep, the body rolled down quickly and was soon at the bank of the river. Su're, carrying the antlers carefully, climbed down slowly. His clothes were stained with the deer's blood. Maqiala, standing beside the deer's body with his hunting knife in hand, started to look it over.

"Let's load it onto the boat first, and find a better place to gut it." Kuyile pulled the deer's front legs while talking to Maqiala and Su're.

"It's so heavy! I bet it weighs more than 150 kilos!" Maqiala said, pulling the back legs.

They painstakingly loaded the red deer onto the boat. The boat drifted downstream a little until they reached a larger beach. After docking there, they unloaded the deer's body quickly.

Kuyile was still in charge of stripping off the deerskin and gutting the deer. With the deer hunted down, Kuyile felt stronger, as he had been several days ago. Su're seemed indifferent, as if he cared nothing about the red deer. It was only when he saw Kuyile cut off the deer's penis that he yelled: "I want nothing but the penis! As for the antlers, you and Maqiala can take them back." Su're had the idea that he had better get something out of a trip of more than ten days, or it wasn't worth the effort.

"Maqiala, light the campfire, please! Don't be so happy that you forget our meal! We'll have fresh deer meat today! Wash this, with more salt." Kuyile gave orders while chopping off the deer ribs and handing them over to Maqiala.

"Hey, listen! It's the sound of a truck, and it's not that far away." Su're said.

Kuyile cut off the deer's hind legs as he replied: "The highway is just over there in the woods on the western bank of the river, downstream. We can pack up our things now, row across the river and return to the road."

Maqiala washed the ribs in the river, put them in water in the black aluminum pot, and hung the pot on the tripod over the campfire. Kuyile finally completed the butchering. Su're kept busy loading the dismembered parts of the deer onto the boat, and finally covered the flesh with the deerskin. Kuyile then went to the river to clean his hands and hunting knife.

Suddenly, some whirlwinds from the river brought rain. It seemed that the drops were not from the sky but from the river, where the winds were sucking up water. They looked at each other in speechless despair. However, after about ten minutes, the rain vanished just as suddenly as it had come. Looking up, the sky was clear, and no clouds were in sight. They were totally astonished.

"Hey, what happened?" Su're asked curiously.

"Whatever it was, it's getting late, so let's have something to eat." Kuyile said, looking at the watch on his left wrist.

It was afternoon, and they had their meal around the black aluminum pot. Kuyile took a kidney, dipped it in some salt, and ate it. Maqiala scrambled for the other kidney, which he also found delicious. Su're didn't want kidney and picked up a rib from the pot instead. While eating, he said: "On the hunting trip to the Baidaoni River with Haxie, we had a lot of deer kidneys to eat. After that, I'm fed up with them. How lucky we are to have a feast like this!"

"You didn't even taste the food!" Maqiala said as he chewed the bloody kidney.

"Since eating the seven eggs we have been out of luck, and I was hoping that everything would get better after seven days. See, it came true!" said Kuyile.

Su're swallowed a piece of meat and said: "I told you! You violated the hunting rules of our elders. That was our god punishing us, wasn't it?"

"Oh, yeah!" Kuyile agreed.

"Or the red deer wouldn't have broken those great antlers with four branches!" Maqiala said while finishing up the kidney.

"Such accidents happened to the elder hunters as well, with even worse outcomes sometimes. They concluded that these accidents must be caused by bad fortune," Su're added.

"What a good meal! Only some alcohol could have made it more wonderful!" Kuyile said while he wiped his mouth.

"Huh! I told you that you should avoid running short on the alcohol. You didn't listen. Do you see now? You are so gluttonous!" Su're teased.

"What can I say?" Kuyile felt embarrassed.

"I also told you not to eat the eggs! The custom of the elder Ewenki hunters was to hunt the right things at the right season, and not to harm innocent creatures. I even witnessed some elder hunters letting go of a doe and its fawn during the season for harvesting antlers. They just wanted the deer to breed more. They were not as greedy as you are!" Su're continued to say.

"All right! Take your food!" Kuyile turned impatient.

As the eating and chatting subsided, they put an end to the last meal of their hunting trip.

Su're, Kuyile, and Maqiala began to put things away. They tied up their bags, extinguished the campfire, got into the boat after everything was checked, and made their way across the river to the western bank. They had left some deer meat and hide that they were unable to bring with them submerged in a deep basin, where it couldn't be washed away.

"Keeping it here is fine. After we reach the Taiping forestry station, I'll ask my two cousins to come and fetch it. We have to take all the meat and hide back!" Kuyile planned.

"What about the boat?" Su're asked.

"Just leave it here. We can't carry it back, anyway." Kuyile responded.

"Anyone who wants it can take it. It's been a great help on our journey. Ah, I hate to throw it away here!" Su're commented.

Maqiala said nothing, his face indifferent. Kuyile finally tied the boat to a pine with a trunk as thick as an arm.

"Okay, let's go!" Kuyile shouldered his semi-automatic, readjusted his bag, and took the lead. All three carried a full bag and a rifle on their backs—more than ten kilos of weight for each of them. They still carried their black aluminum pot and bottle, in case they couldn't catch a car or truck on the road before dark.

They reached the road between Mo'erdaoga and Qiqian and found a milestone on the right side of the road. It was marked "82," indicating this location was eighty-two kilometers away from the road's starting point. The three walked along the gravel road toward the south. The road was quite good and flat, strewn with weathered sand. After about an hour of walking, they arrived at a place that looked almost like a forestry station. There they met a fellow villager, Xu Jiafeng. He recognized Kuyile: "Where have you guys come from, and where are you going?"

Kuyile went over and shook hands with Xu, saying: "Mr. Xu, we came here by boat along the Bei'erci River from Aoluguya! We're heading for the Taiping forestry station."

During the conversation, a Jiefang truck arrived, carrying a full load of furniture. The cab was occupied, and there were also some people seated in the back. The truck halted at the checkpoint outside the station, offering Xu Jiafeng a chance to go over and ask the driver for a lift.

"Done! Get on!" The driver approved.

"Thanks, Xu! Welcome to Aoluguya if you have time!" Kuyile said, shaking hands with Xu Jiafeng again.

Waving his hand, Xu Jiafeng replied: "You're welcome. We're fellow villagers! Please say hi to the other Ewenki people from me!" Xu was from Qiqian Township. Before 1965, the Reindeer Ewenki people had settled in Qiqian on the shores of the E'erguna River, leading a happy life in this land flowing with milk and honey. Xu Jiafeng was now a keeper of the National Defense Highway, in charge of the road that Su're, Kuyile, and Maqiala had just walked.

Su're and Maqiala got onto the truck first, followed by Kuyile. As the truck started, Kuyile waved his hand to Xu, showing his appreciation. From there, the three went straight to the Taiping forestry station and returned to Aoluguya by way of Mo'erdaoga. And that was the end of their hunting trip along the Bei'erci River…

⚙ Glossary of Chinese and Ewenki Terms

Chinese pinyin	Chinese characters	English
Aoluguya ewenke minzu xiang	敖鲁古雅 鄂温克民族乡	Aoluguya Ewenki Ethnic Township
Aoxiangren	敖乡人	people of Aoluguya
bangji	棒鸡	black grouse
ban yidong ban dingju	半移动半定居	seminomadic
caoyuan huifu	草原恢复	grassland restoration
Caoyuan lüse	草原绿色	Grass for Green program
cuoluozi	撮罗子	conical tent (Ewenki tepee)
Daxing'anling	大兴安岭	Greater Hinggan Mountains
dianxing	典型	typical
ding er bu ju	定而不居	settling but not living
dingju	定居	sedentary/sedentarization
E'erguna he	额尔古纳河	Argun River
Elunchun	鄂伦春	Oroqen
Ewenke	鄂温克	Ewenki
Ewenkezu	鄂温克族	Ewenki nationality
feilong tang	飞龙汤	'dragon bird' soup
Gaige kaifang	改革开放	Economic Reforms
guanli	管理	manage/management
guanxi	关系	connections
Heilongjiang	黑龙江	Amur River
hetong	合同	contract

Huanbao ju	环保局	Bureau of Environmental Protection
Jiating chengbao zerenzhi	家庭承包责任制	Household Contract Responsibility System
ke chixu fazhan	可持续发展	sustainable development
lao Aoxiang	老敖乡	old Aoluguya
liemin fang	猎民房	hunter's houses
liemin shenfen	猎民身份	hunter's identity/status
liemin dian	猎民点	hunter's camp
lieye gongsi	猎业公司	hunting enterprise
lieye ju	猎业局	hunting office
lieye lianshe	猎业联社	hunting cooperative
lieye shengchandui	猎业生产队	hunting production brigade
linchang	林场	forest station
linye ditu	林业地图	forestry map
Linye ju	林业局	Bureau of Forestry
luxin xue	鹿心血	reindeer heart blood
Lüyou ju	旅游局	Bureau of Tourism
Minzheng ju	民政局	Bureau of Civil Affairs
minzu	民族	nationality/ethnic group
minzu shibie	民族识别	nationalities identification project
minzu xiang	民族乡	ethnic township
mumin	牧民	pastoralist
Nongmushuili ju	农牧水利局	Bureau of Agriculture, Pastoralism and Water Management
pengyou	朋友	friend
qiqun	起群	harem (during mating season)
shaoshu minzu	少数民族	ethnic minority

shengtai yimin	生态移民	ecological migration/ecological migrant
shilu bu(luo)	使鹿部(落)	reindeer-using tribe
shoulie bu(luo)	狩猎部(落)	hunting tribe
songshuta	松树塔	pinecone
Suolun	索伦	Solon
Tonggusi	通古斯	Tungus
tuihua	退化	degraded (about the environment)
tuimu huancao	退牧还草	converting pasture to grasslands (program)
weifeng zhuanyi	围封转移	pasture fencing (program)
xiang zhengfu	乡政府	township government
mao yan/xun yan	冒烟/熏烟	smoky fire (to protect reindeer from insects)
Xibu da kaifa	西部大开发	Open Up the West (campaign)
xunhua	驯化	domestic/domesticated
xunlu ewenkezu	驯鹿鄂温克族	Reindeer Ewenki nationality
Yakute	雅库特	Yakut
yangluren	养鹿人	reindeer herders
yangzhi	养殖	breed/cultivate
yesheng	野生	wild
yidong weizhu	移动为主	nomads
zaichuliang	载畜量	carrying capacity
zhangpeng	帐篷	tent
Zhonghua minzu	中华民族	Chinese nation
ziran baohuqu	自然 保护区	nature reserve
zuihou de shoulie buluo	最后的狩猎部落	last hunting tribe

Ewenki phonetic or pinyin	Chinese characters where available	English
amin		father
andak	安达	trading partner ('friend' or 'comrade')
bogzor		trade meeting; market (Russian: bazar)
eni		mother
ewo		female relative older than ones father
hala/chala	哈拉	clan
heka		male relative older than ones father
djiu	纠/柱	conical tent (Ewenki tepee); nuclear family inhabiting the tent
kolbo		storage place in a tree
lieba	列巴	pan bread (Russian: khleb)
malu		place directly opposite tent entrance
onko/jagel		reindeer lichen (Latin: *Cladonia rangiferina)*
palatka		ridge tent (Russian: palatka)
sèrukan		wooden structure used for smoky fires
shinmamalen	新玛玛楞	'chief' of a camp or family group
urilen	乌力楞	camp; family group
yasak	亚萨克	fur tribute (claimed by the Russians)

☉)) Contributors

Bai Ying is a painter and an associate research fellow at the Chinese National Museum of Ethnology. He is currently working on a cultural heritage program for five ethnic minorities in Northeast China. In 2009 he curated the exhibition in the Aoluguya Ewenki Reindeer Herders Museum, and he is presently curating the exhibition in the Museum of the Oroqen Autonomous Banner. He is also a council member of the Orochen Foundation (Hong Kong), a nonprofit NGO focused on preserving the cultural heritage of the Orochen ethnic group in China.

Aurore Dumont holds a doctoral degree in anthropology from the École Pratique des Hautes Études (EPHE), affiliated with the Centre de Recherche sur les Civilisations de l'Asie Orientale (CRCAO), Paris, France. Her research interests concern the Tungus nomadic societies of China, especially the Ewenki, with a focus on mobility and adaptation to environmental changes, the domestic economy, and the representation of festivities and religious practices in a touristic context.

Richard Fraser is a postdoctoral researcher at the Mongolia and Inner Asia Studies Unit (MIASU) within the Department of Social Anthropology at Cambridge University. Prior to this he was a PhD candidate in anthropology at Leiden University in the Netherlands. He has carried out fieldwork within Ewenki, Oroqen, and Mongol communities in China's Inner Mongolia Autonomous Region and Heilongjiang province since 2007, as well as Halh and Darhad communities in Mongolia since 2010. His regional specialization is Northern and Inner Asia. His current research project, funded by a Rubicon Fellowship from the Netherlands Organisation for Scientific Research (NWO), explores the impacts on pastoralists of Inner Mongolia's burgeoning wind industry.

Gong Yu was born in 1981 in Aoluguya. She left the settlement after middle school to attend teachers college and eventually obtained a master's degree in ethnic studies from Inner Mongolia Normal University. Since then she has worked as a researcher at the Centre for Ethnicity, Culture and History, Hulun Bei'er College. She has written for newspapers such as *Zhongguo Minzu* (China's Nationalities), *Zhong-*

guo Qingnian Bao (China's Youth Newspaper), and *Guangming Ribao* (Guangming Daily Newspaper).

Gu Xinjun was born in Qiqian, the Ewenki settlement on the Russian border. After graduating from Inner Mongolia Agricultural College he became the head of Aoluguya Ewenki Ethnic Township in 1993. In May 2001 he was assigned to the United Front Work Department of Genhe County. Gu Xinjun is also the deputy head of the Association of Ewenki Studies of Inner Mongolia. He started writing poetry and short stories in 1983 and has published some of his works in the literary journals *Senlin* (Forests), *Ma* (The Horse), and *Shi Bo* (The Wave of Poetry). His short story "Hunting on the Bei'erce River" was originally published in *Aoluguya Feng* (Aoluguya Scenes) in 2010.

F. Georg Heyne, ethnologist, Dr. h.c., was born in 1949 in Lohne, northern Germany. He has worked as a government employee and independent scholar since 1973. His fields of interest are the cultural histories, languages, and religions of circumpolar populations, particularly Manchu-Tungusic hunting, fishing, and reindeer-breeding peoples of East Asia such as the Reindeer Ewenki, Oroqen, and Hezhe. He also engages in research on the eastern groups of the Sámi (Skolt and Kola Sámi) in northern Europe, as well as the Ojibwa and Montagnais-Naskapi Indians in northern North America. Since the early 1970s he has carried out extensive fieldwork in northeastern Fennoscandia, Northeast China (Manchuria), the United States, and Canada. He has published numerous academic articles and treatises in his fields of interest.

Åshild Kolås is a social anthropologist and research professor at the Peace Research Institute Oslo (PRIO). She has authored two books and numerous articles, mainly on Tibetan identity and cultural representation. She carried out fieldwork in Aoluguya in 2008 and 2009. Her work on the Aoluguya Ewenki was conducted under the project "Pastoralism in China: Policy and Practice," funded by the Research Council of Norway and carried out in cooperation with the Institute of Ethnology and Anthropology, Chinese Academy of Social Sciences.

Siqinfu is an ethnic Mongolian from Hulun Bei'er, Inner Mongolia. He holds a doctoral degree in social anthropology from Kanazawa University, Japan, and works as associate professor at the Global Collaboration Center (GLOCOL), Osaka University. Siqinfu has authored four books and numerous articles, mainly on the environment and cultures of Siberia, Mongolia, and North China. The fieldwork he carried out in Aoluguya between 1996 and 2000 amounted to a total of sixteen months. His doctoral dissertation was on the economic life of the Aoluguya reindeer herders.

Tang Ge graduated from China People's University (Renmin Daxue) and works as associate professor in the Department of Sociology at Heilongjiang University. His major research field is anthropology, and the focus of his research is economy and cultural change, marginal culture, and ethnicity. Tang Ge has carried out long-term fieldwork in Hulun Bei'er, mainly on the Aoluguya reindeer herders as well as Russian influences among communities living along the Sino-Russian border in northeastern China.

Weijia was born in 1965 in a tent in the taiga and went to primary and middle school in Aologuya. Thanks to his artistic talent he was accepted as a student in the Department of Arts of the Central University of Nationalities (Minzu Daxue) in Beijing. After studying traditional Chinese painting for two years (1995–97), Weijia returned to the hunters' camps in the Daxing'anling forest. His paintings and poems are inspired by the natural environment of the forest, the lifestyle of its inhabitants, and especially the reindeer.

Xie Yuanyuan holds a doctoral degree in anthropology from Peking University (Beijing Daxue). She is Research Fellow at the National Strategy Institute, Tsinghua University, and Senior Editor and Research Fellow at the Tianda Institute. Xie carried out a year of fieldwork in Aoluguya in 2003–04, just after the resettlement. She is currently working on a new research project on the Aologuya Ewenki, funded by the Chinese National Social Science Foundation.

Zhang Rongde earned a degree in ethnology from the Central University of Nationalities (Minzu Daxue) in 2003 and received his master's degree in sociology from Peking University (Beijing Daxue) in 2012. From 2003 to 2010 he worked at the Chinese National Museum of Ethnology. In 2009 he was a curatorial assistant for the exhibition in the Aoluguya Ewenki Reindeer Herder's Museum. He currently works as an editor at the China Tibetology Research Center, and in his free time he works for the Orochen Foundation (Hong Kong).

𝕯𝖑 Index